FIFTH EDITION

Advanced Harmony
Theory and Practice

ROBERT W. OTTMAN

University of North Texas

PRENTICE HALL, Upper Saddle River, New Jersey 07458

Library of Congress Cataloging-in-Publication Data

OTTMAN, ROBERT W.
    Advanced harmony : theory and practice / Robert W. Ottman.—5th ed.
      p. cm.
    Includes bibliographical references and index.
    ISBN 0-13-083339-8 (pbk.)
    1. Harmony.   I. Title.
  MT50.O923 2000
  781.2′5—dc21   99-042122

Editorial director: *Charlyce Jones Owen*
Publisher: *Norwell F. Therien*
Senior acquisitions editor: *Chris Johnson*
Project manager: *Carole R. Crouse*
Prepress and manufacturing buyer: *Ben Smith*
Copy editor: *Carole R. Crouse*
Marketing manager: *Sheryl Adams*
Cover designer: *Bruce Kenselaar*
Cover design director: *Jayne Conte*

This book was set in 10.5/12 Times Roman by Thompson Type
and was printed and bound by Hamilton Printing Company.
The music was set by MPT Music Engraving.
The cover was printed by Phoenix Color Corp.

ISBN 0-13-083339-8

PRENTICE-HALL INTERNATIONAL (UK) LIMITED, *London*
PRENTICE-HALL OF AUSTRALIA PTY. LIMITED, *Sydney*
PRENTICE-HALL CANADA, *Toronto*
PRENTICE-HALL HISPANOAMERICANA, S.A., *Mexico*
PRENTICE-HALL OF INDIA PRIVATE LIMITED, *New Delhi*
PRENTICE-HALL OF JAPAN, INC., *Tokyo*
PEARSON EDUCATION, ASIA PTE. LIMITED, *Singapore*
EDITORA PRENTICE-HALL DO BRASIL, LTDA., *Rio de Janeiro*

Contents

Preface

Advanced Harmony: Theory and Practice, fifth edition, continues the course of instruction in basic music theory begun in *Elementary Harmony: Theory and Practice,* fifth edition (Prentice Hall, 1998). These two volumes include materials ranging from music fundamentals through twentieth-century music. The contents cover the needs of the usual two-year college music theory program in the subjects of harmony, melody, and form, with applications to analysis, writing (through both exercises employing figured bass and projects in original composition), and keyboard harmony. In addition, they correlate with the author's texts for sight singing and ear training, the other important aspects of the theory program, as discussed at the end of this preface.

Although the studies of harmonic concepts and structures are presented in a traditional and expected sequence, the order of chapters is not inflexible. Some studies can easily be presented at other points in the curriculum, as desired. Chapter 4, "Binary and Ternary Forms," can be introduced almost anywhere. The opening sections of Chapter 5, "Application of Part-Writing Procedures to Instrumental Music," may be used as correlating material as early as Chapter 1, with the rest of the chapter applicable to most of the remaining chapters of the text. Chapter 6, "Diatonic Seventh Chords," which seemingly appears late in the text, can easily follow Chapter 2.

Theory texts tend to present traditional materials in categories, their uses shown as abstract examples or from simple and uncomplicated excerpts from the works of composers. But there are many passages in music where a number of factors operate simultaneously, requiring the ability to isolate those factors and to study their interrelationships. Chapter 11, "Chords and Progressions in Special Situations," provides instruction in this type of analysis through the use of a number of interesting and challenging examples, from the works of Bach through those of late-nineteenth-century composers.

A survey of twentieth-century music covering three chapters concludes the text. A complete volume or several volumes are necessary for a thorough understanding of the subject, but this overview will be found effective in furnishing a solid foundation for later studies. These studies show how music late in the previous century literally used up its resources while at the same time it prophesied the music of the future. A chapter on the music of Debussy shows that he influenced the radical changes occurring at the turn of that century (1800–1900) by using styles of writing markedly different from those of previous years. For twentieth-century music, included first are studies of music that show evolutionary development from the previous century. These are followed by studies of the development of new and original concepts in music composition.

Revision of the text material has been the principal concern of this fifth edition. Most chapters show numerous improvements, but those concerning diminished seventh harmony and the binary and ternary forms have been copiously rewritten. In addition, all chapters with part-writing exercises include additional exercises with only the bass line given. New examples from music literature include excerpts from works of women composers.

A *Workbook* is available as a companion to this text. Though its use is not required, many students will find it helpful, not only for the additional exercises and music excerpts, but especially for those exercises in a semiprogrammed format, by which a student can immediately compare the completed answer with the correct answer. Such exercises are identified in the present text with this statement: *In the Workbook: Answers are given.*

The remaining requirements of the theory program are covered by the author's other titles, *Music for Sight Singing,* fourth edition, 1996, and *Basic Ear Training Skills* (with Paul Dworak), 1991, a comprehensive text serving both as a workbook for the student and as a source of dictation materials for the teacher, together with five supplementary computer disks for independent student practice. Both volumes are published by Prentice Hall.

I would like to acknowledge the invaluable assistance of Professor Alan Swartz of the University of Texas at Tyler in preparing the fifth edition of *Advanced Harmony* for publication.

Robert W. Ottman

1

Modulation

Chapter 1 of this text is a review of the study of secondary dominant harmony and modulation begun in Elementary Harmony: Theory and Practice, *fifth edition (Prentice Hall, 1998). That chapter should be reviewed for its presentation of secondary dominant harmony and for its introductory study of modulation.*

See the Preface of this text, paragraph 2, for alternative placements of presentations for Chapters 4, 5, and 6.

Introduction

Most music compositions, as well as many major sections within compositions, begin and end in the same key. If, for example, the composition starts in the key of A major, it will almost invariably end in the key of A major. The most likely exception is a change of mode: minor to major, or major to minor, but each with a tonic tone of the same letter name—for example A minor to A major, or the reverse.

To remain in the same key for the duration of the composition is satisfactory for many short works, including folk songs, church hymns, dance movements, and familiar pieces such as "America" or "Auld Lang Syne." But for longer or more sophisticated compositions, relief is usually desirable to counteract the constant return to a cadence on the same tonic tone.

The simplest and quickest way to suggest a different tonic is through the use of a secondary dominant chord, which, as you already know, can bestow upon its following chord a temporary feeling of tonic (*tonicization*) different from that of the key of the composition. In Figure 1.1 (key: A major), the two chords identified as V^6_5/vi–vi when heard out of context sound like V^6_5–i of F♯ minor. Similarly, in its context in the example, a temporary and fleeting impression of F♯ is created. It is quickly nullified by the following strong cadence in A major, but this slight excursion into another tonal area enhances the harmonic interest of this particular phrase of music.

FIGURE 1.1

Mozart, Concerto in A Major
for Piano and Orchestra, K. 488, III

Modulation

In contrast to the temporary impression of a new key as effected by a secondary dominant chord, a *modulation* exists when the music provides the listener the aural impression that a new key has been achieved, one that can be identified by a definite and unmistakable cadence in that key.

When you hear the music of Figure 1.2, even without seeing the score, it is obvious that though you first hear a minor key, the excerpt closes in a major key, its tonic a minor third higher than the opening tonic. Looking at the score confirms this impression. The phrase opens with i–V⁷–i in E minor and ends with V⁷–I in G major. To describe what has happened, we say that there has been a modulation from E minor to G major.

FIGURE 1.2

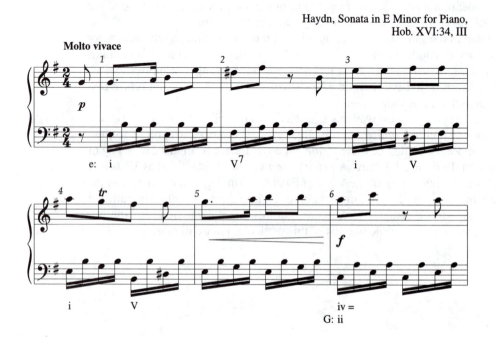

Haydn, Sonata in E Minor for Piano,
Hob. XVI:34, III

V   I

The meaning of the analysis symbols will be discussed under the heading "Modulation by Pivot Chord" on page 6, but first we will discuss the relationship of keys in a modulation.

Relationship of Keys

There are thirty available keys, fifteen in each of the major and minor circles of fifths.[1] So it is possible to modulate from any one key to any of the other twenty-nine keys. Do composers take equal advantage of all of these? Or does their choice produce a range from most used to least used?

Actually, the choices fall into two groups. Those most used are the *closely related* keys. Far more infrequent are the *remote* (foreign) keys. And within each group, some choices are more frequent than others.

Closely Related Keys

A closely related key is one whose tonic triad is one of six diatonic triads of the original key. Note that

1. Diminished triads (vii° in major and ii° in minor) cannot function as tonic triads in a new key, since there is no perfect fifth above their roots, making a tonic–dominant relationship impossible.

2. In minor, diatonic triads are from the natural form of the scale. Note particularly that modulation to the dominant from a minor key is to the *dominant minor*—for example, C minor to G minor (not G major). See Figure 1.10.

[1]Thirty is the number of key signatures. In sound, there are twenty-four key locations because three keys each in major and minor have enharmonic equivalents.

FIGURE 1.3   *The Closely Related Keys with Examples in C Major and G Minor*

FROM C MAJOR

Diatonic triad		Closely related key
ii	D F A	D minor
iii	E G B	E minor
IV	F A C	F major
V	G B D	G major
vi	A C E	A minor
vii°	B D F	—

FROM G MINOR

Diatonic triad		Closely related key
ii°	A C E♭	—
III	B♭ D F	B♭ major
iv	C E♭ G	C minor
v	D F A	D minor
VI	E♭ G B♭	E♭ major
VII	F A C	F major

By examining Figure 1.4 you can readily see that each closely related key either has the same signature as the original key or has one accidental more or less than the original key.

FIGURE 1.4   *Closely Related Keys (identified by key signature)*

	Same signature	+1♯	+1♭
From C major (0♯ or ♭)	C major	G major	F major
	A minor	E minor	D minor
	Same signature	−1♭	+1♭
From G minor (2♭'s)	G minor	D minor	C minor
	B♭ major	F major	E♭ major

There is still a third way to identify these relationships. The closely related keys are found as I, IV, and V (or i, iv, and v) of the original key, and their relative keys.

FIGURE 1.5   *Closely Related Keys (identified by harmonic groupings)*

	I, IV, V (i, iv, v)		Relative keys	
From C major	C E G		A C E	
	F A C	G B D	D F A	E G B
From G minor	G B♭ D		B♭ D F	
	C E♭ G	D F A	E G B♭	F A C

All three ways of calculating the closely related keys produce the same results and each is equally valid, so choose the one easiest for you.

A note of caution: Although the dominant triad in a minor key is usually major—for example, D F♯ A in G minor—the related dominant key is always minor. From G minor, the closely related dominant key is *D minor*.

Though uncommon, modulations from keys with seven sharps or flats to keys with eight sharps or flats are possible. For an example, see Bach's *Well-Tempered Clavier,* volume 2, Prelude No. 3, measures 1–6, for a modulation from C♯ major to G♯ major. There is no signature for G♯ major, so a double sharp is placed on the staff before the leading tone (F✕).

Remote, or Foreign, Keys

Remote keys are any keys not closely related to the original key. For example, G minor (two flats) and F minor (four flats) are remotely related. Generally speaking, the greater the difference in the number of accidentals between the two key signatures, the more remote the relationship. In Figure 1.13, the relationship between A♭ and F♯ minor is seven accidentals. See Figures 1.15 and 1.16, which show remote relationships of three accidentals and eight accidentals, respectively.

Modulations to remote keys are less common than those to closely related keys, their frequency diminishing with the degree of remoteness.

ASSIGNMENT 1.1   Write out or name the five closely related keys to each of the fifteen major keys and the fifteen minor keys.

In the Workbook: Answers are given.

Modulation by Pivot Chord

Figure 1.2 is an example of modulation by pivot chord, the most common of several methods of modulation. When we first hear A C E in measure 6, there is no reason to believe it to be anything but iv in E minor. But listen to the excerpt starting at that point. Now A C E sounds like ii, followed by V^7–I in G major. Therefore, this A C E chord is common to both keys, iv in E minor and ii in G major.

To prove the location of the pivot, play or listen to Figure 1.2 up to and including the pivot, and no further. At this point, there is no question that we are still in the key of E minor. In fact, the music could have continued in E minor as shown in Figure 1.6 (not by Haydn!), where we start at the pivot in measure 6, calling it iv only, and progress to a V–i cadence in the original key of E minor. Compare these measures with Haydn's own, the last three measures of Figure 1.2.

FIGURE 1.6

A chord that functions in two keys simultaneously is known as a *pivot chord* or a *common chord*, and the process whereby the music progresses from one key to another through a pivot chord is called a *pivot-chord modulation* or a *common-chord modulation*. Figure 1.7 shows the harmony of Figure 1.2, measures 5–8, expressed as simple triads, showing the process clearly. Note particularly the method of indicating the pivot, using the equal sign (=) to indicate the common spelling of the two triad functions.

FIGURE 1.7

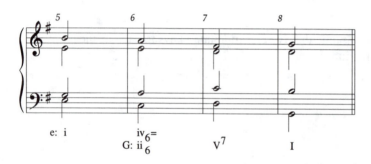

The pivot chord more often than not is the chord immediately preceding the first appearance of V–I in the new key, as in Figure 1.2 or Figure 1.7. But when that chord is not diatonic in the old key, then a preceding chord will probably be the pivot. In Figure 1.8, a modulation from B minor to G major, the new tonic appears at measure 16, preceded by its IV triad, C E G. C E G is not diatonic in the old key of B minor, so we go back one chord to E G B, which proves to be diatonic in both keys, b: iv = G: vi.

FIGURE 1.8

Schumann, *Myrten,* Op. 25,
"Hochländers Abschied"

(My heart is not here, but in the hunting grounds of the Highland.)

Note also in Figure 1.2 that the pivot could logically be placed at measure 5 instead of measure 6. The triad E G B at measure 5 could be e: i = G: vi, followed by ii–V–I. Such alternative analyses occur when each choice produces a commonly used progression in both the old and the new keys, and each is considered equally valid.

Determining the Triads Common to Two Keys

Usually, any chord spelled identically in the two given keys can function as a pivot chord. In Figure 1.9, triad numbers whose roots carry the same letter name in the two keys are aligned vertically. Where each triad in a vertical pair is spelled identically, that pair can function as a pivot chord, as indicated by the X's. The process as shown here produces three X's, indicating three possible pivots.

FIGURE 1.9

C major.	Triad roots:	C	d	e	F	G	a	b	C	d
		I	ii	iii	IV	V	vi	vii°	I	ii
				i	ii°	III	iv	v	VI	VII
E minor.	Triad roots:			e	f♯	G	a	b	C	D
	Possible pivots:			X		?	X		X	

C major to E minor: iii = i, vi = iv, and I = VI

E minor to C major: i = iii, iv = vi, and VI = I

But why isn't V = III an acceptable pivot? Any dominant triad has a "pull" so strong to one tonic that it is difficult to hear it as related to a different tonic at the same time. For that reason, the dominant is unlikely to be considered a pivot in any modulation. The exception is the modulation from a major key to its subdominant where I = V. The dominant (V) is then usually followed immediately by the dominant seventh (V^7), ensuring that the new key will be firmly established.

Figure 1.10 shows a modulation from a minor key to its minor dominant. In this well-known excerpt, the opening tonic triad also serves as the pivot, i = iv. The opening key of A minor is sufficiently established by its duration through four measures. Note again that the new key is E minor and not E major.

FIGURE 1.10

Mozart, Sonata in A Major for Piano, K. 331, III[*]

[*]The figure ♪♩ ♩♩ is played ♩♩♩♩.

After calculating all the possibilities between closely related keys in the same way, we can summarize the results as in Table 1.1. Modulation to a remote key can also be accomplished through the use of a pivot chord but usually requires that one or both of the chords be altered. These modulations will be studied when such chords are introduced.

In actual practice, most commonly found are (1) pivots that include the tonic in either one of the two keys and (2) pivots in which the chord of the new key is ii or IV (iv), these leading easily to a V–I (i) cadence. Use Table 1.1 for reference; memorization is not required.

In the Workbook: Do Assignment 1A. Answers are given.

TABLE 1.1 Available Diatonic Chords in Modulating from a Given Key to a Closely Related Key, Illustrated in C Major and C Minor

(The pivots in **boldface** are those most common and/or easiest to use.)

Modulation from a major key to its . . .		*Modulation from a minor key to its . . .*	
Supertonic key	**ii = i**		
(C major–D minor)	iii = ii*		
	IV = III		
	vi = v*		
Mediant key	**I = VI**	Mediant key	**i = vi**
(C major–E minor)	iii = i	(C minor–E♭ major)	III = I
	vi = iv		**iv = ii**
			VI = IV
Subdominant key	**I = V–V7**	Subdominant key	i = v*
(C major–F major)	ii = vi	(C minor–F minor)	**iv = i**
	IV = I		v = ii*
	vi = iii		VI = III
			VII = IV*
Dominant key	**I = IV**	Dominant key	**i = iv**
(C major–G major)	iii = vi	(C minor–G minor)	III = VI
	vi = ii		v = i
Submediant key	**I = III**	Submediant key	**i = iii**
(C major–A minor)	**ii = iv**	(C minor–A♭ major)	**iv = vi**
	IV = VI		**VI = I**
	vi = i		
		Subtonic key	**i = ii**
		(C minor–B♭ major)	III = IV
			v = vi

*In minor keys ii and IV contain the raised sixth scale step, which ordinarily ascends; v contains the lowered seventh scale step, which ordinarily descends.

Modulation by Sequence

1. Harmonic Sequence

Chords in sequence may be used as a modulating device. The sequence should be so arranged that the last member of the sequence is, or will lead into, the dominant or the tonic six-four of the new key. In Figure 1.11, following a half cadence in D minor, the sequence begins with the secondary dominant of its preceding V and continues with a series of secondary dominants until reaching the V^7 of F major. As a modulatory device, the first chord of the sequence is usually analyzed in the new key.

Note that the melodic motive of the opening half cadence is used antiphonally between the flute and the oboe during the course of the sequence.

FIGURE 1.11

Mozart, Symphony No. 41, K. 551, II

---

* Gr = German sixth chord. Here, the spelling in thirds is G♯ B♭ D F, with the interval B♭ (usually in the bass) up to G♯ resolving to the dominant of the key. See Chapter 8.

2. Formal Sequence

Repetition of a formal pattern, usually a motive or a short phrase, at different pitch levels will accomplish a change of key by stopping the sequence at the desired key. As in any sequence, only a small number of repetitions is desirable. In Figure 1.12, Chopin reaches G major from B major through three successive two-measure motives, each with the same chord progression. Note that the achieved key is *not* closely related to the opening key. Such *remote*, or *foreign*, keys will be observed frequently in the study of chromatic harmony.

FIGURE 1.12

Chopin, Mazurka, Op. 56, No. 1

Direct Change of Key

A new key may be reached simply by going to it directly. Since there is no process involved, the term *modulation* is not entirely appropriate, but it is commonly used.

1. By Phrase

Material following a cadence may simply begin in another key. Figure 1.13 shows a remote relationship, A♭ major and F♯ minor. For a simpler relationship, D major to B minor, see Bach chorale number 120, measures 1–4.

FIGURE 1.13

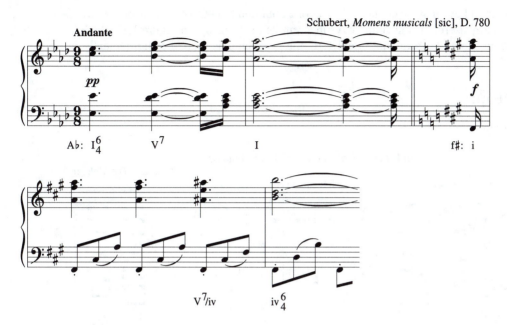

2. By Melodic Chromatic Alteration

This occurs when, during the course of the phrase, there can be found one melodic line (any voice part) that proceeds by chromatically altered half step (two notes of different pitch with the same letter name). In Figure 1.14, the chromatically altered bass line, F–F♯, indicates the location of the direct chromatic modulation. In this example, designating any chord as the pivot will result in an awkward harmonic analysis.

FIGURE 1.14

²The number in parentheses refers to the number of the chorale in the collected editions of J. S. Bach's chorales, such as *The 371 Chorales of Johann Sebastian Bach*, edited, with English texts and with instrumental obbligatos, by Frank D. Mainous and Robert W. Ottman (New York: Holt, Rinehart & Winston, 1966).

3. By Pivot Pitch

Two different keys may be connected by a tone common to both keys. This procedure is particularly useful in connecting keys in a remote relationship. In Figure 1.15, the E is common to both keys, and in Figure 1.16, the pivot pitch is spelled enharmonically, D♭ = C♯.

FIGURE 1.15

E major to
G major
Pivot pitch—E, root of I in E major = 5th of ii, A C E, in G major

Smetana, *The Moldau*

FIGURE 1.16

B♭ minor to
F♯ minor
Pivot pitch spelled enharmonically, D♭–C♯ (D♭, third of tonic triad in B♭ minor = C♯, fifth of tonic triad in F♯ minor)

Wagner, *Tristan und Isolde,* Act I, Scene V

*N₆ or ♭II₆ symbolizes a Neapolitan sixth chord (see Chapter 7).

Secondary Tonal Levels

There are times when a chord within a phrase is tonicized not only by its secondary dominant but also by an additional one or more chords preceding the secondary dominant. Such a series of chords might be called a modulation, but the fact that the series is followed by a cadence in the original key prevents the tonicized chord from achieving any status other than that of a temporary tonic. In measure 2 of Figure 1.17, an analysis of V/V–V/vi–vi could be appropriate. But the aural effect of the two chords preceding vi so strongly reinforces its tonic quality that an alternative symbolization is in order:

$$\frac{\text{IV}_5^6-\text{V}_5^6-\text{i}}{\text{vi}}$$

The symbols above the line indicate the relationship to the single symbol below the line, a secondary tonal progression, spoken here as "IV–V–I on the level of vi."

FIGURE 1.17

Bach, "Wach auf, mein Herz, und singe" (#93)

The next example, Figure 1.18, is the opening phrase of a movement in D minor. It includes a secondary tonal level on F, the length of which might seem to justify a modulation to F major, except that the phrase ends with a Phrygian cadence[3] in D minor, and then continues in that key. An analysis of this excerpt completely within

---

[3] iv$_6$–V in a minor key. Review *Elementary Harmony*, fifth edition, page 351.

the key of D minor produces symbols for an uncommon chord progression (V/VII–VII–III–iv–vii°–III), one that does not sound as such to the ear.

Note that when the harmony of this excerpt is considered without the symbols above the line, the resulting series of chords is i–V–i–III–iv–V–i, a common and regular chord progression.

FIGURE 1.18

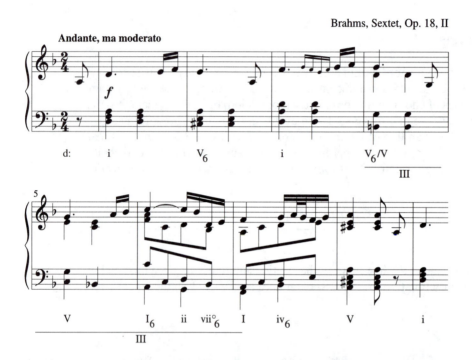

Brahms, Sextet, Op. 18, II

ASSIGNMENT 1.2 *Harmonic analysis.*   In these excerpts, expect to find the following, though not in this order: (1) pivot-chord modulation in which one chord is tonic, (2) pivot-chord modulation in which neither chord is tonic, (3) modulation by pivot pitch, (4) direct change of key, (5) modulation by sequence, and (6) secondary tonal level.

In case of difficulty, it will be helpful to write the chords in block form, without nonharmonic tones, arpeggiation, and so forth, as in Figure 1.7.

(1)

Mozart, Sonata in C Major for Piano, K. 545, I

(2)

Rimsky-Korsakov, *Scheherazade,* Op. 35, III

(3) In the course of this chorale, the passage is repeated, but with a different sequence. Describe the root movement of each sequence. Does either modulate, or does each remain in its key? Opinions may differ.

In the remaining two phrases, describe the difference in the harmonizations of the same melodic line.

Bach, "Eins ist not" (#280)

(4) There are two modulations in this excerpt, one to the new key and a return to the original key, each by a different means.

Beethoven, String Quartet, Op. 59, No. 2, III

(5) Check first the cadence of each phrase. Play the melody alone to determine the length of the second phrase and compare its cadence with that of the first phrase. Where is the cadence in a different key? Is a positive sense of reaching a new key achieved?

Brahms, Sonata for Violin and Piano, Op. 100, III

(6) Determine the name of the new key in excerpt 6. What is the degree of remoteness, expressed as the difference in number of accidentals (review page 5).

How does the circled E♭, the pivot pitch, function in each of the two keys? How does this use of the pivot pitch differ from those in Figures 1.16 and 1.17?

Massenet, *Werther,* Act III, "Ciel ai-je compris"

(7) In measure 42, the chord spelling is obviously enharmonic. What would be its spelling if the use of flats had continued? What would be its key name and its signature in flats (not in the circle of fifths)?

Beethoven, Sonata in C Minor for Piano, Op. 13, II

Part-Writing Modulations

No new part-writing procedures are necessary when writing a modulation. For review of the basic principles of part-writing, consult Appendix A in this volume, where you will find a concise description of each of the basic part-writing procedures.

Part-writing assignments in four voices, such as the assignment immediately following, may also be worked out in open score, (1) using treble, alto, tenor, and bass clefs, and (2) for instrumental combinations using appropriate clefs, key signatures, and transpositions. Review *Elementary Harmony*, fifth edition, Chapter 8, for detailed instruction, and Appendix B, "Instrumentation," in the present volume for specific information concerning each instrument.

ASSIGNMENT 1.3 *Part-writing.*   Add alto and tenor voices. Supply a roman-numeral analysis, identifying the pivot in each key. In other types of modulation, describe the procedure used.

(1)

(2)

(3)

(4)

(5)

(6) Instead of a modulation, look for the opportunity to use a three-chord secondary-level progression.

---

* Review *Elementary Harmony,* fifth edition, page 348, for the simultaneous use of $\flat\hat{7}$ and $\sharp\hat{7}$.

ASSIGNMENT 1.4 *Realizing a figured bass line.*   Follow these steps:

1. Check cadences for location of modulation(s) and identify the new key(s).
2. Write a harmonic analysis below the bass line.
3. Write a soprano line conforming to the spellings indicated by the figured bass.
4. Fill in the alto and tenor voices, adding nonharmonic tones where appropriate.

ASSIGNMENT 1.5 *Part-writing.*   Write the following chord progressions in four voices. Devise a satisfactory rhythmic pattern within each measure. Other keys may be used.

(a) G minor. $\frac{3}{4}$i | VI ii$^{\varnothing6}_{5}$ V |i$_6$ iv = |
                  i | VI ii°$_6$ V | i ‖

(b) E♭ major. $\frac{4}{4}$V$^6_5$ | I V^7 vi V$^4_2$ | i$_6$ iv i V | I$_6$ IV I$^6_4$V | I ‖
                  $\underline{\hspace{2cm}}$
                       ii

(c) F♯ major. $\frac{6}{8}$I | ii$^4_2$ V$^6_5$I I$_6$ | IV I$^6_4$ VI iii |
                  vi =
                  iv   V$^4_2$i$_6$ ii$^{\varnothing6}_{5}$ V | i ‖

Melody Harmonization

To harmonize a phrase containing a modulation, follow this procedure:

1. Analyze the cadence. Is it in a key different from that of the beginning of the phrase? If so, determine that relationship between the two keys. Use Table 1.1 to find the possible pivot chords.

2. Locate a place for the pivot chord. Look for melody tones that imply V–I or I_4^6–V–I in the new key. Does the first or second chord preceding this progression function in both keys? If so, it can be the pivot. Place the pivot numbers below the note for that chord.

3. Choose the harmony for the rest of the phrase.

4. Write the bass line first, using inversions where appropriate. Fill in alto and tenor voices. In all voices, use nonharmonic tones to enhance their melodic quality.

Observe this process in Figure 1.19.

FIGURE 1.19   *Harmonizing a Modulation*

1. The melody modulates from B♭ major to its submediant key, G minor, as indicated by the melodic cadence F♯–G.

2. The first indication of G minor is A–B♭ in the melodic line, suggesting V–i in G minor.

3. Preceding this A–B♭ is the pitch C, which can represent the triad C E♭ G, a likely harmony for the pivot ii = iv.

   In this melody, there is also another pivot location available. It is on the note B♭ in measure 2, I = III.

4. Harmonize the remainder of the melody. Here are two possibilities:

   B♭:   I | iii IV I I | ii =

   　　　　　　　　g: iv V i   ii$_6^\circ$ | i$_4^6$ V i ‖

   B♭:   I | iii IV I I | ii V I =

   　　　　　　　　g: III ii$_6^\circ$ | i$_4^6$ V i |

Always consider the possibility that your first harmonization could be improved upon through further experimentation. Look again at the chorale, excerpt 3 in Assignment 1.2. The melodic lines of measures 1–2 and 5–6 are identical. Measures 1–2 are diatonic, all in the key of D major. Measures 5–6 make use of simple chromaticism (as you have already analyzed) and include a modulation to B minor.

As an example of more imaginative writing, try, in Assignment 1.6, this progression in measures 7–8 of melody 5,

b: IV vii$_6^\circ$ I VI | ii$_5^{\varnothing 6}$ V i i |
　　　　　‾‾‾‾
　　　　　　III

instead of the easiest possibilities:

$$\text{b: i - - - | V - i - |}$$

or

$$\text{b: i - - VI | ii}^{\circ 6}_{5}\text{ V i - |}$$

ASSIGNMENT 1.6 *Melody harmonization.*   Harmonize one or more of these melodies as assigned. After completing your harmonization, it will be both interesting and instructive to compare your version with that of Bach, as found in the *371 Chorales*. Where Bach has provided more than one harmonization,[4] study each one. Additional settings for these chorale tunes are (1) 102, 343; (2) 121, 233, 350, 365; (3) 41, 120, 265. Note changes in the melodic lines, and especially the use in some cases of both quadruple and triple meter for the same hymn tune.

---

[4]Bach made as many as nine different harmonizations of some chorales. In the Mainous-Ottman edition, cross-references to all the harmonizations are given with each chorale.

ASSIGNMENT 1.7 *Writing modulations.*   Select an opening key, major or minor. From Table 1.1, choose a key relationship and one of the pairs of pivot chords indicated for that modulation; for example, E minor, modulation to the submediant, iv = vi. Write an example in four voices or for four instruments. Be sure that the original key is firmly established by at least one cadential progression, as in the examples in Assignment 1.5, and that the chords leading up to and away from the pivot chord are good, acceptable progressions. Strive for a good soprano melody line.

Keyboard Harmony

The harmonic progressions of Figure 1.20, written for keyboard practice, present modulations from both major and minor keys to each closely related key. For each example, the pivot chord chosen provides one of the easier ways of progressing from one key to another.

FIGURE 1.20

(9) to the mediant

i   iv   V   i

i =
VI   IV   V   I

(10) to the subtonic

i   iv   V   i

i =
ii   vii°₆   I

ASSIGNMENT 1.8 *Playing modulations to closely related keys.*   Play progressions from Figure 1.20. Note that each begins with I–IV–V–I (i–iv–V–i) to establish the original key.

(a) Play each progression in all keys. Any progression may be played beginning with the first chord in a different soprano position—positions of following chords will be determined by basic part-writing procedures.

(b) Modulate to a closely related key and return to the original key. For example, modulate from C major to the submediant and return to C major. Follow these steps:

1. Modulate to the submediant (a minor) as in progression 3.
2. Determine relationship of new key (A minor) to original key (C major)— C major is the mediant of A minor.
3. From A minor, modulate to the mediant as in progression 9.

TO PLAY A MODULATION FROM A MAJOR KEY TO:	PLAY PROGRESSION NO.	FOLLOWED BY PROGRESSION NO.
dominant and return	1	2
subdominant and return	2	1
submediant and return	3	9
supertonic and return	4	10
mediant and return	5	8

TO PLAY A MODULATION FROM A MINOR KEY TO:	PLAY PROGRESSION NO.	FOLLOWED BY PROGRESSION NO.
dominant and return	6	7
subdominant and return	7	6
submediant and return	8	5
mediant and return	9	3
subtonic and return	10	4

ASSIGNMENT 1.9 *Playing modulations, using other harmonic patterns.* Modulations can be played with pivots other than those shown in Figure 1.20. Choose a pivot from Table 1.1, establish the original key with I–IV–V–I, and follow the pivot with a common progression in the new key. If necessary, write out the chord progression first.

Figure 1.21 shows a modulation from a major key to its supertonic key using the less common pivot vi = v. The pivot in the new key is the minor dominant, requiring that its seventh scale step descend (C–B♭). v–VI is a logical choice, followed by the common progression ii $^{\varnothing}_{^6_5}$ –i$^6_4$–V–i.

FIGURE 1.21   *Example of a Modulation with a Less Common Pivot*

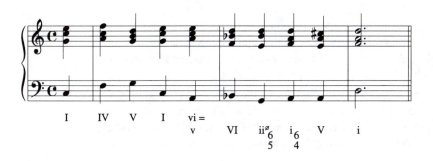

ASSIGNMENT 1.10   Play exercises from Assignment 1.3 at the keyboard.

ASSIGNMENT 1.11   Harmonize at the keyboard melodies chosen from Ottman, *Music for Sight Singing,* fourth edition (Prentice Hall, 1996), Chapters 5, 7, 8, 10, and 11, or from other sources.

Summary

A modulation occurs when music progresses from one key to another. Modulations can be classified in two ways: (1) by the relationship of the two keys and (2) by the method of achieving the new key.

There are two groups of key relationships:

1. *Closely related keys.* Two keys are closely related when the tonic of the new key is a diatonic triad in the original key. For calculation in minor keys, triads built on the degrees of the natural (pure) minor scale are used. Therefore, there are five closely related keys to each major and each minor key. (There are no related keys from vii° in major and ii° in minor, since a diminished triad cannot function as a tonic triad.)

   A close look at the five closely related keys shows that each has either the same signature as the original key or a signature with one accidental more or less than the signature of the original key. Also, the triads representing the tonic, subdominant, and dominant triads and the relative minor for each (or from a minor key, the relative major for each) are the tonic triads of the closely related keys.

2. *Remote, or foreign, keys.* Any key not closely related is in a remote relationship to the new key.

A modulation can be achieved in several ways, that by pivot chord being the most common.

1. *Pivot chord* (common chord). To be a pivot, a chord is spelled identically in both keys. Therefore, it has a dual function as the last chord of the original key and the first chord of the new key.

2. *Sequence.* In a harmonic sequence, the progression may end at a chord that can function as the tonic of the new key or that can lead to V or I of the new key. Also, a melodic/harmonic pattern such as a short phrase can be repeated at different pitch levels until the desired key is reached.

3. *Direct change of key.* A direct key change is accomplished (a) by simply stopping in one key and starting in another, (b) by chromatic alteration of a scale step in one of the voice lines, using the same letter name, and (c) by pivot pitch, in which a single pitch in the original key assumes a different function in the new key.

A *secondary tonal level* is a progression within a phrase that seems to achieve a tonic but instead immediately progresses to a cadence in the original key or another key.

2

Diminished Triads and Seventh Chords, Including Secondary Leading-Tone Functions

The importance of the dominant relationship has been stressed from the beginning of our study of harmony and has included consideration of

1. the dominant triad and the dominant seventh chord
2. the leading-tone triad
3. the secondary dominant triads and their seventh chords

Our continuing study of the dominant relationships will include the use of diminished triads in a secondary function, and diminished seventh chords in both primary and secondary functions.

Secondary Leading-Tone Triads

Just as the tonic triad can be approached by vii° in a dominant–tonic relationship, so can other major and minor triads in a key be tonicized by their secondary leading-tone triads. Figure 2.1 shows, in C major, the following:

At (*a*), the familiar diatonic leading-tone triad, vii°, and its resolution to tonic

At (*b*), the diminished triad F♯ A C (°/V) used as the secondary leading-tone triad to G B D (V)

At (*c*), this same progression (*b*) as used by Bach, which includes a suspension, G–F♯, in the diminished triad

FIGURE 2.1   *Comparison of the Diatonic and Secondary Leading-Tone Triads*

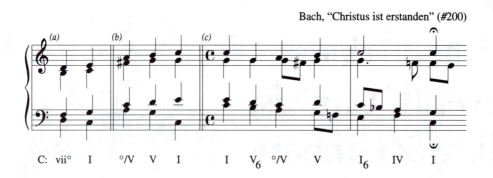

Figure 2.2 shows, in root position, the secondary leading-tone triad to each diatonic triad in major and minor keys. The figure shows two sets of identifying symbols. The first set correctly describes the function of each triad, but the symbol is lengthy to the point of being cumbersome.

In the second set, the simplified symbol "°/" means "vii°/." As an example, "°/III" means "vii°/III," spoken "seven of three." It is understood, of course, that like all diminished triads, these are ordinarily used only in first inversion; therefore, "°/" implies "$^\circ_6$/".

We will use the simplified symbols in this text, but both are acceptable.

FIGURE 2.2   *The Secondary Leading-Tone Triads*

(*a*)   Major keys

(*b*)   Minor keys

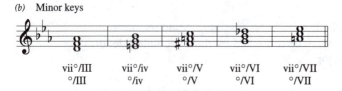

Observe that all the secondary leading-tone triads except °/III include accidentals not in the key signature. This single exception is spelled the same as the diatonic ii°. The chords °/III and ii° are differentiated by their resolutions as shown in Figure 2.3. Although at (*b*) the progression may appear to be ii°–III, the *aural impression* is more likely to be a tonicization of E♭ G B♭, just as in Figure 2.1*c* where F♯ A C tonicizes G B D.

FIGURE 2.3   *The Triad D F A♭ Used as ii°–V and as °/III–III in C Minor*

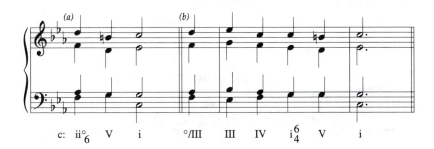

ASSIGNMENT 2.1   Spell each of the secondary leading-tone triads in any major or minor key. For example, to spell °/iv in E minor, (1) the root of iv is A, (2) the leading tone to A is G♯, and (3) a diminished triad spelled on G♯ is G♯ B D.

In the Workbook: Answers are given.

Uses of the Secondary Leading-Tone Triads

The simplest and most common use of secondary leading-tone progressions is found within the phrase as shown in the representative examples, Figures 2.1*c* and 2.3. In addition, the °/V–V may function as a cadence in the same way as the V/V–V discussed in Chapter 1, and shown here as Figure 2.4. The alternative analysis indicates the less likely presence of a modulation.

FIGURE 2.4   *The °/V at the Cadence*

Whereas V/V frequently progresses to the tonic six-four, use of the triad °/V with the same destination is quite uncommon. Bach, in Figure 2.5, neatly solves several problems with the °/V–I$_4^6$ by imaginative use of nonharmonic tones.

The secondary leading tone D♯ (of D♯ F♯ A) reaches the next harmonic tone, C (of A C E), without sounding an actual augmented second. D♯ is followed by an upper neighbor (E), the resolution of which is an accented passing tone (D). In this way, the necessary upward resolution of D♯ is accomplished, after which the melodic line can incorporate the ♭$\hat7$–♭$\hat6$ of the descending minor scale.[1]

Note also the series of first inversions, with the upper voice either in thirds or in sixths with the bass (review *Elementary Harmony*, pages 209 and 376).

FIGURE 2.5   °*V–I$_4^6$ at the Cadence*

Bach, *English Suite II,* BWV 807, "Sarabande"

Frequently seen is the use of a secondary leading-tone triad between a triad and its inversion, or the reverse, like the progression I–vii°–I$_6$ already studied. Figure 2.6 shows two such occurrences, on the levels of vi and ii in A major. These could be symbolized as i vii$_6^\circ$ i and i vii$_6^\circ$ i, respectively.
             vi   ii

FIGURE 2.6   *Examples of °/vi and °/ii*

Schumann, *Album for the Young,* Op. 68, No. 43

---

[1]The symbol ^ means "scale step." $\hat5$ means "fifth scale step." This symbol, continued from *Elementary Harmony*, will be used throughout this text.

Compared with diminished seventh chords, these triads are used quite infrequently, in spite of many possibilities offered by the variety available.

Diminished Seventh Chords

Adding a seventh above the root of a diminished triad will produce a diminished seventh chord. There are two varieties, depending upon the size of the seventh.

1. The *diminished-diminished* or *fully diminished seventh chord* includes the interval of a diminished seventh between the root and the seventh of the chord. The name of the chord is commonly shortened to *diminished seventh chord*, adding the adverb "fully" when necessary to distinguish it from the other variety. The symbol °7 will mean "fully diminished seventh chord," as in Figure 2.7a.

2. The *diminished minor seventh chord* includes the interval of a minor seventh between the root and the seventh of the chord. It is usually called a *half-diminished seventh chord* (only the triad is diminished). The symbol ø7 will mean "half-diminished seventh chord," as in Figure 2.7b.

FIGURE 2.7   *The Two Varieties of Diminished Seventh Chords*

ASSIGNMENT 2.2   Spell diminished seventh chords above these pitch names:

E, C♯, A, G♯, C×, E♯, D♯, G, B♭

Spelling can be easily accomplished by adding a minor third above the fifth of the diminished triad. *Example:* B D F + m3 (A♭) = B D F A♭.

In the Workbook: Answers are given.

ASSIGNMENT 2.3   Spell half-diminished seventh chords above these pitch names:

B, E, F♯, A G♯, F×, C, G, B♭, D♯

Spelling can be easily accomplished by adding a major third above the fifth of the diminished triad. *Example:* D♯ F♯ A + M3 (C♯) = D♯ F♯ A C♯.

In the Workbook: Answers are given.

Characteristics of the Diminished Seventh Chord

The diminished seventh chord (referring to the diminished-diminished variety) displays features unlike other chords studied thus far. Composers have taken copious advantage of its many unique features, as will be shown later in this and other chapters.

1. *Construction.* The chord is made up exclusively of minor thirds. The interval from the seventh up to the root is written as an augmented second, the enharmonic equivalent of the minor third.

FIGURE 2.8   *Intervals in the Diminished Seventh Chord*

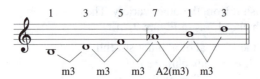

In addition, every interval located by skipping a member of the chord is a tritone: a diminished fifth or its enharmonic equivalent, an augmented fourth. For these reasons, the diminished seventh chord lacks any semblance of stability; it is a "restless" chord, which must seek its resolution.

FIGURE 2.9   *Tritones in the Diminished Seventh Chord*

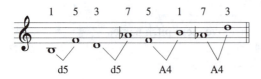

2. *Inversions.* Though on paper the chord can be inverted, its sound remains the same, regardless of the arrangement of the tones. The equal division of the octave prevents any inversion from having a characteristic sound of its own, in contrast to inversions of most other chords. In fact, each inversion can be spelled enharmonically, so that the lowest sounding note could serve in turn as root, third, fifth, or seventh. In Figure 2.10, the lowest note of each inversion serves as the root of an enharmonic spelling.

FIGURE 2.10   *Inversions of the Diminished Seventh Chord*

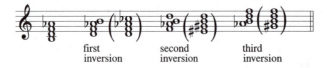

3. *Sonorities.* In terms of *sound*, there are only three different diminished seventh chords (Figure 2.11 *a, b,* and *c*). At *d*, the chord, though spelled differently from *a,* is simply the inversion of *a*. Any other possible spelling of any diminished seventh chord will also prove to be a respelling of one of the three sounds represented by *a, b,* or *c*.

FIGURE 2.11   *The Three Possible Sounds*

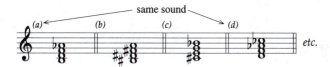

4. *Expression of function.* Different spellings of the same sound are necessary in the score to indicate differing functions of the same sound. For example, the two chords in Figure 2.12 sound the same, but they are spelled differently to express different functions of that sound: vii°⁷ (B D F A♭) progresses to I whereas °⁷/vi (G♯ B D F) progresses to vi.

FIGURE 2.12   *Same Sound but Different Function*

5. *Resolution of the seventh.* The seventh of the diminished seventh chord may resolve in either of two ways:
   a. With a change of harmony at the point of the resolution of the seventh (Figure 2.13*a*, showing such a resolution in both the V⁷ and the vii°⁷).
   b. With no movement in the other three voices (*early resolution*), resulting in a major-minor seventh chord at the point of resolution (Figure 2.13*b* and *c*). In such cases, the apparent seventh can usually be considered a nonharmonic tone. (See also Figure 2.18.)

FIGURE 2.13   *Resolutions of the Seventh*

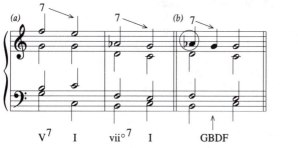

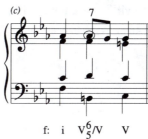

Terminology Variant

In an alternative analysis, both the diminished triad and the diminished seventh chord may be considered dominant chords, each with its root missing. In this view, the vii° triad is V^7 with a missing root, symbolized V°_{7}, and the diminished seventh chord is a V^9 with its root missing, symbolized V°_{9}. This concept will be helpful in certain analyses.

FIGURE 2.14   *Alternative Symbols*

A minor: V^7 V°_{7} or vii° V^9 V°_{9} or vii°^{7}

The Leading-Tone Seventh Chord

These are the useful seventh chords built on the leading tone of a key (Figure 2.15):

1. vii°^{7} in a minor key is a diminished seventh chord built on the leading tone, $\sharp\hat{7}$ (Figure 2.15*a*).

2. vii°^{7} in a major key is spelled identically to the vii°^{7} in a minor key. For this spelling to be achieved in major, $\hat{6}$ must be chromatically lowered one half step (Figure 2.15*b*, where A has been lowered to A♭).

3. vii$^{\o7}$ in a major key is a half-diminished seventh chord built on the leading tone (Figure 2.15*c*). It is used far less frequently than the vii°^{7}. In a minor key (Figure 2.15*d*), its seventh, which should descend, is also $\sharp\hat{6}$, which should ascend. The same note cannot, of course, resolve both ways at once.

FIGURE 2.15   *The Leading-Tone Seventh Chords*

c: vii$^{\o7}$ i   C: vii°^{7} C: vii$^{\o7}$ c: vii$^{\o7}$

ASSIGNMENT 2.4   (*a*) Spell the vii°^{7} in each major and minor key.
     (*b*) Spell the vii$^{\o7}$ in each major key.

In the Workbook: Answers are given.

Examples of Uses of the Leading-Tone Seventh Chords

The leading-tone seventh chords almost invariably progress to tonic. When used as a dominant function in any other way, such as in a deceptive cadence, the chord is ordinarily respelled, even though the sound is the same.

The use of any diminished seventh chord in any inversion is acceptable and, indeed, common. Figures 2.16 and 2.17 show the vii°⁷ in first inversion and in second inversion, respectively. Note the resolutions, the descending seventh, and the ascending root (leading tone).

FIGURE 2.16   *vii°⁷, First Inversion*

Bach, "Ist Gott mein Schild und Helfersmann" (#122)

FIGURE 2.17   *vii°⁷, Second Inversion*

Mozart, Sonata in C Major for Piano, K. 279, II

The seventh, B♭, in Figure 2.18 resolves to A while the harmony is static, an example of the early resolution of the seventh. The B♭ is quite obviously a simple upper-neighbor tone, so the harmony is best analyzed as the first inversion of V⁷.

FIGURE 2.18   *Early Resolution of the Seventh*

Bach, "Jesu, meine Freude" (#356)

Slightly more complex is the explanation for the repeated E♭'s in the bass clef of Figure 2.19. Above each "V" in the analysis, the early resolution of E♭ before a change of harmony indicates the use of neighbor tones. The E♭ above "i" usually functions in the same way, even though there appears to be a VI triad. The latter is an excellent example of the "consonant" nonharmonic tone described in *Elementary Harmony*, fifth edition, page 273.

FIGURE 2.19   *Neighbor Tones in V and i*

Chopin, Nocturne, Op. 37, No. 1

The less common vii°⁷ is found in the next example at the point of a dramatic climax in the theme of this scherzo movement.

FIGURE 2.20   *The vii$^{\varnothing 7}$ Chord*

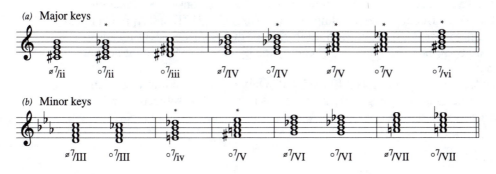

Schubert, Sonata in A Minor for Piano, D. 845, III

Secondary Leading-Tone Seventh Chords

Figure 2.21 shows all the possible diminished secondary leading-tone seventh chords, but note that those with the asterisk (*) are by far more common than the others. A fully diminished seventh chord is possible above each root.

A secondary leading-tone chord may be either fully diminished (°7) or half-diminished (°7). The principal function of each is to tonicize its following triad. Whereas the °7 can tonicize both major and minor triads, the $^{\varnothing 7}$ is limited to the tonicizing of major triads, for the same reason as that described for the vii$^{\varnothing 7}$. (On page 40, review item 3 and Figure 2.15.)

FIGURE 2.21   *The Secondary Leading-Tone Seventh Chords*

(a) Major keys

$^{\varnothing 7}$/ii $^{\circ 7}$/ii $^{\circ 7}$/iii $^{\varnothing 7}$/IV $^{\circ 7}$/IV $^{\varnothing 7}$/V $^{\circ 7}$/V $^{\circ 7}$/vi

(b) Minor keys

$^{\varnothing 7}$/III $^{\circ 7}$/III $^{\circ 7}$/iv $^{\circ 7}$/V $^{\varnothing 7}$/VI $^{\circ 7}$/VI $^{\varnothing 7}$/VII $^{\circ 7}$/VII

In the analysis symbols, "vii" is again omitted in the interest of simplification. Therefore, for example, "°7/ii" means "vii°7/ii."

For inversions, use ° or ° with the appropriate figured bass symbol. For example, °$^6_5$/ii means "the first inversion of the vii°7/ii."

In a series of secondary dominant chords where one or more of these is replaced by a secondary leading-tone chord, analysis symbols may be abbreviated by use of connecting arrows (*Elementary Harmony*, page 388). In C major, for example, the second line below the chord spellings shows abbreviated symbols:

	E G B	C♯ E G B♭	D F♯ A	G B D	C E G
	vi	°7/ii	V/V	V	I
or	vi	°7/	→ V/V →	V	I

See Figure 2.24*b*, measure 19.

ASSIGNMENT 2.5   Spell the secondary leading-tone seventh chords in any given major or minor key.

In the Workbook: Answers are given.

Regular Resolution of Secondary Leading-Tone Seventh Chords

The secondary leading-tone seventh chords shown in sequence in Figure 2.21 resolve in the same manner as the vii°7, also shown; that is, their roots resolve up a half step and their sevenths resolve down a half step.

Some note groupings visually similar to °7 chords may at times be better described as groups of nonharmonic tones. At ① in Figure 2.22, the E♯ and the G♯ clearly sound as chromatic lower neighbors. Even when the bass (D) is included, forming E♯ G♯ (B) D, the impression of individual dissonances remains.

At ②, we see a complete °7. It is unlikely that we would consider its function to include four nonharmonic tones, reading down as App, UN, UPT, and App. On the other hand, in Figure 2.29, the three tones in each of the sonorities identified as ct° will be heard by some to function as a °7 chord, and by others as a group of nonharmonic tones.

How are these two concepts differentiated? Only by the aural impression upon the listener. Analyses, including those given in this text, must be subjective and will differ from person to person.

FIGURE 2.22   *ii°7, °7/IV, °7/V*

Schumann, Concerto in A Minor
for Piano and Orchestra, Op. 54, I

Figure 2.23 includes five diminished seventh chords. Two of these are half-diminished and are included in a three-chord harmonic sequence. This example includes several features of interest, two of which are fully discussed later, as indicated.

1. In the sequence, two of the diminished seventh chords are ^{ø7} and one is ^{o7}. Why did Mozart choose the ^{o7} rather than the ^{ø7}?

2. Why can ♮7 and ♯7 sound simultaneously? (Review *Elementary Harmony*, page 348.) Remember that the small note F♮ is the appoggiatura that receives half the value of its following note—in this case, a sixteenth note sounding on the beat.

3. Successive diminished seventh chords will be examined later. See Figure 2.30 and accompanying discussion.

4. Resolution of ^{o7}/V to I_4^6 will also be examined later in this chapter. See Figure 2.26 and accompanying discussion.

FIGURE 2.23   *vii^{ø7}, ^{ø7}/IV, ^{o7}/V, ^{o7}/vi*

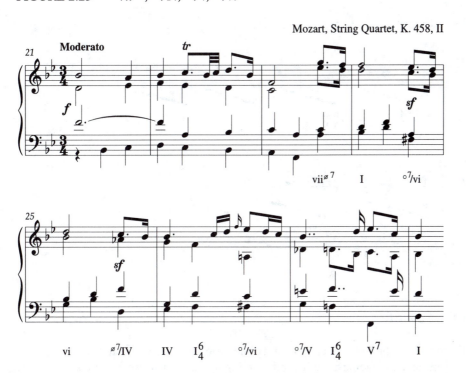

Mozart, String Quartet, K. 458, II

There is usually no change of spelling in diminished seventh chords when they are found in inversion, even though to the ear the lowest sounding note could be the root of the chord. The spelled root and seventh resolve exactly as in the root position of the chord. In Figure 2.24, these resolutions are necessarily implied because of the arpeggiation. Note in the final two measures that V/V progresses not to V but to its substitute, vii^{o7}.

FIGURE 2.24   *°⁷ Chords in Inversion*

Brahms, Intermezzo, Op. 76, No. 7

Early Resolution of the Seventh

The early resolution, described in this chapter in connection with the vii°⁷, applies equally well to the secondary leading-tone sevenths. In Figure 2.25, measure 3, the E♭ of F♯ A C E♭ resolves to D, resulting in a D F♯ A C chord, V⁷/iv. The simpler analysis is that of a V⁷/iv for two beats with appoggiatura E♭. In measure 5, the pattern is repeated in the V⁷ chord.

However, when the aural impression of a diminished seventh sonority is as positive as that in Figure 2.25, analysis as a diminished seventh progressing to a dominant seventh cannot be ruled out. When an objective analysis is difficult, either solution is acceptable.

FIGURE 2.25   *Early Resolution of the Seventh*

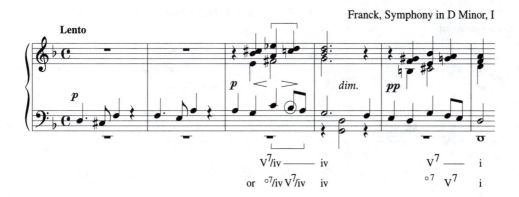

Franck, Symphony in D Minor, I

Resolution of °7/V to Tonic Six-Four, Major Keys

It has been established in earlier studies that the tonic six-four functions as a dominant chord, containing two nonharmonic tones. Therefore, just as the V⁷/V can resolve to V through the tonic six-four, so can the °7/V.

When °7/V resolves to V (Figure 2.26*a;* C major, F♯ A C E♭), its seventh makes
the usual downward resolution, E♭ to D. But when the tonic six-four is placed between °7/V and V (Figure 2.26*b*), the E♭ must resolve *up* to E before reaching D of
the V triad. Many composers let this stand, as can be seen in Figure 2.23, measure 27,
where the D♭ of E G B♭ D♭ resolves up to D.

But other composers prefer to spell the °7/V enharmonically. In Figure 2.26*c*,
D♯ F♯ A C replaces F♯ A C E♭, so that D♯, instead of E♭, resolves to E. Although the
chord appears to be spelled as °7/iii, it functions as °7/V. This sonority is shown in another key in Figure 2.27 as used by Haydn. What is the °7/V spelling of this chord?

Another explanation of this progression is found following Figure 2.29.

FIGURE 2.26   *°7/V–I⁶₄, Alternative Spelling*

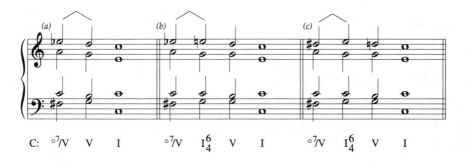

FIGURE 2.27

Haydn, Quartet in G Major, Hob. III:81, I

* Note the deceptive resolution of $\text{V}\frac{7}{}$/vi in progressing to IV, more graphically stated in the symbol $\frac{\text{V}^7\text{–vi}}{\text{IV}}$.

Nondominant Diminished Seventh Chords

Two additional diminished seventh chords (in major only) do not function as leading-tone chords. They differ in that each has a tone in common with its chord of resolution; thus they are often called *common-tone diminished seventh chords*. The common tones are the tonic (1) and the dominant (5). From this information, these chords many be symbolized as ct°$\hat{1}$ and ct°$\hat{5}$. In score analysis, ct° will serve for both, since the common tone will be obvious in the music. The addition of "1" and "5" will be helpful in text materials when necessary for differentiation.

Each common tone is the seventh of its chord. Spelling downward in minor thirds reveals that the chords are built on the roots $\sharp\hat{2}$ and $\sharp\hat{6}$, respectively, each of which moves up one half step to its chord of resolution. Figure 2.28*a* shows the single regular resolution of ct°$\hat{1}$ to I; Figure 2.28*b* shows the resolution of ct°$\hat{5}$ to V and to V^6_5.

Note that the spelling of ct°1 (D♯ F♯ A C) is also the spelling of °7/iii. They are easily distinguished by their resolutions. There is no spelling conflict with ct°$\hat{5}$.

FIGURE 2.28   *Resolutions of ct° Chords*

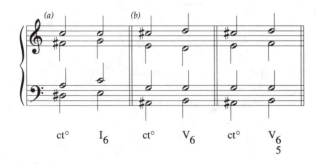

Figure 2.29 shows both ct° chords in successive measures as used by Beethoven. That ct° chords can be used freely in inversion is shown in measure 2 by the first inversion of ct°5̂. Regardless of the inversion, the common tone is held, the "root" of the ct° rises one half step, and the other voices fall easily into place.

FIGURE 2.29   *Typical Use of the ct° Chords*

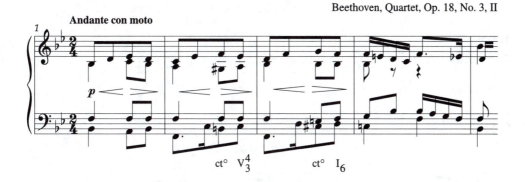

In figure 2.26*c*, the °7/V in C major, F♯ A C E♭, was replaced with its enharmonic spelling D♯ F♯ A C, thus avoiding an upward resolution of E♭ to E in progressing to tonic six-four. It so happens that D♯ F♯ A C is also the spelling of the ct°1̂ in C major. Thus, there appear to be three alternative explanations for the progression °7/V–I$^6_4$:

1. The "regular" spelling in Figure 2.26*b*
2. The substitute spelling in Figure 2.26*c*
3. Considering the tonic six-four a chord in its own right, identification of the °7 as ct° because of the common tone between the two chords

ASSIGNMENT 2.6   Spell in each major key the two ct° chords. Here is a simple method:

ct°1̂: 1̂ is the seventh of the chord. Spell downward in minor thirds.

ct°5̂: 5̂ is the seventh of the chord. Spell downward in minor thirds.

In the Workbook: Answers are given.

Successive Diminished Seventh Chords

Diminished seventh chords are often used freely in succession and without concern for resolution of sevenths or of altered tones. In such a succession, any feeling for a specific key is often lost until the final diminished seventh chord, which usually resolves normally. In this situation, roman-numeral symbols are without value, except to identify the spelling of the chord. In Figure 2.30, four successive diminished seventh chords effectively eliminate a sense of key until the last of the four, C♯ E G B♭, assumes the role of a °7/V chord in resolving to i$^6_4$.

FIGURE 2.30   *Successive Diminished Seventh Chords*

Bizet, *Les Pêcheurs des Perles,*
Act II, No. 8, "Duo"

Descending Resolution of the Root
of a Diminished Seventh Chord

In all previous chords of dominant function, including V, V^7, vii°, and vii°^{7}, we have seen that the leading tone of the chord can resolve down by half step, always using the same letter name, when progressing to a chord with a different spelling. The same is true with the secondary leading-tone seventh chords. Figure 2.31, measure 156, shows the root B, of B D F A♭ (°^{7}/V), moving down by half step to B♭ of C E G B♭.

This movement does not occur in the nondominant diminished seventh chords.

FIGURE 2.31

Haydn, Quartet in F Minor *(Razor),* Hob. III:61, II

The Melodic Augmented Second

When diminished seventh chords are used, the melodic interval of the augmented second may sometimes appear, especially when the chord is arpeggiated or repeated in different positions, as in Figure 2.30, measures 93, 94, and 96.

Composers occasionally use this interval other than in a diminished seventh chord. In a minor key, a scale passage displayed prominently in the musical texture may include all or part of the harmonic form of the scale, ascending or descending.

FIGURE 2.32   *The A2 in a Scale Line*

Beethoven, Quartet,
Op. 59, No. 3, II

The two descending scale lines of Figure 2.32 display the descending harmonic minor scale, including the augmented second, leading to an authentic cadence in D minor. Obviously, the V triad requires a C♯. Use of the descending melodic form of the scale, using C♮, would imply the minor v triad, while at the same time, each ♭$\hat{6}$ must progress down. There is no choice but a melodic line including C♯–B♭.

The interval is also used as an appoggiatura figure where the second note of the augmented second is the dissonant tone (Figure 2.33, measure 63, E–F𝄪).

FIGURE 2.33   *The A2 in a Nonharmonic Tone Pattern*

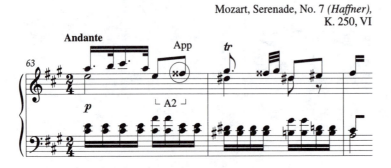

Mozart, Serenade, No. 7 *(Haffner),*
K. 250, VI

Any other melodic augmented second you are likely to encounter will have its own particular reason for its use, to be determined by the use of the interval in its context.[2]

ASSIGNMENT 2.7 *Harmonic analysis.*   Each excerpt contains one or more of the various uses of diminished sonorities described in this chapter. Make a roman-numeral analysis below the staff and describe the use of the diminished sonorities.

---

[2]The melodic second used to imply scale lines of eastern Europe or the Orient was discussed and illustrated in *Elementary Harmony*, page 132. For an example in this volume, see Assignment 7.4 (6).

(1)

Bach, "Ich dank dir, Gott" (#223)

(2)

Mozart, Sonata in D Major for Piano, K. 311, II

(3)

Clara Schumann, Sonata in G Minor
for Piano (1841), I, II

(4)

Beethoven, Symphony No. 5, Op. 67, IV
(incomplete score)

(5)

Schumann, *Nachtstücke,* Op. 23, No. 2

Markiert und lebhaft M.M. ♩ = 76

(6) This example has a key signature for A major, and begins and ends with A major triads. But does it begin in the key of A major? If not, what other key? Try analyses under both conditions. Which one is more satisfactory?

The F♯ A C triad in measure 2 is an altered form of F♯ A C♯. See Chapter 7.

Brahms, "Dein Herzen mild," Op. 62, No. 4

(7)

Haydn, Quartet, Hob. III:71, I

(8) This excerpt is noteworthy for its use of dissonance in conjunction with diminished seventh chords. In each group of four sixteenth notes, which notes sound dissonant, either as a nonharmonic tone or as a seventh of a chord?

At measure 217, the three lower notes spell C E B♭, seemingly a major-minor seventh chord. The aural effect, like that in the previous measure, is a nonharmonic approach to the triad on the second beat. The appoggiatura B♭ resolves to A and the passing tone C to C♯. Usually, this C is written as B♯ to emphasize visually its nonharmonic function, but that is not practical here because of the B♭ above it. This is another good example demonstrating that it is the sound of the notation that we are analyzing, and not its appearance.

In measure 218, why do C♮ and C♯ sound simultaneously? (Review *Elementary Harmony*, Figures 16.3 and 16.4.) Where else in this excerpt do similar clashes occur?

Mozart, Quartet for Strings, K. 499, I

Part-Writing Diminished Triads and Seventh Chords

Procedures listed here consist of a review both of known practices and of others unique to the part-writing of diminished triads and seventh chords.

1. Secondary leading-tone triads are almost invariably in first inversion.
2. The seventh of a seventh chord resolves down.
3. The secondary leading tone (the root of the triad or seventh chord) will ascend. Exception: The root may descend a half step to a pitch of the same letter name. Review Figure 2.31.
4. When diminished seventh chords are used in succession, altered tones may move in any direction.
5. A cross-relation is acceptable when one of the tones is a member of a diminished seventh chord. The characteristic sound of the chord distracts the ear from the usual unpleasant effect of the cross-relation.

6. In the half-diminished seventh chord, root in bass and seventh in soprano, care must be taken to avoid parallel fifths, as in Figure 2.34*a*. Doubling the third or the fifth of the triad of resolution is usually effective, as in Figure 2.34*b* and *c*. See Mozart's solution in Figure 2.23.

FIGURE 2.34

7. In the nondominant chords, the seventh is held over while other tones move up a half step. See Figures 2.28 and 2.29.

ASSIGNMENT 2.8 *Part-writing secondary leading-tone triads.*   Fill in alto and tenor voices. Write in harmonic analysis.

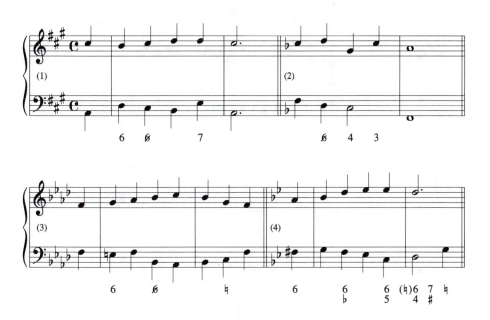

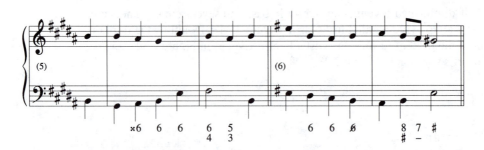

In the Workbook: Answers are given.

ASSIGNMENT 2.9 *Part-writing diminished seventh chords.*   Fill in alto and tenor voices. Make harmonic analysis.

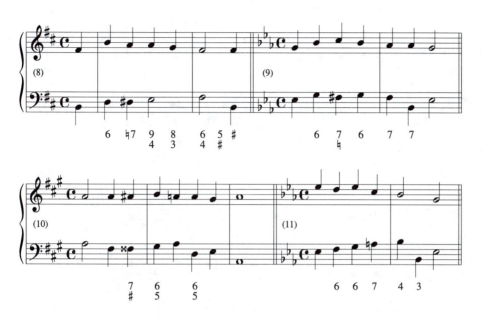

In the Workbook: Answers are given.

ASSIGNMENT 2.10 *Part-writing extended exercises.*

ASSIGNMENT 2.11 *Realizing a figured bass line.*   Follow these steps:

1. Determine the harmony. Place chord symbols below each bass note.
2. Write the soprano line.
3. Fill in inner voices, using nonharmonic tones as appropriate.

(1)

(2)

(3)

(4)

(5)

(6)

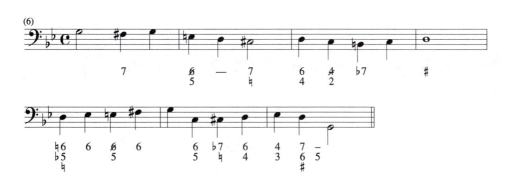

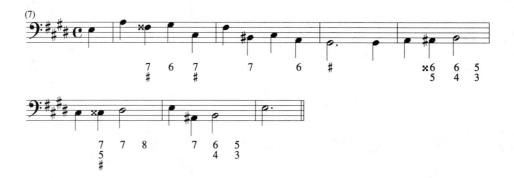

Additionally, exercises from Assignment 2.14 can be used here. First, choose a particular item and a particular key. Then write out the bass line in accordance with the roman numerals and their inversion indications. The bass line of exercise 1, if in D major, would be D F♯ G F♯ E D.

Use a time signature and a rhythmic pattern of your choosing. The final tonic triad should occur on a strong beat, preferably the first beat of the measure.

ASSIGNMENT 2.12 *Melody harmonization.*   In harmonizing each melody, use vii°⁷ and any other diminished seventh chord at appropriate places. Include a harmonic analysis.

Keyboard Harmony

ASSIGNMENT 2.13   *Playing diminished seventh chords.*

(*a*) Play the C major tonic triad followed by a diminished seventh chord, choosing from Figure 2.21 a chord marked with an asterisk. Follow the diminished seventh chord with its resolution and a common progression back to tonic, as in Figure 2.35.

(*b*) Continue as in *a*, using other keys as chosen or assigned.

(*c*) Continue as above, but experiment with various inversions of the diminished seventh chord, as in Figure 2.36.

FIGURE 2.35

Example: Play the °7/vi in C major.

FIGURE 2.36

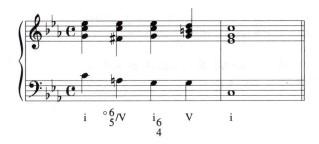

ASSIGNMENT 2.14   Play these harmonic progressions in keys as chosen or assigned. Some choices of the position of the initial tonic triad may lead to difficult part-writing. In such cases, start over with a different initial soprano position.

1. I   °7/V   V$_2^4$ I$_6$ vii$_6^°$ I
2. I   °7/V   vii°$_3^4$ I$_6$ vii$_6^°$ I
3. I   °7/vi   vi   °7/V   V$_2^4$ I$_6$ V/V   V   I
4. I   °7/ii   ii   °7/iii   iii   V$_3^4$ I
5. i   °$_5^6$/V   V$_5^6$ i   °7/iv   iv   V   i
6. i   ii$_2^{ø4}$ vii°7   i   °7/VI   VI   ii$_5^{ø6}$ V   i
7. I   ii   ct°$\hat{1}$ I$_6$ ^{ø6}/V   I$_4^6$ V   I
8. I   vi   ct°$\hat{5}$ V$_5^6$ I   ii$_5^6$ V   I

Summary

A secondary leading-tone triad tonicizes its triad of resolution in the same manner as the vii° triad progressing to tonic. Any major or minor triad may be so tonicized.

Diminished seventh chords are of two varieties, each based on a diminished triad: (1) the diminished-diminished (or fully diminished) seventh chord with the interval of a diminished seventh above its root, and (2) the diminished minor (or half-diminished) seventh with the interval of a minor seventh above its root.

The fully diminished seventh chord displays these features: (1) The distance from one of its members to the next is always a minor third, or its enharmonic equivalent, the augmented second; (2) any pair of successive thirds produces a tritone; (3) the chord sounds the same in any inversion; and (4) there are but three different diminished seventh chord sounds.

Resolution of the seventh in either variety of the chord can occur in two ways: (1) The seventh resolves together with the other members of the chord, and (2) the seventh resolves alone, resulting in a major-minor seventh chord.

The leading-tone seventh chord in a major key is either vii°7 or viiø7, whereas in a minor key only vii°7 is used.

The secondary leading-tone seventh chord tonicizes its following major or minor triad just as the secondary leading-tone triad does, its root ascending one half step to the following root.

There are two nondominant diminished seventh chords, identified as ct°$\hat{1}$ and ct°$\hat{5}$ and commonly called *common-tone diminished seventh chords*. The seventh of each has a tone in common with its chord of resolution, the tonic and the dominant, respectively. As spelled in thirds, the root of each is ♯$\hat{2}$ and ♯$\hat{6}$, respectively, each rising by half step in resolving a $\hat{3}$ and $\hat{7}$.

Diminished seventh chords in succession may follow each other in no particular order, thus temporarily confusing the sense of key. The last in the series usually resolves as described above.

Like the third of secondary dominant chords, the root of the diminished seventh chord may resolve down by half step to a tone using the same letter name.

3

Modulation with Diminished Seventh Chords

The $^{\circ7}$ as a pivot chord is more versatile than any other chord that could be used for this purpose. Any $^{\circ7}$ can follow a given chord in the original key and then become a usable function in any other major or minor key from the circle of fifths. You might liken the $^{\circ7}$ pivot to the Neutral position in a stick-shift automobile transmission: You can leave any gear (original key), go into Neutral ($^{\circ7}$ pivot), and shift into any other gear (new key). See Figure 3.1.

FIGURE 3.1   *The $^{\circ}7$ as a Pivot Chord*

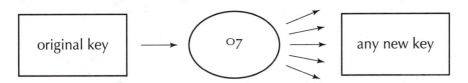

These characteristics of the $^{\circ7}$ chord allow this versatility:

1. When inverted, its sound is no different from any other position of the chord.
2. Any $^{\circ7}$ chord and each of its inversions can be spelled enharmonically. The chord E♯ G♯ B D, for example, can be spelled enharmonically as F A♭ C♭ E♭♭, and the first inversion of either of these as G♯ B D F. Any enharmonic respelling that produces a root that can function as a leading tone can be useful as a pivot. Thus, any chord with a flatted note serving as a root, except B♭, is not useful.[1]

---

[1]The spelling B♭ D♭ F♭ A♭♭ serves for the vii$^{\circ7}$ of C♭ major. Other uses of the $^{\circ7}$ chord with a flatted note as the root are rare and, when required, are most likely to be found spelled enharmonically.

Schubert's modulation from B♭ major to F♯ minor in Figure 3.2*a* shows the process. It is a particularly good illustration because it shows the °7 as spelled in both keys, whereas in most instances the composer writes the °7 pivot only in the new key. Reducing this harmonic progression to block chords as in Figure 3.2*b* helps to clarify the procedure.

FIGURE 3.2   *The °7 as Pivot, Both Spellings Shown*

B♭ major, °7/ii, B D F   A♭ =

F♯ minor, vii°7,   E♯ G♯ B D (both spellings shown)

Schubert, Sonata in B♭ Major for Piano, D. 960, I

*The bass movement, G♯ to C♯, creates an ambiguous harmony, vii °7 or V9.

Bb: I_4^6 V $^{\circ 7}/ii$ =
f#:   vii$^{\circ 7}$ V^7 i

Follow the composer's procedures step by step.

1. B D F Ab was chosen as the pivot, appearing first in second inversion and followed by third inversion. It is not necessary to justify a "good" harmonic progression from the preceding V^7 chord. The V^7 (or any other chord) is simply moving into neutral territory; any $^{\circ 7}$ in any inversion could have been used, assuming a satisfactory part-writing connection between the two.

2. B D F Ab is repeated in its enharmonic equivalent of E# G# B D with the seventh as its highest tone.

3. The seventh, D, resolves early to C#, the V^7 of F# minor.

Modulating to All Keys from a Single $^{\circ 7}$ Chord

Table 3.1 (page 72) shows how a single diminished seventh chord, B D F Ab, can be used to modulate to all keys. (A similar table can be made based on any $^{\circ 7}$ spelling.) Although the chart offers almost endless possibilities, those used by composers are relatively limited. But for many musicians, including keyboard players and arrangers for instrumental ensembles, this knowledge is particularly valuable in making rapid changes of key.

The table is intended principally for reference and need not be memorized. However, a careful perusal will facilitate understanding of the modulatory process. In studying the table, keep these facts in mind:

1. The enharmonic spellings of B D F Ab are

   D F Ab Cb   F Ab Cb Ebb   G# B D F

   Cx E# G# B   E# G# B D

2. In this table, $^{\circ 7}$ chords in the new key are limited to vii$^{\circ 7}$, $^{\circ 7}/IV$ (or iv), and $^{\circ 7}/V$. These represent common uses of the three different $^{\circ 7}$ sounds. Also common is the use of nondominant diminished seventh chords—for example, B D F Ab, vii$^{\circ 7}$ in C = ct$^{\circ}$ in Ab major (common tone, Ab).

TABLE 3.1   Modulation from C Major and C Minor to All Keys Using a Single °7 Chord, B D F A♭ and Its Enharmonic Spellings

C, c	vii°7, B D F A♭	G♭	vii°7, F A♭ C♭ E♭♭
C#, c#	°7/IV (iv), E# G# B D	G, g	°7/IV (iv), B D F A♭
D, d	°7/V, G# B D F	g#	°7/V, C× E# G# B
d#	vii°7, C× E# G# B	A, a	vii°7, G# B D F
E♭, e♭	vii°7, D F A♭ C♭	a#	°7/iv, C× E# G# B
E, e	°7/IV (iv), G# B D F	B♭, b♭	°7/IV (iv), D F A♭ C♭
F, f	°7/V, B D F A♭	B, b	°7/V, E# G# B D
F#, f#	vii°7, E# G# B D	C♭, c♭	°7/V, F A♭ C♭ E♭♭

ASSIGNMENT 3.1 *Spelling enharmonic °7 chords.*   Respell a given °7 chord.

1. Use each member of the given chord as a root.

2. Respell any °7 chord enharmonically, choosing those spellings whose roots can be used as a leading tone. Do not use a flatted note as a root (B♭ excepted; review footnote 1 of this chapter). Disregard any complete chord using more than one double sharp or double flat, since these have little or no practical application.

3. Each given °7 chord will provide five additional °7 chords, as shown in this example. Configurations may differ from that shown.

   Example: Given, F# A C E♭

F#	A	C	E♭
	A	C	E♭	G♭
G×	B#	D#	F#
	C	E♭	G♭	B♭♭
	B#	D#	F#	A
	D#	F#	A	C

(Note that in this particular case, the roots of F# A C E♭ and D# F# A C when spelled enharmonically, G♭ and E♭, cannot act as leading tones.

   Provide similar enharmonic spellings for (1) B D F A♭, (2) A# C# E G, and (3) E# G# B D, or other spellings as assigned or chosen.

In the Workbook: Answers are given.

Using the °⁷ as a Pivot Chord

Figure 3.3 demonstrates a very simple modulation to the dominant[2] where the °⁷ chord happens to be spelled identically in both keys. You may wonder why the pivot was not assigned to the preceding chord, I = IV. Remember from Figure 3.1 that the °⁷ is in a neutral area, or think of it as being at a fork in the road where many paths are available. In hearing, until the °⁷ resolves, the direction it will take is unknown. This feature of modulation was demonstrated in Figures 1.2 and 1.6. It will also be shown in Figure 3.4.

FIGURE 3.3   *Use of the Secondary Leading-Tone Chord as the Pivot*

D major, vii°⁷/ii, D♯ F♯ A C =
A major, vii°⁷/V, D♯ F♯ A C (same spelling in both keys)

Haydn, Symphony No. 101 *(Clock)*, III

D: I

---

[2]The analysis of measures 93–95 of Figure 3.3 is one of several interpretations of a harmonic progression to the dominant, as described and illustrated in *Elementary Harmony*, pages 396–98. Whether this cadence concludes *in* the dominant key of A or *on* the dominant tone of D is a subjective evaluation. An analysis for the latter interpretation is shown below the measures in question.

Most commonly, the °⁷ chord is spelled in the new key only, as in measures 13 and 17 of Figure 3.4*a*. Figure 3.4*b* shows the °⁷ chord of measure 13 in its A major spelling and how it might have progressed had it remained in the same key.

In measure 17, the analysis indicates the pivot to be °⁷/V in the old key of C♯ minor. What is its spelling in that key?

Note that in the °⁷ chord, measure 13, the two notes B♯ and D♯ might be considered simply as chromatic lower-neighbor tones. But in the parallel situation, measure 17, there is little doubt about the °⁷ harmony. Since the aural harmonic effect is the same at each point, °⁷ chords at these points seem logical, but either analysis is appropriate.

FIGURE 3.4   *The °⁷ Pivot Chord as vii °⁷*

Schumann, Concerto in A Minor for Piano, Op. 54, III

Looking ahead to Figure 3.9, we see that measure 153 shows this enharmonic pivot:

°7/V in C♯ minor, F𝄪 A♯ C♯ E =
°7/V in G major, C♯ E G B♭

The Nondominant Diminished Seventh Chord as Pivot

The two nondominant diminished seventh chords (ct°) are also commonly used as pivot chords. In Figure 3.5, measure 15, G♯ B D F in its first appearance can easily be identified as vii°7 of the first key. Upon its repetition on beat 3, the common tone F with the following F A C identifies the °7 as ct° in F major. (The D F A in second inversion between the two appearances of the °7 should be considered a passing six-four chord. The B♭ D F chord labeled N_6 is presented in Chapter 7.

FIGURE 3.5   *Use of the Nondominant °7 Chord as the Pivot Chord*

A major, vii°7, G♯ B D F =
F major, ct°,   G♯ B D F

Brahms, "Dein blaues Auge," Op. 59, No. 8

A most common modulation is the progression of the $^{\circ 7}$ to I_4^6–V of the new key with the tonic note held over. As discussed in Chapter 2, if the tonic six-four is considered a "legitimate" chord, then the $^{\circ 7}$ is a ct°. On the other hand, if the tonic six-four is considered a V with nonharmonic tones, the $^{\circ 7}$ is $^{\circ 7}$/V. The analysis in Figure 3.6 shows both possibilities.

FIGURE 3.6   *Progression of $^{\circ 7}$ to Tonic Six-Four*

Schubert, Sonata in A Minor, D. 537, I

Alternative Spellings of the $^{\circ 7}$ Pivot Chord

Any diminished seventh chord may at times be found with a spelling not in accordance with its function in its particular key. Contrary to the usual careful harmonic spellings that clearly indicate harmonic functions, composers are often quite casual in the spelling of $^{\circ 7}$ chords, especially when used as pivots.

Figure 3.7 shows the very remote modulation B♭ minor to B major, a difference of ten accidentals. The $^{\circ 7}$ chosen for the pivot is spelled in the score D♯ F♯ A C, progressing to F♯ A♯ C♯ E (V^7). Immediately noticeable is the common tone F♯, identifying the $^{\circ 7}$ chord as a ct°, in B major usually spelled G𝄪 B♯ D♯ F♯.

To identify the $^{\circ 7}$ in the old key, B♭ minor, observe first that there is no common tone with its preceding B♭ minor triad. Next, look for a pitch in the $^{\circ 7}$ chord that is a half step below the root of B♭, D♭ F. That note is A, indicating the enharmonic spelling for vii$^{\circ 7}$ in B♭ minor, A C E♭ G♭.

As we look at the score and keep in mind the "correct" spellings we have derived above, it should be obvious that clarity and simplicity justify the respelling of the pivot chord. But in analysis, the symbol used *must always* represent the *sound* and the *function of* the harmony, in this case vii$^{\circ 7}$ = ct°, rather than its appearance on paper.

FIGURE 3.7   *Alternative Spelling of the °⁷ Chord*

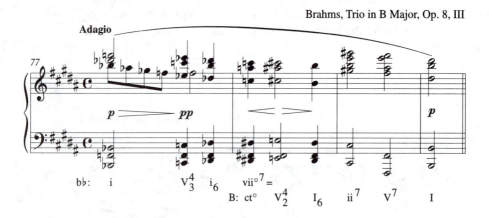

Brahms, Trio in B Major, Op. 8, III

Modulation by Resolving Early One Member of the °⁷ Chord

We have already seen the seventh of the °⁷ chord resolve before the remaining members of the chord, resulting in a V^6_5 chord (Figures 2.18 and 2.25.) This principle can be extended to any member of the °⁷ chord, increasing the potential possibilities for modulation. When any member of the °⁷ chord is lowered one half step (using either the same letter name or the next lower letter name), that lowered tone becomes the root of a major-minor seventh chord. Figure 3.8, using B D F A♭ as an example, shows those resulting major-minor seventh chords that are useful as dominant seventh chords or secondary dominant seventh chords. (In the B D F A♭ chord of Figure 3.8, chords built on F♭ and A♭♭ are not useful.) Note that the new spellings are sometimes expressed enharmonically.

FIGURE 3.8   *Lowering Members of the °⁷ Chord, B D F A♭, by One Half Step*

Member lowered	to	Resulting major-minor seventh
root—B	B♭	B♭ D F A♭
root—B	A♯	A♯ C𝄪 E♯ G♯
third—D	D♭	D♭ F A♭ C♭
third—D	C♯	C♯ E♯ G♯ B
fifth—F	E	E G♯ B D
seventh—A♭	G	G B D F

An example from Haydn is shown in Figure 3.9, where the change of key is from G major to the remote key of C♯ minor. At measure 146, the A of D♯ F♯ A C resolves down to G♯ while C is enharmonically respelled as B♯. The result is the chord G♯ B♯ D♯ F♯.

So spelled, it appears to be V^7 in C♯ minor. That key is not firmly established, but the C♯ minor triad also functions as a location for the beginning of a chromatic line in the viola part (measures 151–154, G♯–A–B♭–B♮). Reaching B♭ opens the possibility for the °7 chord, one that can progress to tonic six-four in G major (Figure 3.9b).

In this case, the chromatic melodic line is more responsible than the °7 chord for the return to G major. But should that chord be considered a pivot, then the °7/V, F𝄪 A♯ C♯ E in C♯ minor = °7/V, C♯ E G B♭ in G major.

FIGURE 3.9   *Modulation by Resolution of a Single Tone of the °7 Chord*

Haydn, Quartet, Hob. III:72, II

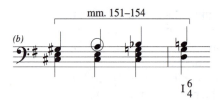

In the excerpt from *Siegfried*, Figure 3.10, the composer uses this device repeatedly in short motives in close succession, using both half-diminished and fully diminished seventh chords. In the first of these motives, the A of B D F A moves down a half step to G♯, creating G♯ B D F, the D of which moves down a half step to C♯, creating a dominant seventh chord requiring an enharmonic spelling of C♯ E♯ G♯ B.

Note that no attempt is made to resolve the achieved dominant seventh in each case, except to proceed to a similar motive. At this point in the score, this process continues for a total of nineteen measures, during which the listener feels time after time that the music is arriving at a new key, only to start over at another tonal level.

FIGURE 3.10   *Single-Tone Resolutions in Series*

Wagner, *Siegfried*, Act III, Scene I

* denotes the beginning of a similar figure, each either two or three chords in length.

ASSIGNMENT 3.2 *Altering °7 chords.*   Alter °7 chords to become major-minor seventh chords. Make a list of chord members, as found under *member lowered* in Figure 3.8. Use the °7 chord spelling of your choice or as assigned, and complete the second and third columns as in Figure 3.8.

In the Workbook: Answers are given.

ASSIGNMENT 3.3 *Harmonic analysis.*   Describe the process used for each modulation, either by roman-numeral symbols or by discussion, as appropriate.

(1)

Beethoven, Sonata in C♯ Minor for Piano,
Op. 27, No. 2, I

(2) The circled note, E (measure 69), though consonant at the moment it sounds, is dissonant in the context of the entire second beat.

Beethoven, Quartet, Op. 18, No. 5, III, Variation 4

(3) The diminished seventh chord is not spelled according to its function. In each of its two appearances, spell the chord according to its function and identify it by its harmonic symbol. Why was the chord spelled this way?

Beethoven, Symphony No. 7 in A Major, Op. 92, II

A: ii₆

(4)

Beethoven, Quartet, Op. 18, No. 2, IV

(5)

Wagner, *Lohengrin,* Act II, Scene 2

Gb: vi

(6)

Schubert, Trio for Piano and Strings in Bb Major, D. 898, I

ASSIGNMENT 3.4 *Part-writing.*   Part-write these modulations with diminished seventh chords as pivots.

Writing a Modulation Using the °7 Chord as the Pivot

For this project, we will write a modulation between two given keys using the °7 chord as the pivot. In Figure 3.11, these keys are C major and B♭ minor, and the pivot is vii°7 in both keys. This is the procedure:

1. Begin with the tonic chord in the chosen key; assume this chord to have been preceded by music in that key.

2. On the next beat, write the °7 pivot in the new key, choosing root position or an inversion that will more easily connect with the next chord.

3. Resolve the °7 and continue to a cadence. In Figure 3.11*a*, °7/iv proceeds to iv, followed by V–i. Had the pivot been °7/VI in the new key, it would have been followed by iv (or ii°)–V–i.

4. In Figure 3.11*b*, we have added nonharmonic tones, both to add to the musical interest and to cover any weak places—the unequal fifths on beats 1 and 2, for example.

5. This same example could have progressed to A♯ minor (enharmonic with B♭ minor). Simply change the pivot to its enharmonic equivalent C𝄪, E♯ G♯ B, and continue.

FIGURE 3.11   *Modulation, C Major to B♭ Minor with the °7 Pivot*

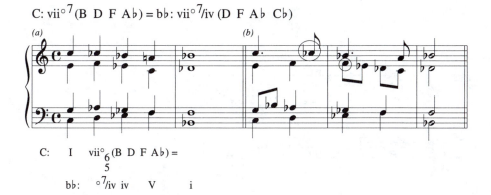

C: vii°7 (B D F A♭) = bb: vii°7/iv (D F A♭ C♭)

C: I   vii°65 (B D F A♭) =

bb: °7/iv iv   V   i

ASSIGNMENT 3.5 *Writing modulations.*   Write a modulation between any two keys of your choice or from the list below, or choose any other °7 or ct° as pivot. The following given pivots are as spelled in the new key.

1.	C major to A♭ major	vii°7	6.	B major to E♭ major	ct°1̂
2.	C major to F major	°7/V	7.	F♯ minor to C minor	°7/VI
3.	G minor to F major	°7/iv	8.	E♭ minor to F minor	°7/V
4.	B minor to D minor	vii°7	9.	F♯ major to A major	ct°5̂
5.	A major to G♭ major	°7/ii	10.	A♭ minor to B♭ major	vii°7

In the Workbook: Do Assignment 3A. Answers are given.

Modulations Making Use of Early Resolutions

This procedure was shown in Figures 3.8 and 3.9 and the accompanying discussion. In Figure 3.12, the $°7$/ii in the original key is chosen as the pivot, and its root, third, and fifth are lowered in turn to become a V^7 chord in the new key. In examples *a–c,* its spelling, C♯ E G B♭, is found in root position. In *b* and *c,* note that enharmonic tones are required in the V^7.

These examples can also modulate to parallel minor keys—for example, in *b,* G♯ minor with V^7–i spelled D♯ F𝄪 A♯ C♯ to G♯ B D♯.

Figure 3.12*d* shows the $°7$ of the original key in inversion. In any inversion, each member of the $°7$ may be treated as above.

FIGURE 3.12

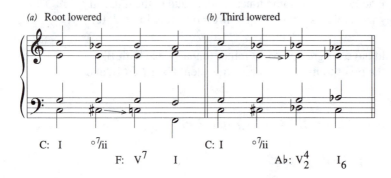

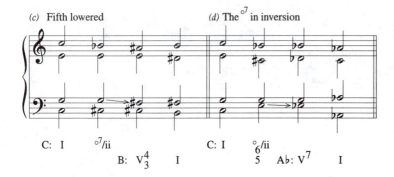

ASSIGNMENT 3.6 *Writing modulations.*   Write modulations by making use of the early resolution of the root, the third, or the fifth of the diminished seventh chord.

Using Figure 3.12 as a model, choose a beginning key and a diminished seventh chord in that key, and lower the root, the third, and the fifth in turn to create a major-minor seventh chord, using the new spelling as V^7 in the new key. Use root position or any inversion of the $°7$ chord.

In the Workbook: Do Assignment 3B. Answers are given.

ASSIGNMENT 3.7 *Realizing a figured bass line.*   The bass line only is given. Follow directions from Assignment 2.11. Always identify the pivot chord in both the old and the new keys.

Keyboard Harmony: Improvising Modulations

If you have acquired keyboard skills as presented in earlier chapters and are fluent in spelling diminished seventh chords, you can improvise modulations with the $^{\circ 7}$ as a pivot with a minimum of difficulty. These are the steps:

1. Determine an opening key and the key to which you will modulate.
2. Choose and spell the °7 pivot chord in the new key. The choices are
   a. Major keys: vii°7, °7/ii, °7/iii, °7/IV, °7/V, °7/vi
   b. Minor keys: vii°7, °7/III, °7/iv, °7/V, °7/VI
3. Establish the opening key by playing a simple progression such as I–IV–V–I, i–ii$^6_5$–V–i.
4. Follow the opening progression with any °7 chord. Based on the function chosen, resolve it to the appropriate chord in the new key, and complete the exercise with a simple cadence in the new key.

In Figure 3.13, the modulation from C major to A♭ major utilizes vii°7 in the new key, G B♭ D♭ F♭. What is the spelling of C: °7ii? Also try

1. Other pivots between the same two keys. In A♭, °7/IV is C E♭ G♭ B♭♭, °7/V is D F A♭ C♭, and so forth.
2. Placing the pivot in inversion as in Figure 3.12*d.* Remember to resolve the seventh by half step.

FIGURE 3.13   *Example of a Keyboard Modulation*

$$\begin{array}{l}\text{C:} \quad \text{°7/ii} =\\ \text{A♭: } \text{vii°7}\end{array}$$

ASSIGNMENT 3.8 *Playing modulations.*   At the keyboard, improvise modulations from the list in Assignment 3.5. Figure 3.13 is the first exercise from the assignment.

ASSIGNMENT 3.9 *Playing modulations, continued.*   Continue as in the previous assignment, but upon playing the °7 chord, resolve any one of its members down by one half step, as illustrated in Figures 3.12 and 3.14. Call the resulting major-minor seventh chord a V7 chord, or a secondary dominant seventh chord, and resolve it to its appropriate key.

FIGURE 3.14

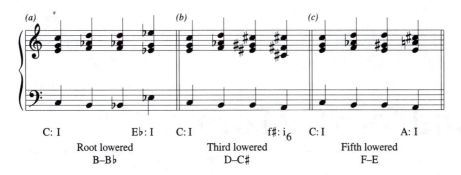

| C: I | Eb: I | C: I | f#: i₆ | C: I | A: I |

Root lowered   Third lowered   Fifth lowered

B–Bb   D–C#   F–E

Summary

The diminished seventh chord offers greater versatility in modulation than any other chord, since a single °7 chord in the original key will function in some way in any of the other twenty-nine major and minor keys. This versatility is the result of two characteristics of the °7 chord: (1) Its sound is the same in all positions and inversions, and (2) with enharmonic spellings of the chord, any member of the chord can assume the function of root (or any other member) with no change in the sound.

As a pivot to the new key, any °7 chord of the old key can function as vii°7, as the °7 of any other major or minor triad, or as a nondominant °7 in the new key.

In some situations, simplified spellings of diminished seventh chords are used—for example, D♯ F♯ A C instead of G𝄪 B♯ D♯ F♯, as in Figure 3.7.

Modulation may also be accomplished by lowering any one note of the °7 chord by one half step, thereby creating a major-minor seventh chord, one that can be used as the V7 or any secondary dominant seventh chord in the new key.

4

Binary and Ternary Forms

Chapters 4 and 5 are independent presentations. They may be interpolated in any order and at any time between other chapters of the text. The presentation of harmonic materials resumes in Chapter 6.

Our study of musical form began in *Elementary Harmony*. Chapter 7 of that text presented phrases and periods, and Chapter 15 presented the phrase group, the double period, phrase extension, and thematic development. Following is a brief review of these smaller structures. For more detail, consult the chapters in *Elementary Harmony*.

Review of the Smaller Forms

A *phrase* is a group of notes, often four measures in length, leading to a cadence, as in the marked phrases of Figure 4.1 and the first three phrases of Figure 4.2. Phrases may be shorter, usually not less than three measures, or they may be longer, usually by extension, which is displayed in the final phrase of Figure 4.2.

   A *period* consists of two phrases, called "antecedent" and "consequent," the first usually ending with a half cadence, though any cadence but a perfect cadence is possible. The second phrase ends with a perfect cadence, usually authentic (V–I).

   In the *parallel period,* the melodic line of each phrase is similar, whereas in the *contrasting period,* the two phrases differ. Figure 4.1 shows a contrasting period.

FIGURE 4.1   *Contrasting Period*

Beethoven, Bagatelle, Op. 119, No. 1

A *double period* consists of two periods. Only the last of the four phrases has a perfect cadence. Thus, the last cadence of the first period is usually a half cadence, in contradiction to the definition given earlier. The first and third periods are usually identical or similar, and the second and fourth may be similar or different. Figure 4.2 shows a double period in which the fourth phrase differs from the second and is extended to a length of eight measures before the final cadence.

FIGURE 4.2   *Double Period, a b / a c (extended)*

In the *phrase group,* each phrase is different and only the final phrase ends with a perfect cadence. Commonly, the length of a phrase group is three phrases, as in Figure 4.3.

FIGURE 4.3   *Phrase Group*

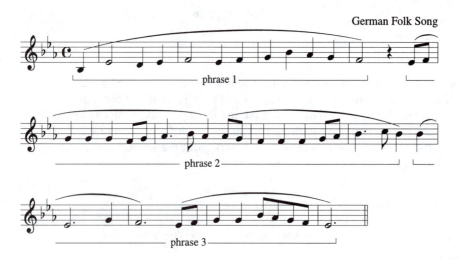

Binary and Ternary Forms Defined

The terms *binary* and *ternary*[1] refer to larger structures that may be divided into two or three parts, respectively. In general, they include the features enumerated below. This chapter will attempt to present the basic constructions used in these forms through the use of clearly defined examples. It should be understood that composers are not so restricted, their music displaying a wide variety of exceptions, extensions, and interpolated development devices.

1. Each part of a binary or ternary structure in itself consists of one of the smaller forms: a phrase (uncommon), a period, a phrase group, or a double period. Extensions of phrases are commonly used in any of these smaller forms.

2. The succession of parts is characterized by a relationship of keys, especially in the ternary forms, often tonic and dominant, or tonic and the relative major or minor.

3. There is a definite contrast in the nature of the thematic material between the first and second parts, and in ternary form, a return in the third part to the material of the first part.

Each example is preceded by a diagram outlining its formal structure. The two parts of binary form are indicated by A and B, and the three parts of ternary form by A B A. Lowercase letters, such as *a* and *b,* refer to phrases. The prime symbol, as in *a′*, indicates a phrase similar but not identical to *a.*

The relationship of keys is indicated by a roman-numeral designation, such as I–V, meaning in this case that the part begins in the tonic key (but not necessarily on

---

[1]Terminology for some of the forms described in the remainder of this chapter is not completely standardized. Terms used in this text may not appear in other souces. Alternative terminology will be noted as appropriate.

the tonic chord) and ends in the dominant. The use of "V" and "dominant" in this context indicates either that the part actually modulates to the dominant key or that the cadence is considered a secondary dominant progression V/V–V in the original key.

Binary Form

The term *binary form,* as its name denotes, refers to a composition divided into two distinct sections. The simplest binary form, that shown in Figure 4.4, appears strikingly similar to the *double period* shown in Figure 4.2.

FIGURE 4.4   *Binary Form*

A   B
a a' b c
A = period, I–V; B = period, I–I

*In the original, this phrase is repeated. No change of analysis results.

There are two principal differences between these two examples.

1. *Cadences.* In the double period (Figure 4.2), the first period ends on a simple half cadence in the tonic key. In the binary structure, the first period ends with a strong impression of dominant tonality, whether its cadence is considered a full cadence *in* the dominant or a transient cadence *on* the dominant. The IV–I$_4^6$–V–I of Figure 4.4 establishes a key feeling of A♭, whether that of a transient cadence or a more permanent closure.

   In binary form, a cadence on a different closely related key is possible, especially the relative major of the opening minor key.

2. *Melodic line.* In the double period, the melody of the second period usually opens with a repetition (actual or varied) of the first phrase, emphasizing the "oneness" of the total structure. At the same place in the binary form, the melody differs from preceding material, emphasizing the separation of the two parts.

The binary form just described is far less common than another binary structure, known as the *two-reprise form.*

The Two-Reprise Form

The *two-reprise* is the most common of the binary forms.[2] As its name implies, each of the two sections is repeated, indicated in the score with repeat signs: ‖ ‖ ‖. The Baroque period is a fertile source of examples, since music for many of the various dances of that period (*allemande, gigue, minuet, sarabande,* and so forth) were cast in the two-reprise form. Easily available sources for examples are the *French Suites* and the *English Suites* of J. S. Bach.

The two-reprise structures are further defined by the nature of the cadence at the close of the first part. When that cadence is in the tonic key, it is known as a *sectional two-reprise form.* When the cadence is in another key, it is known as a *continuous two-reprise form.* As might be expected, modulation from a major key to its dominant and from a minor key to its relative major are those most commonly used.

The two-reprise minuet of Figure 4.5 is perfectly regular, consisting of two eight-measure periods. There is no question that the cadence of Part I is in the dominant key, the tonic triad of B♭ major having been reached twice in the final measures. The quick introduction of the pitch A♭ after the cadence prepares for the V^7 chord of E♭ major introducing Part II.

[2]In other terminology, the two-reprise is not identified as such but is included in the general designation of binary form.

FIGURE 4.5   *Two-Reprise Form (Continuous)*

‖: A :‖: B :‖
  a   b   c   d
A = period, I–V; B = period, V–I

Bach, *French Suite IV*, BWV 815, "Minuet"

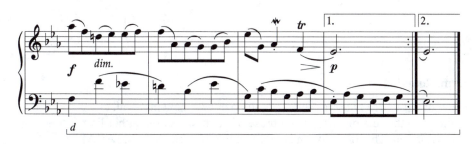

A late use of the two-reprise form, this time sectional, is seen in Figure 4.6. Brahms, though a nineteenth-century composer, made frequent use of this and other older forms and devices, such as the medieval modes and the hemiola. Compared with A, the B section includes three phrases with one extended. This longer B section is more typical of the construction of the two-reprise form than are the equal sections of Figure 4.5.

The work is written for vocal duet and piano, four hands. Space requirements, unfortunately, do not allow a complete reproduction. We have added harmonic analysis symbols. Note that all the harmonic progressions, except the uncommon V/iii–V, are familiar ones from previous study. It will be worth your while to use your keyboard-harmony skills with the study of this example.

FIGURE 4.6   *Two-Reprise Form (Sectional)*

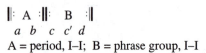

A = period, I–I; B = phrase group, I–I

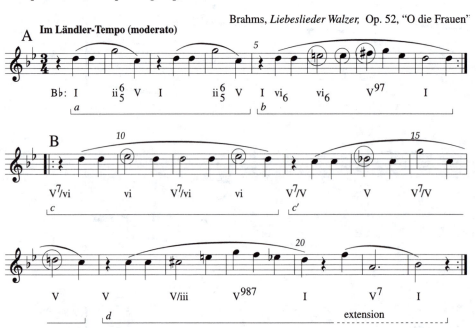

Two-Reprise Form, Rounded

The second section of a rounded two-reprise form will open with new material, as expected, but will then end the section with the *a* phrase of the first section, either literally or with some variation. This description actually is that of ternary form (ABA), except that ternary is free of repeat signs and that B and A are more free to exceed the length of the opening A.[3]

---

[3]The form described here as rounded two-reprise is also known simply as *rounded binary*. At the same time, because of its ternary characteristics, it is known as *incipient ternary*.

The music of Figure 4.7 falls somewhere between two-reprise and its rounded form. At measures 12–13, where A should be repeated, we find measures 3–4 from A. The immediate aural impression is that of a thematic connection with A (ternary) but too short to actually be so.

FIGURE 4.7   *Two-Reprise with Partial Rounding*

‖: A :‖: B :‖
　a a'　b c
A = period, i–III; B = period with extension, i–i

Haydn, Sonata in E Minor for Pinao, Hob. XVI:34, III

A complete rounding is seen in Figure 4.8. The music consists of four four-measure phrases, the fourth of which is the repeated *a*, slightly altered, to complete the B section.

FIGURE 4.8   *Two-Reprise, Rounded*

Ternary Form

Ternary form is often called simply "ABA form," reflecting its construction as a statement of a principal idea, a contrasting idea, and a return to the principal statement. It differs from the rounded binary form in that there is nothing in the score to indicate a repeat.

The simplest ternary form is that in which the two A's are identical, very often indicated by a *da capo* at the end of the B section. In operatic literature, especially from its beginnings through the mid–nineteenth century, this form is known as a *da capo aria*. The familiar aria in Figure 4.9 shows this device, in which both A and B are extended periods.

FIGURE 4.9   *Ternary Form (the "Da Capo" Aria)*

A   B   A
a b c d (da capo)

(Can I live without my Euridice? In my woe, where can I go without my love? Forever, I am your true love.)

Ternary Form, the Return Written Out

Writing out all three parts of the ABA form allows the composer to vary the material of the opening A section when it reappears in the closing A section. When the composition incorporates this choice, its structural identification is A B A′. The change in A′ can range from minor to so substantial that the section only minimally resembles the original A.

In Figure 4.10, Chopin begins the return of A (measure 17) with only three melodic tones of the original A section, and these with a new harmonization. In addition, the rhythmic similarity in the melody continues for only two measures (17–18), but the rhythmic pattern of measure 18 (compare with measure 2) continues for another two measures. These shortened melodic and rhythmic references to the opening A are sufficient to establish the closing section as A′.

The harmony of this work is of more than passing interest.

Part I   Measures 1–8: C minor–G minor

Measures 5–8: Opens in E♭ major; at measure 6, modulates to G minor via chromatic step, B♭–B♮.

Part II   Measures 9–16: C minor–(E♭ major)

Measures 9–12: A♭ C E♭ G♭–D♭ F A♭. The progression is c: V^7/N–N, with descending stepwise bass line (N = Neapolitan sixth; see Chapter 7), followed by c: V–i, with ascending stepwise bass line. Melody line of measures 11–12 is a variation of that in measures 9–10.

Measures 15–16: Modulation to E♭ major begun but not completed, ending on B♭: V. Pivot is c: iv = E♭: ii. In measure 16, bass line B♭–B♮ leads back to C minor.

Part III   Measures 17–24: C minor

Measures 17–20: Opens with sequence (up fourth–down fifth) beginning with G B D F of previous measure extending to G B D F of measure 20, resolving to VI.

Measures 21–23: Ascending stepwise bass line, as in Part I.

FIGURE 4.10   *Ternary Form*

Chopin, Nocturne, Op. 48, No. 1

Larger Ternary Forms

Although this chapter is limited to discussion of the smaller forms in music, it is of interest to note the uses of even larger three-part structures. They can be identified as **A B A** (here using boldface letters rather than the previously presented A B A). In such large structures, **A** is composed of one of the binary or ternary forms; **B** may be another such form or one of the smaller forms; and the final **A** or **A′** ranges from a literal repetition to a complete reworking of the initial **A** section.

In a diagram, an ABA at both levels appears thus:

A   **B**   **A**

A B C   C D C   A B A

Note that C D C represents new material not found under **A**. If the music under **B** were a separate composition, "C D C" would be identified as A B A.

One source for the simplest version of this extended ABA is found in the classical minuets from such works as the Haydn and Mozart piano sonatas. In Figure 4.11, the complete minuet movement consists of successive rounded two-reprise forms, called Menuetto I and Menuetto II. The final **A** is indicated by *Men. I da Capo.*

FIGURE 4.11   *Minuet Form with Da Capo*

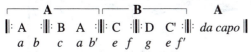

Menuetto I (**A**)

Mozart, Sonata in E♭ Major for Piano, K. 282, II

Menuetto II **(B)**

A more complex example, that with the final **A′** written out with significant changes, can be seen in the complete nocturne from which the initial **A** was shown as Figure 4.10. The final C major chord of the figure is the opening chord of the **B** section (Part II), in itself a three-part structure, C D C′:

C = period

D = phrase

C′ = as C, octave higher with extensive doubling and extended to thirteen measures

The final **A′** (Part III) is similar to the opening **A** but with a considerable amount of added figuration, plus a six-measure coda.

FIGURE 4.12   *Thematic Material from Chopin, Nocturne, Figure 4.10:*
B (Part II), themes C and D, and A′ (Part III)

B (Part II):

A′ (Part III):

Further Use of Larger ABA Forms

Although the purpose of this text does not include a complete coverage of the subject of form, there are two further expanded uses of the ABA idea that deserve mention.

The *rondo* form is one in which the theme first stated is repeated after one or more interruptions of new material. In this sense, the Chopin nocturne analyzed earlier (Figure 4.10) is a simple rondo form, A B A. A second and different interpolation results in the formal structure A B A C A, sometimes known as a "five-part rondo." An example can be seen in Beethoven's Piano Sonata in G major, Op. 49, No. 2, last movement.

This brief analysis marks the beginning of each of the structural themes and their key relationships in the Beethoven sonata. You should be able to determine the smaller forms within each major section and to recognize extensions and transitional materials.

Measure	Theme	Key
1	A	G
28	B	D
48	A	G
68	C	C
88	A	G
108 (Coda)		

Further extension of this structure, such as A B A C A D A, is infrequent.

More likely is the form A B A C A B A, sometimes known as a "sonata-rondo" form or a "seven-part rondo." Its balanced structure, consisting of two ABA forms on either side of a center C statement, has had great appeal to composers. An excellent example is Beethoven's Piano Sonata in A major, Op. 2, No. 2, last movement. Look for smaller forms, extensions, and transitional materials as above.

Measure	Theme	Key
1	A	A
26	B	E
41	A	A
57	C	a
100	A	A
124	B (modified)	E
135	A and Coda	A

Finally, the *sonata-allegro*, the form most frequently used for the first movement of a sonata or a symphony in the eighteenth and nineteenth centuries (including works by composers from Haydn through Brahms), is usually considered a variety of an **ABA** form:

A (*Exposition*), based on two themes, in the tonic key and a related key, respectively. In a major key, the second theme is usually in the key of the dominant; in a minor key, the relative major.

B (*Development*), wherein the themes of **A** are treated in new and various ways, along with optional new material.

A′ (*Recapitulation*), the return of the themes from **A**, both in the key of the tonic. But there are exceptions. For example, in Brahms's third symphony, the principal theme is in F major, whereas the second theme sounds first in A major, then in the recapitulation in D major. But note that the relationship of a fifth between the two appearances of the second theme is maintained.

Interestingly enough, a double bar line with repeat signs often appears at the close of the exposition, **A** :‖ **B A** ‖, and in many cases, the development and the recapitulation are bounded by repeat signs as well, **A** :‖: **B A** :‖. Definitely a binary concept, this practice recalls the problems of terminology encountered in the small binary and ternary forms of the early part of this chapter.[4]

A Small Three-Part Form

A three-part form consisting only of phrases, contrary to our opening definition, is occasionally seen. It appears in children's songs such as "Twinkle, Twinkle, Little Star" and in folk music. Figure 4.13 shows an example by Schubert. Look for another example in the excerpts for analysis in Assignment 4.1.

[4]An easily available example of a simple sonata-allegro is the first movement of Mozart's Piano Sonata in C major, K. 307. Exposition: measure 1, first theme in C; measure 35, second theme in G. Development: measure 59. Recapitulation: measure 94, first theme in C; measure 129, second theme in C.

FIGURE 4.13

Schubert, *Die schöne Müllerin*, D. 795, "Wohin"

muß – te auch hin – un – ter mit_ mei – nem Wan – der – stab,

(repeated)

ASSIGNMENT 4.1 *Formal analysis.*   Each of these examples illustrates one of the binary or ternary forms. Analyze these forms using Figure 4.6 as an example. Procedure:

1. Locate the beginning of each major section, marking it with an A or a B.

2. Locate each smaller form within the larger sections, identifying it with a lowercase letter—*a, b, c,* and so forth.

3. Bracket each of these smaller forms with a horizontal solid line below the music. When extensions, codas, and so forth, occur, continue the bracket with a dotted line (as in Figure 4.6, final three measures).

4. Summarize your findings, including key relationships, in a chart similar to the one preceding Figure 4.6.

In the Workbook: Do Assignments 4A and 4B. Answers are given.

(1)

Schubert, *Die Winterreise,* D. 911, "Der Lindenbaum"

Am Brun – nen vor dem To – re   da steht   ein Lin – den – baum;   ich

(By the well at the gate stands a lime tree. I dreamt in its shadow many a sweet dream. In joy and sorrow I felt ever drawn to it.)

(2)

Couperin, Gavotte, "La Bourbonnaise"

(3)

Haydn, Sonata in G Major for Piano, Hob. XVI:6, II

(4) Observe how the cadence chord of each phrase functions also as the first chord of the following phrase.

Elgar, *Enigma Variations* (Theme)
(piano reduction)

(5)

Schubert, Theme and Variations, D. 156

(6)

Beethoven, Sonata in E♭ Major for Piano, Op. 27, No. 1, I

(7)

Fauré, *Poëme d'un jour,* Op. 21, "Adieu"

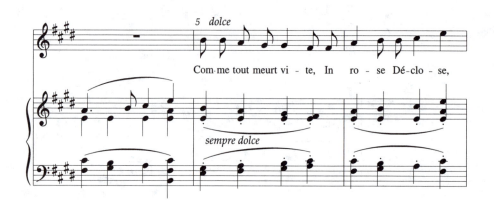

Com-me tout meurt vi – te, In   ro – se Dé-clo – se,

Mais hé – las!   les plus longs a – mours   Sont courts!

cresc.

Et je dis   en quit-tant vos char – mes, Sans lar – mes.

dolce   **pp**

Pres-qu'au mo-ment de mon a – veu._____   A –

pp *sempre*

dieu!

(The flowers of the meadow, the long sighs, our beloved ones,—how quickly every-
thing dies. In this fickle world, change is faster than the waves on the sand or the
frost on the flowers. The longest loves are short, and leaving your charms without
tears, I say "Adieu.")

(8) Three of the forms from this chapter are included in this movement. Be sure
to watch for small italicized words below the score.

Mozart, *Eine kleine Nachtmusik*, K. 525, III

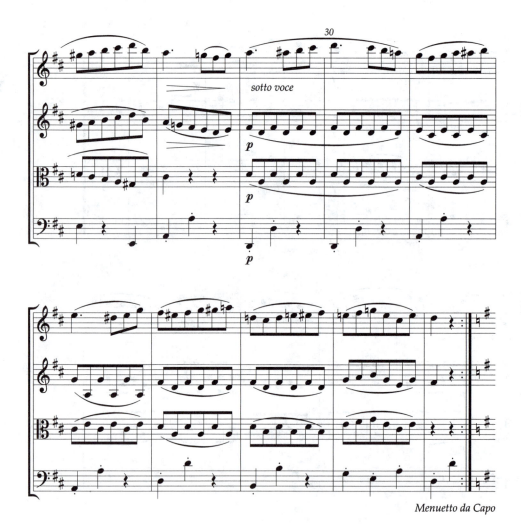

Menuetto da Capo

(9) In what way is the theme at measure 9 similar to measure 1? How do you justify measure 9 as the opening of a new part?

Mozart, Quintet for Strings, K. 593, III

Summary

Binary forms are commonly found with each of their two sections marked with repeat signs: ‖: :‖ :‖. When found thus, they are referred to as *two-reprise binary forms,* reflecting the fact that each part is repeated. The two-reprise was widely used in many dance forms in the Baroque period.

The material within each bracketed group determines its classification.

1. *Sectional two-reprise.* The cadence closing the A section is in the tonic key.
2. *Continuous two-reprise.* The cadence closing the A section is usually in the dominant key, interpreting dominant as either an indisputable modulation or a closing dominant harmony preceded by its secondary dominant.
3. *Two-reprise, rounded.* In Part B, the final phrase or period is a repetition of the first section of Part A:

$$\|{:}A \quad {:}\|{:}B \quad {:}\|$$
$$a \ b \qquad c \ a'$$

Binary forms without the repeat indications are far less frequently used. They can be more easily found in vocal literature.

Larger forms also utilize the ternary (ABA) principle. In one, *rondo* form, its A returns after each new presentation, as in A B A C A. This alternation is infrequently carried further. The *sonata-rondo* form, diagrammed as A B A C A B A, is in itself a large ternary form:

$$\textbf{A} \qquad \textbf{B} \qquad \textbf{A}$$
$$\text{A B A} \quad \text{C} \quad \text{A B A}$$

The *sonata-allegro form,* usually the first movement of the classical sonata or symphony (and occasionally other movements), displays ternary form in these sections:

A (*Exposition*): Two themes, the first in the tonic key. In major, the second is usually in the dominant key; in minor, the relative major.

B (*Development*): Ideas from the exposition varied in many ways and, usually, with unrestricted use of varying tonal areas

A′ (*Recapitulation*): Return of A, this time with both themes in the tonic key, frequently closing with an extended coda

5

Application of Part-Writing Procedures to Instrumental Music

Introduction

In our study of part-writing, the four-voice chorale style[1] of writing has been used to illustrate procedures and to serve as a medium for students' efforts. But at the same time, in studying harmonic progression, we have investigated and analyzed music in many different styles, ranging from the four-voice chorale to excerpts from symphonic literature. It is now time to discover the relationship of part-writing procedures to music other than four-part vocal music.

Composition of almost all the music of the common practice period follows the basic principles of part-writing that you have already learned. These principles evolved through the years preceding the seventeenth century, a time when most music was written for vocal ensemble and a time in which instruments were at liberty to double the vocal parts in performance, or even to perform the parts without vocalists. Thus, early music written for instruments alone usually looked and sounded like vocal music, but without words.[2]

As composers concentrated more on the unique qualities of both solo instruments and ensemble combinations, styles of writing for nonvocal music looked and sounded different from music written for vocal ensemble. In spite of this difference in look and sound, the principles of vocal part-writing continued as a basis for most music composition through most of the nineteenth century. How instrumental writing of the common practice period utilized these basic part-writing techniques while at

---

[1]The meaning of the term *style* in reference to music is not constant. Here, it refers to various vocal and instrumental solos or groupings, such as "piano style" and "chorale style." See *The New Harvard Dictionary of Music,* ed. Don Michael Randel, "Style" and "Style Analysis."

[2]Review in *Elementary Harmony* the articles "The Theory of Inversion (Chapter 9) and "Another Metrical Concept" (Chapter 15).

the same time exploiting unique instrumental capabilities is the subject of this chapter. For our purposes, we will concentrate on writing for the keyboard, where a single instrument must produce all the voice lines of a composition.

Similarities between Vocal and Instrumental Writing

Figure 5.1 certainly doesn't look like chorale-style writing, but its instrumental character is created by making only minor changes from four-voice chorale writing. Although the appearance is that of three-voice writing, the inner voice actually functions as two voices (alto and tenor) by means of the arpeggiation.

FIGURE 5.1

Note carefully these details:

Measure 1, beat 1:	Major triad (alto a♭, tenor e♭), usual doubling
beat 2:	V$_2^4$: no note doubled, the seventh displays its usual resolution down by step
Measure 2, beat 1:	Major triad, first inversion with the usual soprano doubling
beat 2:	Another major triad in first inversion, also with usual soprano doubling; the passing seventh displays its usual resolution
Measure 3, beat 1:	Similar to previous measure, beat 1
beat 2:	Minor triad, F A♭ C, common doubling of its third; seventh chord, B♭ D F A♭, all notes present, usual resolution of the seventh

You could easily rewrite this example in four voices and it would look exactly like four-voice chorale style.

Figure 5.2*a* shows an excerpt with the common Alberti-bass figure (arpeggiated chords below the melodic line). Figure 5.2*b* is the same composition with all nonharmonic tones or repeated harmonic tones in the melody eliminated. Note the careful consideration given to voice leading, and the use of expected doublings and resolutions.

Measures 71, 73:   Minor triad with doubled third

Measure 71:   Triad in first inversion with doubled soprano tone

Measures 72, 75, 76:   With nonharmonic tones, no doubling of the note of resolution

Measures 72, 74, 75:   In seventh chords, all complete, no note doubled, and each seventh resolved down by step

FIGURE 5.2

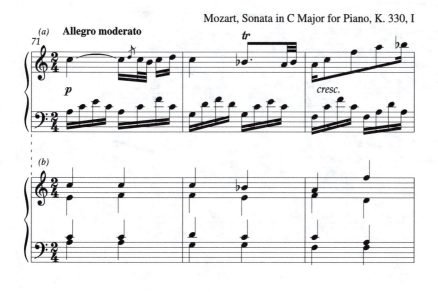

Mozart, Sonata in C Major for Piano, K. 330, I

This excerpt differs from four-part chorale style only in the arpeggiation and in the distance between the soprano and alto lines, freedom warranted by the range of the piano keyboard.

In Figure 5.3*a*, arpeggiation for more than an octave in a single chord produces notes that must be considered duplicates of those in the four-part texture. When both the duplications and the nonharmonic tones have been eliminated, the remaining four-part texture is very clear.

FIGURE 5.3

Differentiating Instrumental from Vocal Writing

1. *Extended harmonies.* In harmonic chorale style, chord changes are frequent, often on every beat or even on a beat division. (This feature was appropriate to the study of harmonic progression, allowing many chord changes in a short space.) But in other styles, including instrumental music and other varieties of vocal music, a single harmony is often of a longer duration, such as the tonic triad of Figure 5.4.

FIGURE 5.4

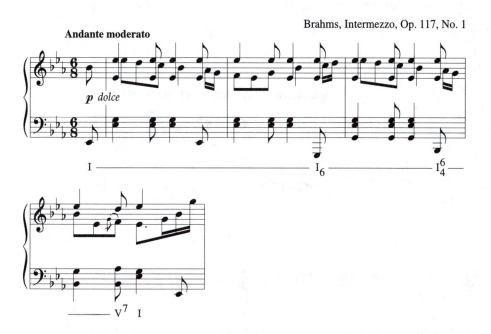

Brahms, Intermezzo, Op. 117, No. 1

Extended harmonies such as those in Figure 5.4 are effective when written in conjunction with other compositional features that highlight the continuous single harmony. A few of these are[3]

- *a.* Striking melodic motive or theme (B. Op. 2, No. 1, first movement, measures 1–4)
- *b.* Strong rhythmic pattern (B. Op. 14, No. 2, "Scherzo," last seventeen measures)
- *c.* Change in inversion of chord during duration of single harmony (B. Op. 7, third movement, measures 1–4)
- *d.* In passages of rapid tempo (B. Op. 31, No. 2, last movement, measures 1–4)
- *e.* Long melodic line implying a single harmony (M. Op. 53, No. 2, measures 1–2; also, Figure 5.4)

[3]In this section (*Differences*), musical excepts cited but not quoted will be found in three sources: B—Beethoven, Sonatas for Piano; M—Mendelssohn, *Songs Without Words;* S—Schumann, *Album for the Young,* Op. 68.

  f. Melodic line in which the interest lies in the use of nonharmonic tones or chromatic scale passages (B. Op. 2, No. 2, fourth movement, measures 57–58)

  g. In introductions, codettas, or cadenzas (B. Op. 7, first movement, measures 1–4; M. Op. 62, No. 4, measures 1–4, and last four measures)

 2. *Free voicing.* In keyboard music, it is not necessary that a given number of voice lines be maintained throughout a composition. A glance at any keyboard composition of the eighteenth and nineteenth centuries will show a vertical texture of any number of voices from one to as many as eight or more, and a constant change in the number of voice lines as the composition progresses.

FIGURE 5.5

Mozart, Sonata in B♭ Major for Piano, K. 281, III

 3. *Sonority doubling.* Voice lines in music written for keyboard or for any instrumental ensemble are often doubled at the octave to produce a richer sound. At the keyboard, the octave naturally fits the hand position, so the device is used frequently in either or both hands. In instrumental ensemble music, two or more different instruments may play in parallel unisons or octaves, producing a combined sound differing from that of any of the individual instruments.

 A sonority doubling is always an octave reinforcement of a single voice line, such as a bass line or a soprano line. Octaves between two different voice lines can never be considered sonority doubling; these are simply undesirable parallel octaves.

 Examples of sonority doubling follow.

  a. Bass line doubled in octaves.

FIGURE 5.6

b. Doubling in inner voices.

FIGURE 5.7

c. Soprano voice doubled (see also Figure 3.7, where both soprano and bass are doubled).

FIGURE 5.8

Brahms, Romanze, Op. 118, No. 5

4. *Arpeggiated harmonies.* This very common device is used most often in writing for piano. It helps keep the music in motion for the duration of a single chord or for each in a series of chords. Almost any piano composition will provide an example of this device, ranging from simple arpeggiation of the basic triad to extended arpeggiation over a wide range (see Figure 5.9). The use of common part-writing procedures in arpeggiated harmonies has been described in connection with Figures 5.2 and 5.3.

FIGURE 5.9   *Typical Examples of Triadic Arpeggiations*

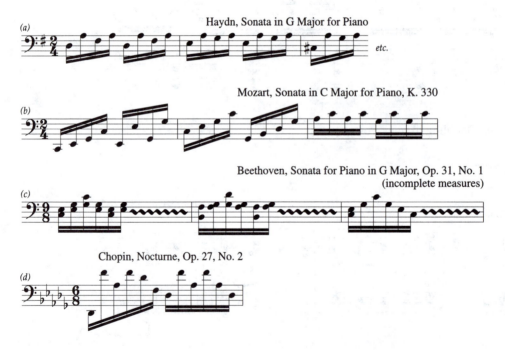

5. *Pedal point.* This device is common in instrumental music. Several varieties of the pedal point exist; the following are among them.

a. Single pedal tone in the bass (see also Figure 5.18).

FIGURE 5.10

b. Double pedal in the bass, usually the interval of a fifth.

FIGURE 5.11

c. Inverted pedal (pedal in an upper voice).

FIGURE 5.12

Mozart, Sonata in F Major for Violin and Piano, K. 377, III

d. "Interrupted pedal," in which the pedal tone is repeated at frequent (and usually regular) intervals of time to help create the effect of a sustained pedal tone, particularly in music performed at a fast tempo.

FIGURE 5.13

Bach, *Well-Tempered Clavier,* Vol. 1, Prelude No. 2

For examples showing pedal points of longer duration, see

B. Op. 22, "Allegro con brio," measures 4–7

M. Op. 19, No. 6, measures 7–14; Op. 102, No. 3, last twelve measures

S. No. 31, measures 34–40; No. 18, measures 1–4

See also Chopin, Prelude, Op. 28, No. 15; the entire piece is built on a pedal tone, A♭ and G♯, alternating in the keys of D♭ major and C♯ minor.

6. *Melody in a voice line other than the soprano.* The melody line can be found as an inner voice (see Figure 5.4) or as the lowest voice line (Figure 5.14), or it can be divided between two voice lines (Figure 5.15).

FIGURE 5.14

Schumann, *Album for the Young,* No. 10

FIGURE 5.15

Beethoven, Sonata in C Minor for Piano, Op. 13, I

7. *Melody doubled in thirds or sixths.*

   a. Melody doubled at the tenth (an octave plus a third).

FIGURE 5.16

Mendelssohn, *Songs Without Words,* Op. 85, No. 2

   b. Melody doubled in thirds, plus additional sonority doubling.

FIGURE 5.17

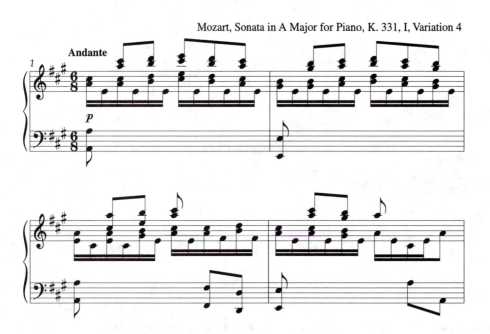

Mozart, Sonata in A Major for Piano, K. 331, I, Variation 4

   c. Melody doubled in sixths.

FIGURE 5.18

Chopin, Mazurka, Op. 67, No. 3

8. *Range and spacing of voices.* In four-part chorale style, the upper and lower limits of each vocal line were determined by the average range of each of the four classifications of the human voice. Similarly, in instrumental music, the range of a particular instrument will determine its pitch limits, high or low. Most instruments have a much wider range than the human voice and, depending upon the mechanics of a given instrument, provide opportunities for melodic lines less confining than those in chorale style. Figure 5.19 shows in dramatic fashion such a melodic line. The very wide leaps are not difficult to perform because of the clarinet's keying mechanism. But note that otherwise, traditional principles of melodic and harmonic writing still apply.

FIGURE 5.19   *Wide Melodic Leaps*

Mozart, Quintet for Clarinet and Strings, K. 581, II

A vocal line other than in chorale style can also demonstrate considerable flexibility in range, especially in large vocal works such as operas and oratorios, as in Figure 5.20.

FIGURE 5.20   *Wide Vocal Range*

Mozart, *Così fan tutte,* K. 588,
Act I, "Come scoglio"

(Secure as in a marble tower, guarded from every foe and power.)

The keyboard has the widest range of any of the instruments. The performer, playing the instrument with two hands, can produce close spacing with hands close together, or wider spacings as the hands move farther apart. Figure 5.2, measures 73 through 76, show a moderately wide spacing by this means while, as described at that point, maintaining usual part-writing and harmonic procedures.

Projects in Writing for the Keyboard

For the purpose of developing the ability to write for the keyboard, a series of projects will be presented in this chapter and continued in future chapters. The order of the projects will allow slow and steady progress, beginning with easier examples in which a maximum amount of material is given and continuing to the ultimate goal of composing with no prestated material.

Order of projects

1. Realization of figured basses from the works of Baroque composers. Both the melodic line and the bass line, with figuration, are given. These resemble the figured bass part-writing exercises of previous chapters.

2. Harmonizing a melodic line, using folk songs. The melody line is given, and the accompaniment written without the aid of figured bass, resembling melody harmonization assignments of previous chapters.

3. Original composition: Setting a poem to music. The poem helps suggest a melodic line, which is then harmonized and written for keyboard as above.

4. Composing for piano solo or for an instrument with a piano accompaniment.

In succeeding chapters, activity in these projects can be continued as follows.

Project I: Figured bass realizations will be included under "Assignments."

Projects II and III: Continue by using the same melodic and poetic materials given in the present chapter, or with similar materials chosen by the instructor or the student. To these, add the new harmonic materials of the particular chapter under study.

Project IV: Continue at the discretion of the instructor and through the initiative of the individual student.

Project I. Realization of Seventeenth- and Eighteenth-Century Compositions for Solo Instrument or Voice and Figured Bass

Figured bass is used almost universally today as an aid in teaching part-writing. Its original function was quite different.[4] In the seventeenth and early eighteenth centuries (the *Baroque* era), much of the music for vocal solo, instrumental solo, or those instrumental ensembles that included a keyboard instrument, was written by the composer with only a figured bass line for the keyboard player. (This practice was also known as *thorough bass,* and the bass line itself was known as the *continuo.* In ensemble music, the continuo was used by both the cellist and the keyboard player.) It was the responsibility of the keyboard player to improvise from the figured bass line. But after 1750, the continuo was little used, replaced by music for the keyboard fully written out. Thus, there is little demand today for the skill of improvising from a figured bass. So the editions of such music in current publication usually include a keyboard part written out by someone at a later date, using the composer's figuration as a basis.

Composing such keyboard parts is known as "realizing a figured bass." No two persons will realize a given bass in the same way, since the figured bass symbols do not indicate chord position or the character of any of the melodic lines above the bass. To illustrate, Figures 5.21*a* and 5.22*a* each show an excerpt from a violin sonata by Handel, exactly as written by the composer. Parts *b* and *c* of each figure show two different realizations of Handel's figured bass as found in current publications of these sonatas.

---

[4]Review the article "Figured Bass" in *Elementary Harmony,* page 202, for a brief history of the origin and use of figured bass.

FIGURE 5.21

Handel, Sonata in G Minor for Violin and
Figured Bass, Op. 1, No. 10

FIGURE 5.22

Handel, Sonata in D Major for Violin and
Figured Bass, Op. 1, No. 13

Realization by A. LeMaitre from Haendel, Sonates pour Violon et Piano, *Paris. © Heugel S. A.
Used By Permission.*

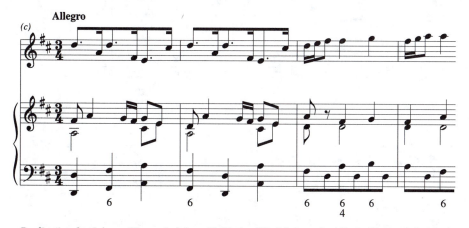

Realization by Johann Hinnenthal from Hallische Händel-Ausgabe, *Serie IV, Band 4, "Sechs
Sonaten für Violine," Kassel, Bärenreiter-Verlag, 1955. Reprinted by permission.*

Figures 5.23 and 5.24 show, from the many possibilities, two more ways to accomplish a realization. Again, only the melody and the figured bass of these were supplied by the composers.

FIGURE 5.23

Telemann, Partita 5

FIGURE 5.24

Lully, *Cadmus et Hermione* (1673),
Act III, Scene 6

It can easily be seen that various styles of writing can be employed in the realization. From Figures 5.21–5.24, here are some of the devices used:

1. Block chords.
   a. In all four voices: Figure 5.22*b*, measures 1–2.
   b. In the three upper voices: Figure 5.21*b*.
2. Block chords with occasional nonharmonic tones: Figure 5.24. Note that the addition of sevenths and nonharmonic tones is permissible and even desirable even when not indicated in the figured bass. Should the added nonharmonic tone coincide with another in the melody line, the two nonharmonic tones should be consonant with each other.
3. Melodic line in the realization: Figures 5.21*c*, 5.22*c*, and 5.24.
4. Rhythm pattern in the keyboard part in contrast to that in the melodic line: Figure 5.22*c*.
5. When the given bass line is melodic, often another voice can be written in parallel thirds (tenths) or sixths: Figure 5.23, measures 1–2.
6. Parallel first inversions: Figure 5.23, measures 3–4.

Special doubling procedures are common for realizations in some circumstances.

1. Triads in the realization are usually complete, even if this means doubling the third of a major triad, the leading tone of the key, or any altered tone, when that tone appears in the solo instrumental melody. In Figure 5.24, measure 3, the leading tone, C♯, appears simultaneously in the melody and in the accompaniment.
2. In a dominant seventh chord or another major-minor seventh chord, the leading tone may be omitted when that tone is in the melody.

While working with the realizations of Assignment 5.1, you will find it helpful to locate further examples of realized figured basses in your library. Look especially for sonatas for violin, flute, or oboe, and for trio sonatas (usually for violin, cello, and continuo) by Corelli, Vivaldi, Bach, Handel, and Telemann, among others.

ASSIGNMENT 5.1 *Realizing a figured bass.*   Four examples from the Baroque period are provided.

(1) Prepare three staves as in Figures 5.21–5.24, placing the melody on the top staff and the continuo on the lowest staff. Write your realization of the figured bass on the two lower staves (treble and bass).

The long line in the figured bass, as in measures 2 and 4, indicates that the same harmony is to be maintained during the bass line's movement.

Telemann, Sonata für Blockflöte und Basso Continuo,
No. 1, "Largo"

(2) The composer of this example did not include all figured bass symbols on the assumption that the performer would understand from the context of the music what figured bass was required. In measure 3, below the C♯ a "6" is understood. The B♮ is a passing tone, and below the A, "7" is understood. In measure 18 and similar measures, a single triad is appropriate above the florid bass line, or another voice may sound in parallel thirds (tenths) or sixths, as in Figure 5.23.

Vivaldi, Concerto in Fa, "Allegro alla Francese"

(3) The composer furnished no figured bass for this song. We have placed appropriate symbols up to the first double bar, after which you should furnish your own. When a sequence occurs in the melodic line, be sure to write a harmonic sequence to accompany it. When the bass line is melodic, as in the last eight measures, do not attempt to harmonize each note.

Purcell, Song: "I Envy Not a Monarch's Fate"

Ce - lia,   in   you,   my   Ce - lia,   I   have   all.

(4) This example is the second half of a binary form. The first half began in G minor and modulated to D minor.

Marcello, Sonata in G Minor for Flute or Violin

Project II: Harmonizing a Folk Song as Vocal Solo with Accompaniment

Harmonizing a folk song in instrumental style combines the skill of choosing a harmonic background, as studied beginning in the early chapters of *Elementary Harmony,* and the skill of writing an accompaniment, as just studied in Project I. Following are three examples of published folk-song arrangements, ranging from easy to moderate in difficulty.

Figure 5.25 shows a common procedure in harmonizing folk tunes, that of including the melody in the accompaniment. Parts *a* and *b* of this figure are the first and last phrases of this setting, with the same melody but with differences in the accompaniment to provide variety.

FIGURE 5.25

Welsh Folk Song: "The Ash Grove,"
arr. Robert Ottman

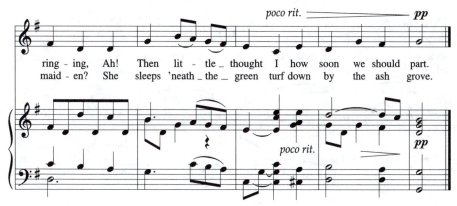

From Basic Repertoire for Singers *by Robert Ottman and Paul Krueger.* *Copyright 1959 by Southern Music Company, San Antonio, Texas.* *Used by permission.*

In Figure 5.26, measures 4–8, the folk tune is modified when placed in the accompaniment. Observe also the piano interlude that appears between stanzas. Short introductions and postludes for piano are also common. In *Elementary Harmony*, Figure 18.5, a complete folk-song setting by Brahms includes a postlude.

FIGURE 5.26

German Folk Song: "Soll sich der Mond,"
arr. Johannes Brahms

Figure 5.27 is the third stanza of a folk-song setting. In the first, the melody is included in the piano part, but for this stanza, the soprano line of the accompaniment is a completely independent melody.

FIGURE 5.27

Russian Folk Song: "The Jackdaw and the Falcon,"
arr. Kurt Schindler

From Sixty Russian Folk Songs, *by Kurt Schindler. Copyright © 1918 (Renewed) by G. Schirmer, Inc. International Copyright Secured. All Rights Reserved. Used by Permission.*

The preceding examples show but a few of the countless ways of creating a keyboard harmonization for a melodic line. Before embarking upon assignments in Project II, you should examine, play, and sing many additional folk-song settings. Numerous volumes of such materials are available in most music libraries. Especially recommended are those of Brahms, found in two collections, *48 German Folk Songs* and *28 German Folk Songs,* available in performing editions and in the complete works of Brahms, volume 26 (Brahms, *Sämtliche Werke*, Leipzig, Breitkopf and Härtel).

Some students, especially those with previous experience in composition, may wish to investigate twentieth-century folk-song settings, including Ravel (*Five Greek Folk Songs*), Bartók, Kodály, Britten, Vaughan Williams, and Copland, among others. All or many of these should be available in most music libraries.

ASSIGNMENT 5.2 *Harmonizing a folk melody and writing an accompaniment for piano.*   Using three staves, as in Figures 5.25–5.27, harmonize the folk tune with a keyboard accompaniment. The following steps will be helpful in planning the harmonization.

1. Sing or play the melody; read the text carefully. Folk songs usually have no tempo indication; choose a tempo appropriate to the character of the melody and the text.

2. Choose a harmonic progression, just as you did in harmonizing a chorale melody or a melody at the keyboard in earlier chapters. Be sure that each melody note is either part of a triad or a nonharmonic tone as previously defined.

3. Choose a style of accompaniment (arpeggiated, block chord, and so on) appropriate to the melody being harmonized. It is not necessary that the same style be maintained throughout the composition, but there should not be an abrupt change from one style to another.

4. Give special attention to the movement between the soprano and bass lines, just as in harmonizing a chorale.

5. Consider the possibility of adding a short (two- or four-measure) introduction and/or a coda to your harmonization.

6. Edit your manuscript. This includes tempo markings, dynamic markings, and phrasing in the piano score. Phrasing marks are used to indicate melodic motives and places where *legato* is desired. Study Figures 5.25–5.27 and examples from published harmonizations.

If you wish a wider choice of melodies or need additional material for practice, select melodies from your sight-singing book or from the many collections of unharmonized folk songs usually available in music libraries.

though with her na - ture it did not a - gree, which __

made her re - pent, And so of - ten la - ment, Still __

wish - ing a - gain in the North for to be. O the

oak and the ash, and the bon - ny i - vy tree do __

flour - ish at home in my own coun - try.

(3)   English Folk Song

Love me lit - tle, love me long, __ is the _ bur - den of __ my _ song.

Love that is too hot and strong _ burn - eth soon to waste.

Still I would not have thee cold, Nor too back - ward nor too bold; __

Love that last - eth 'til 'tis old, __ Fa - deth not in haste.

(4)   Czech Folk Song

Good-night be-lov - ed, good night, good night;   God keep you safe in His watch-ful sight.

Good-night, dear,   soft - ly sleep;   Sweet be the dreams of your slum - ber deep.

Good-night, dear,   soft - ly sleep;   Sweet be the dreams of your slum - ber deep.

Project III: Original Composition and Setting a Poem to Music

A piece of composed music is regarded by many people, even some musicians, as the direct result of inspiration or intuition. Although there are such instances, for most composers, inspiration and musical knowledge go hand in hand. At this point in your studies, you certainly have enough knowledge to write music ranging from very simple to quite sophisticated.

As for inspiration, many beginners in composition find it easier to start by setting a poem to music. The text can often present just the inspiration needed, while its structure suggests the musical form in which the piece will be set.

Composing an original song combines the skill of writing a good melodic line, as studied in previous chapters, and the ability to write an accompaniment, as studied in Project I and Project II. In addition, knowledge of combining a text with a melodic line is necessary.[5]

1. *Meter.* A poem, which, like music, has meter and rhythm, is usually chosen as a text for a song. The melodic line is composed to accommodate the metrical considerations of the poem. Therefore, it is first necessary to scan the poem to determine its strong and weak accents. These generally conform to like accents in the music. In the scansions following, "-" indicates a strong accent, and "˘" indicates a weaker accent.

FIGURE 5.28

Sleep   my child and   peace   at-tend thee,   All   through the night.

---

[5]See also *New Harvard Dictionary of Music,* "Text and Music."

The meter of a poetic line does not necessarily indicate a specific musical meter. In Figures 5.29 and 5.30, the same poetic lines have been set in both simple and compound time, but in both cases, the metrical accents of music and poetry coincide.

Ĭ wālk ĭn thĕ gār- dĕn eār- lĭy

Jŭst āt thĕ brēak ŏf thĕ dāy.

Thĕ flŏw-ĕrs āll whĭs- pĕr tŏ- gēth- ĕr.

Nēv- ĕr ă word Ĭ sāy.

FIGURE 5.29

FIGURE 5.30

Figure 5.31 shows three different settings of the first line of "Nur wer die Sehnsucht kennt," each with a different time signature. Note again how the accents in the melodic line conform to the accents in the poetic line.

FIGURE 5.31

2. *Form.* The form of a song is usually dictated by the form of the poem being set. In simple poetry, where the meter is constant and all lines are of equal length, a simple setting may result—one phrase of music (regular) for each line of poetry. Such well-known songs as "Auld Lang Syne" and "The Blue Bells of Scotland" illustrate this procedure. Any of the forms previously studied can be utilized: phrases, periods, double periods, and so on.

In addition, the devices of extension may be used. In Figure 5.32, part of the last line of the poetic stanza is repeated to extend the phrase.

FIGURE 5.32

In Figure 5.33, phrase 1, a short poetic line is extended to make a full four-measure musical phrase; in phrase 2, the same short line is extended to make a five-measure phrase:

The post brings you no note today,
   my heart,
So now why act in this strange way,
   my heart?

FIGURE 5.33

Schubert, *Die Winterreise,* D. 911, "Die Post"

3. *Syllabic and melismatic methods of text setting.* When one syllable of the text is set to one note of the melody, the result is known as a *syllabic* setting. (See Figures 5.28–5.29.) When more than one note is assigned to a single syllable, the result is *melismatic,* and the group of single notes sung to a single syllable is called a *melisma.* Most art songs use syllabic settings with occasional short melismas, usually two or three notes, but sometimes longer, as in Figure 5.32.

4. *Strophic and through-composed songs.* In the *strophic* songs, each stanza of the poem is sung to the same melody. Most church hymns are strophic. See also Schubert, *Die schöne Müllerin,* Op. 25, Nos. 1, 7, 8, 9, 10, 13, 14, 16, 20.

   More sophisticated songs, such as the German *lied,* the French *chanson,* or art songs of any nationality, are more often than not *through-composed;* that is, the melodic line at any moment is an expression of or a reaction to the sentiment of the poem. Therefore, although the song is made up of phrases as dictated by the cadential points of the poem, these phrases do not necessarily combine into larger formal structures such as period and double periods.

5. *Vocal notation.* In syllabic settings, eighth notes and smaller are traditionally not beamed, each carrying its own flag with each syllable (Figure 5.34*a*).

In current compositional practice, as well as in newly revised editions of earlier vocal music, beaming is generally used (Figure 5.34 *b*). Note in both *a* and *b* that the melisma is identified by a phrase mark from its first to its last notes.

FIGURE 5.34   *Vocal Notation*

ASSIGNMENT 5.3 *Setting a poem as vocal line and accompaniment.*   Any poem of short or moderate duration can be set as a song. For the first attempts, choose something short and to your liking. A number of poems are provided here, not as requirements, but as possibilities.

The finished composition should be fully edited, including tempo indication, dynamic markings, and phrasing. Be sure to follow the procedures of vocal notation as seen in the preceding music examples.

> Ye flowery banks o'bonny Doon.
>   How can ye blume sae fair?
> How can ye chant, ye little birds,
>   And I sae fu' of care?
>
> Thou'll break my heart, thou bonny bird,
>   That sings upon the bough;
> Thou minds me o' the happy days,
>   When my fause love was true.
>   —*Robert Burns*

> Of a' the airts the wind can blaw;
>   I dearly like the west,
> For there the bonnie lassy lives,
>   The lassie I lo'e best;
> There wild woods grow, and rivers row,
>   And mony a hill between;
> But day and night my fancy's flight
>   Is ever wi' my Jean.
>   —*Robert Burns*

The sun, above the mountain's head,
A freshening lustre mellow
Through all the long green fields has spread,
His first sweet evening yellow.
                    —*William Wordsworth*

Pack clouds away, and welcome day,
    With night we banish sorrow;
Sweet air, blow soft; mount, lark, aloft,
    To give my love good morrow.

Wings from the wind to please her mind.
    Notes from the lark I'll borrow;
Bird, prune thy wing, nightingale, sing,
    To give my love good morrow.
                    —*Thomas Heywood*

Ask me no more where Jove bestows,
When June is past, the fading rose;
For in your beauties orient deep,
These flow'rs as in their causes sleep.

Ask me no more whither do stray
The golden atoms of the day;
For in pure love heaven did prepare
Those powders to enrich your hair.

Ask me no more where those stars light
That downwards fall in dead of night;
For in your eyes they sit, and there
Fixed become as in their sphere.
                    —*Thomas Carew*

Away delights, go seek some other dwelling,
For I must die.
Farewell false love! thy tongue is ever telling
Lie after lie.
Forever let me rest now from the smarts;
Alas, for pity, go
And fire their hearts
That have been hard to thee! Mine was not so.
                    —*John Fletcher*

Four ducks on a pond,
A grass-bank beyond,
A blue sky of spring,
White clouds on the wing;
What a little thing
To remember for years—
To remember with tears!
                    —*William Allingham*

Jenny kissed me when we met,
   Jumping from the chair she sat in.
Time, you thief! Who love to get
   Sweets into your list, put that in.

Say I'm weary, say I'm sad;
   Say that health and wealth have missed me;
Say I'm growing old, but add—
   Jenny kissed me!
                  —Leigh Hunt

Project IV: Composing for Piano Solo or for an Instrument with a Piano Accompaniment

At this point, specific instruction in music composition through a book is usually not satisfactory. In your work in this chapter, you have started with the maximum amount of given material (realizing figured bass compositions) and have gone on to projects with less and less given material. By this time, your imagination should have been stimulated sufficiently to make good use of the theoretical material presented in previous chapters.

Assignments in original composition may be assigned by the instructor. Additionally, you should find that personal creative composition can be a most worthwhile experience.

Remember that writing music is comparable to original work in any art form in that success is usually not immediate. Continually rework your ideas when at first they do not seem to be exactly what you want. You might keep in mind the notebooks of Beethoven. In these, he constantly rewrote and revised his original ideas. For constructive criticism of your work, consult with your instructor or with other students more advanced in this activity.

6

Diatonic Seventh Chords

Throughout the previous chapters, you have already become acquainted with the most common and the most useful of the diatonic seventh chords. Though appearances of the remaining chords as single sonorities are quite limited, all diatonic seventh chords are used freely and frequently as members of the popular harmonic sequence root movement by fifth.

All the diatonic seventh chords are shown in Figure 6.1. Chords marked with an * are the ones you have already studied. Take special note of the chords built on $\hat{6}$ and $\hat{7}$ of the minor scale. In the ascending form, $\sharp\hat{6}$ and $\sharp\hat{7}$ produce $vi^{\varnothing 7}$ and $vii^{\circ 7}$, whereas in the descending form, $\flat\hat{6}$ and $\flat\hat{7}$ produce VI^7 and VII^7.

FIGURE 6.1   *Diatonic Seventh Chords*

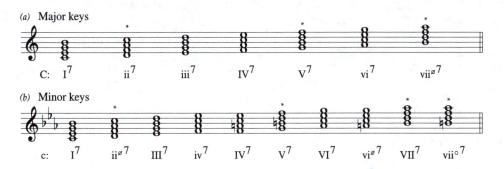

The Major Seventh Chord

Although Figure 6.1 contains many seventh chords not yet studied, as based on their roman-numeral identification, only one type of chord construction, the major-major seventh, remains to be accounted for. Usually referred to simply as a major seventh chord, it consists of a major triad and the interval of a major seventh between its root and its seventh. The diatonic major seventh chords are these: major keys, I^7 and IV^7, and minor keys, III^7 and VI^7.

FIGURE 6.2   *The Major Seventh Chord*

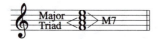

ASSIGNMENT 6.1   Spell each diatonic seventh chord in any major or minor key.

In the Workbook: Answers are given.

Uses of Single Diatonic Seventh Chords

Of those chords in Figure 6.1 not marked with an *, the sonority most commonly used nonsequentially is the subdominant seventh in its resolution to a chord of dominant function, iv⁷–V (Figures 6.3 and 6.5) and IV⁷–vii° (Figure 6.4), or to the supertonic triad (Figure 6.5).

FIGURE 6.3   *iv⁷–V: Minor Key*

FIGURE 6.4   *IV₂⁴–vii°₆: Minor Key*

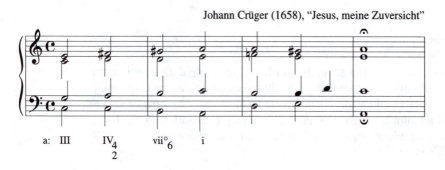

FIGURE 6.5   *IV$_5^6$–V$_5^6$; IV$_5^6$–ii$_6$: Major Key*

The IV^7 (a major-minor seventh chord) in a minor key has a dual function. Not only can it resolve to a dominant function—to V in Figure 1.17, measure 2, and to vii° in Figure 6.4—but it can also function as a secondary dominant, V^7/VII. In Figure 6.6, it serves as the opening chord in a short harmonic sequence.

The vi^{ø7} is uncommon and appears only in a minor key, above $\sharp\hat{6}$ in the bass. In Figure 6.7, it appears in a chromatic bass line between V$_6$ and V. It is obvious that the chromatic line is the important aspect of this progression and that the use of the vi^{ø7} is only coincidental. See Figure 6.11 for a different use of this sonority.

FIGURE 6.6   *The Subdominant Seventh as V^7/VII*

FIGURE 6.7   *The Submediant Seventh, vi*$^{\varnothing7}$

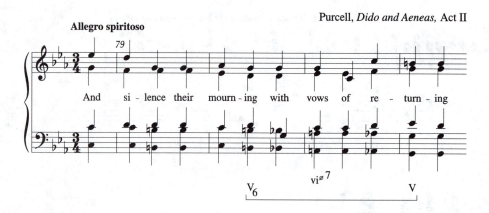

Most other single uses of these sonorities strongly suggest analysis of the seventh as the simple use of an ordinary nonharmonic tone. In Figure 6.8, the apparent seventh is probably better analyzed as an accented lower-neighbor tone.

FIGURE 6.8

Diatonic Seventh Chords in Sequence, Three Voices

In contrast to the paucity of individual uses of these chords, their frequency in the harmonic sequence is very high. Most often they appear in that sequence, where the successive roots are down a fifth and up a fourth. In this sequence, a chain suspension in each of two voices creates a seventh above each root (Figure 6.9). The seventh alternates between each of the two voices. Each resolves to the third of the next chord and becomes the preparation for the next seventh.

In a minor key, the descending melodic lines require the use of the descending form of the scale. When the bass line reaches $\hat{5}$–$\hat{1}$ and a cadence occurs, the harmony is V^7–i, but if the sequence continues past that point, the harmony is v^7–i (Figure 6.11, measure 2). The minor dominant seventh, v^7, is rarely used elsewhere.

FIGURE 6.9

(a) Major keys

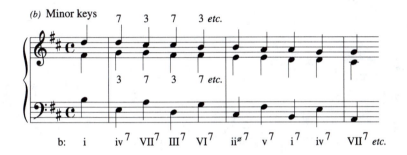

(b) Minor keys

This same three-voice structure is seen in Figure 6.10, where each seventh is decorated by a four-note melodic figure.

FIGURE 6.10

Mozart, Sonata in F Major for Piano, K. 533, III

An interesting variation of this three-voice texture is seen in Figure 6.11. In measures 1–3, each quarter rest in the bass voice appears to have replaced an expected bass note of the sequence. Supplying the notes A, F♯, and D for these rests completes the sequence stucture. In measures 7–8, the composer has held the bass notes A and G for two beats each, instead of dropping down a fifth to the expected notes D and C, respectively.

This lengthy sequence of seventh chords is interrupted in measure 4 by V⁷–i of the opening key, followed by a continuation of the sequence leading to a cadential pattern, IV–vii°–i, in A minor (measure 6). But A minor is only weakly established, if at all, since there is no pause in the continuing movement to E minor. Therefore, the excursion away from E minor is probably best considered a secondary tonal level over iv of the original key after which the sequence continues to cadence in the original E minor.

Note (1) the use of the minor dominant seventh (v⁷) in measure 2 (review Figure 6.9*b*) and (2) the rare use of viᵒ⁷ in measure 4, where, no doubt, the composer chose C♯ for the bass note to avoid the ascending tritone, C–F♯.

FIGURE 6.11

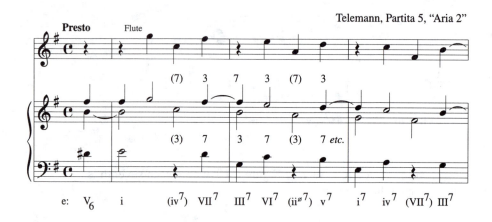

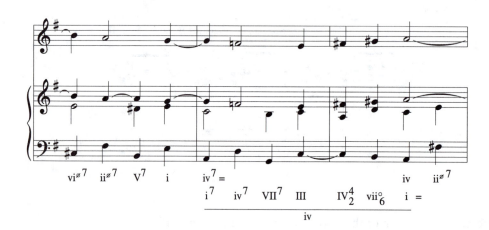

V^7	i	iv^7 (VII^7)	III^7 (VI^7)	$ii^{ø7}$	V^7	i	iv	V		i
		or $ii^{°}_6$	i_6							

Although this sequence, roots down a fifth and up a fourth, commonly begins with roots on $\hat{1}-\hat{4}-\hat{7}$, as seen in Figures 6.9–6.11, it can also begin on any other roots. In Figure 6.13, the root movement $\hat{5}-\hat{1}-\hat{4}$ ($V^4_2-I^7-iv^4_3$) opens the sequence.

Diatonic Seventh Chords in Succession and in Sequence, Four Voices

In the study of dominant and supertonic seventh chords, we learned that when these chords are used in succession with roots in the bass, one chord is complete and the other incomplete. The same is true for a succession or for a sequence of seventh chords in four voices. Figure 6.12 uses the series seen in Figure 6.9*b,* but with a fourth voice added. Note in this case that the first, third, and fifth seventh chords are complete, and those between incomplete. Also note the same pattern of alternating suspensions as shown in Figure 6.9.

FIGURE 6.12 *Seventh Chords in Succession*

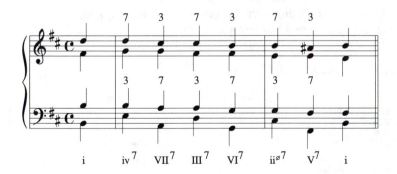

i iv^7 VII^7 III^7 VI^7 $ii^{ø7}$ v^7 i

In inversion, seventh chords of any variety are usually complete, as shown in Figure 6.13, where the sequence shows alternating second inversions with root positions ($_3^4$ 7). The pattern of alternating suspensions is seen in the upper two voices, one decorated in eighth notes. For the sequence $_5^6 \, _2^4$, see Figure 6.21.

FIGURE 6.13   *Inversions in a Sequence*

A sequence may consist of a pattern of root movements different from the one shown so far, and any sequence may be found with the seventh chord alternating with a triad. Both of these possibilities are shown in Figure 6.14, where the root movement, down a third and up a second, utilizes alternating triads and seventh chords. Also review Figure 2.23, which includes three diminished seventh chords resolving to triads in a harmonic sequence, roots up a second and down a fourth.

FIGURE 6.14   *Alternating Triads and Seventh Chords*

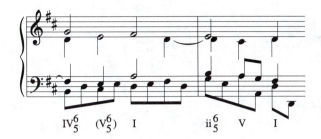

Although most of the seventh chords of the sequence in Figure 6.15 are secondary dominants, three seventh chords are without chromatic alteration, as indicated by the * above each. What does the resolution of each have in common with the others?

FIGURE 6.15

Mozart, Concerto in F Major for Piano and Orchestra, K. 459, I

In instrumental writing, more freedom in the treatment of the seventh is commonly seen. In Figure 6.16, each circled seventh resolves on the second eighth note following. This example actually includes two sequential patterns, connected so smoothly that it is easy to mistake the entire passage for a single harmonic sequence. Where is the break between sequences and how is it accomplished?

FIGURE 6.16   *Delayed Resolution of Sevenths*

ASSIGNMENT 6.2 *Harmonic analysis.*   Analyze each example, taking particular note of the use of the seventh both in single seventh chords and in sequences.

(1)

Franck, *Symphonic Variations*

(2)

Purcell, *The Virtuous Wife,* "Minuet II"

(3)

Bach, *Christmas Oratorio,* No. 41, BWV 249

(4) This passage in C minor from a concerto in C major includes two harmonic sequences, ending on a Picardy third that leads back to C major. In the melody line, at each appearance of an eighth rest, calculate the chord spelling by including the pitch name immediately following the rest.

In addition to doing a roman-numeral analysis, answer these questions:

1. First sequence
   a. What is the root movement?
   b. Which measures contain two different spellings above the same root?
   c. Why does the bass line of the first and third measures differ from that in the second and fourth measures?

2. Second sequence
   a. What is the root movement?
   b. What did the composer accomplish by using crossed voices?

Mozart, Concerto in C Major for Piano, K. 503, I

(5)

Schumann, *Dichterliebe,* Op. 48,
"Das ist ein Flöten und Geigen"

(6) In measure 8, consider the D♭ and its duplication in the arpeggio as a non-harmonic tone against A C E♭ G♭. Note its resolution at the end of measure 9.

Brahms, Intermezzo, Op. 117, No. 2

Andante non troppo e con molto espressione

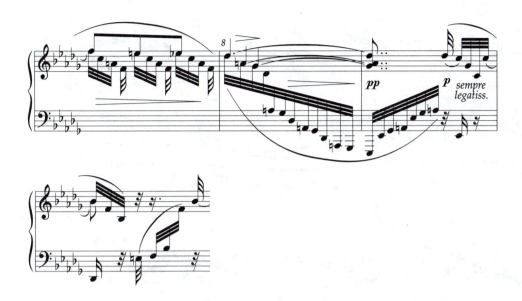

(7) This excerpt from a twentieth-century work includes a harmonic sequence markedly similar to the typical earlier sequence. Locate the sequence, describe its root movement, and explain the function of tones that are not members of the harmonic sequential pattern.

Walton, Concerto for Viola and Orchestra, I

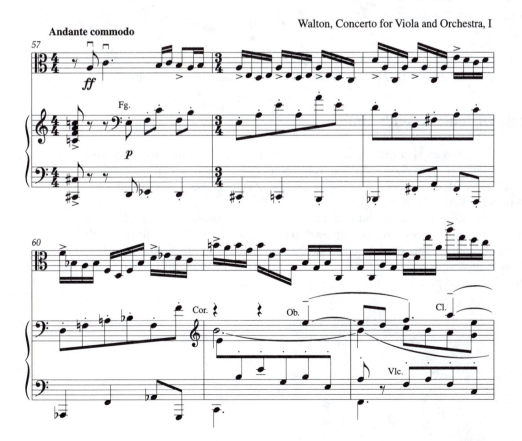

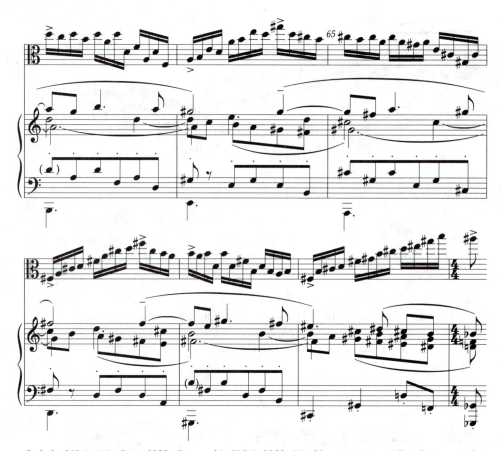

Writing Single Diatonic Seventh Chords

The procedures already learned for the part-writing of seventh chords apply equally to the remaining seventh chords. In four-voice nonsequential writing, all four voices are usually present, thereby avoiding any ambiguity of sound (does B D A stand for B D F A or B D F♯ A?).

Only the subdominant seventh chord requires special treatment, caused by the fact that its root movement is usually up by step to V rather than down by fifth as with most seventh chords. This resolution can easily produce parallel fifths, but only when the chord's seventh is above its third, as in Figure 6.17. When the third is above the seventh, there is no problem.

FIGURE 6.17   *Incorrect Resolution of IV⁷*

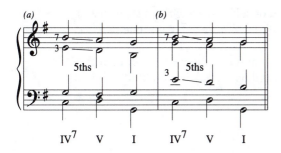

To avoid the fifths, any resolution that does not include parallel octaves or augmented seconds is acceptable. Usually, it is the third that moves unconventionally, often down by fifth or by third as in Figure 6.18. The downward approach to the seventh in *b* is acceptable in this particular progression.

FIGURE 6.18   *Resolution of IV⁷*

In the Workbook: Do Assignment 6A. Answers are given.

Writing Harmonic Sequences in Three Voices

Figure 6.9 demonstrates clearly the suspension figure alternating between the upper and middle voices. Although Figure 6.9 shows the sequence entered by the progression I–IV⁷ (i–iv⁷), the tonic can also progress to any other chord to begin the sequence, such as I–ii⁷–V⁷–I⁷ and so forth, or another appropriate chord may proceed to the first chord of the sequence, such as I–V–vi⁷–ii⁷ and so forth.

ASSIGNMENT 6.3   *Writing the sequence roots down a fifth and up a fourth in three voices.*

(a) Using any major or minor key, assigned or self-chosen, write a sequence in three voices patterned after Figure 6.9. Begin with I–IV^7 or i–iv^7. Continue past the roots $\hat{5}$–$\hat{1}$ until the next appearance of the roots $\hat{5}$–$\hat{1}$.

(b) Write a sequence in which the first chord of the sequence is other than IV^7 (iv^7). Should your sequence end with the tonic chord on a weak beat, add ii$^6_5$–V–I or ii$^{\varnothing6}_5$–V–i to complete the exercise.

Writing Harmonic Sequences in Four Voices

The basic four-voice pattern for writing the common harmonic sequence roots in the bass down a fifth and up a fourth is shown in Figure 6.12. The sequence can be written with either the root or the fifth as the first soprano note, as well as with the third shown in the example. (See Figure 6.19 for an example beginning with the fifth in the soprano.)

Figure 6.13 shows that when inversions are used in this sequence, each seventh chord is complete while other conditions remain the same. Note also that here the sequence is introduced not with iv^7 but the V^7. Examples of each of the inversion patterns are shown in Figures 6.20 and 6.21. Though in keyboard style (three notes in the right hand), they can easily be converted to four-voice chorale style.

In review, these conditions apply no matter what the inversion or the soprano position:

1. With root movement down a fifth and up a fourth, roots in the bass, seventh chords are alternately complete and incomplete. With the use of inversions, all seventh chords are complete.

2. Alternating suspension figures will occur between any two voices, the seventh of the chord resolving to the third of the next chord, while simultaneously the third is held over to become the seventh of the next chord.

3. The sequence may begin with any member of the series.

ASSIGNMENT 6.4 *Writing the harmonic sequence roots down a fifth and up a fourth in four voices.*   As before, to continue past the tonic chord in major, use I^7, or in minor, v^7–i^7. If the final tonic triad ends on a weak beat, add ii$^6_5$–V–I (ii$^{\varnothing6}_5$–V–i).

For further practice, use other keys.

1. E major, I–IV^7–vii$^{\varnothing7}$–(to I)

2. G minor, i–iv^7–VII^7–

3. C# minor, i–ii$^{\varnothing4}_2$–v$_6$–

4. B♭ major, I–vi–ii$^6_5$–V$^4_2$–

5. E minor, V–i–iii^7–VI$^4_3$–

6. The sequence down a third and up a second, as in Figure 6.14: F minor, i–ii$^{\varnothing6}_5$–VII$_6$–i$^6_5$–

ASSIGNMENT 6.5 *Figured bass exercises including diatonic seventh chords and harmonic sequences.* For the practice of writing in the C clefs, use a brace of four staves with the alto clef and the tenor clef on the second and third staves.

ASSIGNMENT 6.6 *Realization of a figured bass.*   *(a)* The bass line only is given. Supply the three upper voices.

The keyboard exercises of Assignment 6.7 can also be used here. Follow the directions given in Assignment 2.14 (page 67).

(b) Examples from music literature are given. Using three staves, write a piano accompaniment based on the composer's bass line and figuration. The first example is the first part of a binary form.

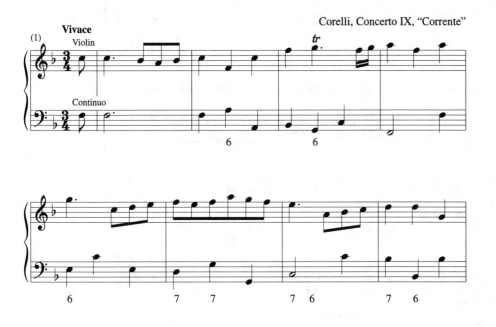

Corelli, Concerto IX, "Corrente"

Bach, Sonata No. 1 in C Major for Flute and Continuo

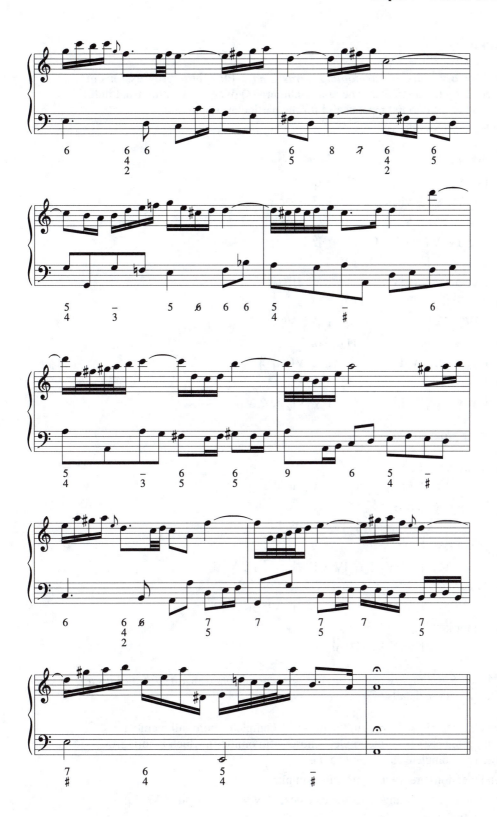

Keyboard Harmony

ASSIGNMENT 6.7 *Playing harmonic progressions.* Play these progressions in keys as directed by the instructor. The arabic numeral(s) over the opening triad indicate(s) the soprano position(s) most useful for the particular progression.

(a) Short progressions

Major keys	Minor keys
(1) 1 or 5	(7) 1 or 5
I I^7 IV V (or vii$^\circ_6$) I	i i^7 iv V i
(2) 1 or 5	(8) 1
I I$^6_5$ IV V (or vii$^\circ_6$) I	i i$^6_5$ iv V i
(3) 1	(9) 1
I vi iii^7 IV V I	i VI III^7 iv V i
(4) 3	(10) 1, 3, 5
I IV$^6_5$ V$^6_5$ I	i IV$^6_5$ V$^6_5$ i
(5) 5	(11) 3 or 5
I V$_6$ vi^7 ii$^4_3$ V I	i v$_6$ VI^7 ii$^{\varnothing 4}_{3}$ V i
(6) 5	(12) 1 or 5
I V vi$^4_2$ ii$^6_5$ V I	i V VI$^4_2$ ii$^{\varnothing 6}_{5}$ V i

(b) Longer progressions

(13) Major key: 1

     I I$^6_5$ IV$^4_2$ vii$^\circ_6$ iii$^4_2$ vi$_6$ ii V I

(14) Major key: 5 or 3

     I iii vi^7 ii V I$^6_5$ IV vii$^\circ_6$ I

(15) Major key: 1

     I ii$^4_2$ V$^6_5$ I I$^6_5$ IV vii$^{\circ 6}_{5}$ I$_6$ vi^7 ii$^4_3$ V^7 I

(16) Minor key: 1

     i ii$^{\varnothing 4}_{2}$ V$^6_5$ i i$^6_5$ iv vii$^\circ_6$ i$_6$ VI^7 ii$^{\varnothing 4}_{3}$ V^7 i

(17) Minor key: 1, 3, or 5

     i vii$^{\circ 7}$ v$_6$ vi$^{\varnothing 7}$ ii$^{\varnothing 4}_{3}$ V i

ASSIGNMENT 6.8 *Playing the harmonic sequence roots down a fifth and up a fourth.* Observe these details:

1. When each chord has its root in the bass, the complete chord (all members present) progresses to an incomplete chord (fifth omitted), which in turn progresses to a complete chord, and so on.

2. When inversions are used, chords are complete.

3. In a major key, to continue past the cadence, play V^7–I^7 instead of V^7–I. In minor, play v^7–i^7 instead of V^7–i .

4. If the tonic triad of the cadence falls on a weak beat, continue with ii$^6_5$–V–I or ii$^{\o6}_5$–V–i.

5. This sequence need not always start with the progression I–IV^7. The opening tonic may progress to a different seventh chord—for example, I–ii^7–V^7–I^7 and so on, or another chord may progress to a seventh chord, as I–V–vi^7–ii^7 and so on. There are almost limitless possibilities for experimentation.

   (a) Play the sequence, each chord with its root in the bass.

FIGURE 6.19

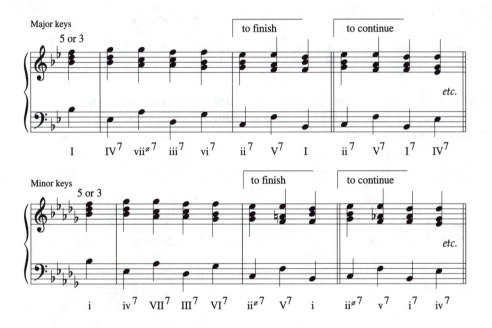

   (b) Play the sequence using inversions, figured bass pattern $^4_3$ 7. With three sharps, Figure 6.20 can be played in A major.

FIGURE 6.20

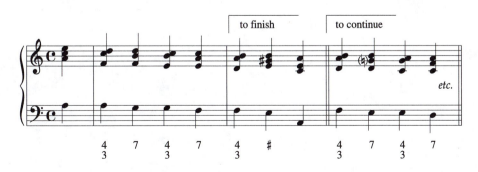

(*c*) Play the sequence using inversions, ⁶₅ ⁴₂. This sequence can also be played in a major key.

FIGURE 6.21

ASSIGNMENT 6.9 *Playing the sequence roots down a third and up a second.*   The sequence in Figure 6.22*a* is the same as in the Bach example, Figure 6.14. At *b,* in a different version, the figured bass is ⁴₃ ⁴₂.

FIGURE 6.22

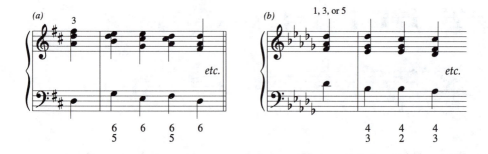

ASSIGNMENT 6.10 *Improvising an accompaniment from a figured bass.*   In this example from Handel (Figure 6.23), an accompaniment for the first two measures is given.

FIGURE 6.23

Handel, Sonata in B Minor for Flute and Continuo

Summary

A seventh chord may appear on any scale step in both major and minor keys. Those studied in previous chapters—seventh chords on the dominant, supertonic, and leading tone—are those most commonly used. The remaining seventh chords are found mostly in harmonic sequences, especially that with roots down a fifth and up a fourth. Except for the subdominant seventh, the remaining seventh chords are not commonly seen used other than in a sequence.

In a minor key, seventh chords built on $\hat{6}$ and $\hat{7}$ have varied uses. The VI^7, built on $\flat\hat{6}$, functions similarly to other diatonic seventh chords. The vi$^{\varnothing7}$, built on $\sharp\hat{6}$, is used only when the melodic line in the bass requires a $\sharp\hat{6}$. VII^7, built on $\flat\hat{7}$, functions as the secondary dominant of III, whereas vii$^{\circ7}$, built on $\sharp\hat{7}$, is the diminished seventh chord commonly used to precede the tonic triad.

7

Chromatic Chords

modal mixture; the Neapolitan sixth; the augmented triad

The remaining triads and seventh chords in the catalog of regularly used harmonic structures are found in this chapter and the one following. All are chromatically altered chords, but without secondary dominant functions.

The term *chromatic* means "pertaining to color," so these harmonies are sometimes referred to as *color chords*. Certainly they break up the homogeneity of diatonic harmony and inject color when ranging from a single chord to progressions of length.

We have already had experience with chromatic harmonies, all of which have added color to the musical canvas. But those previously studied have had more important functions: the Picardy third to avoid a final minor tonic triad, and secondary dominant and secondary leading-tone chords to temporarily tonicize the harmony following. Modulation also provides color when we hear tones in the new key that would have been chromatic in the original key.

The remaining chromatically altered chords serve only the purpose of adding color. These chords generally function exactly as their unaltered counterparts do, or as pivot chords in modulation, easily opening the way to keys unavailable through diatonic pivots.

Modal Mixture

Modal mixture refers to the practice of using chords of one mode (major or minor) in music written in the opposite mode[1] and is specifically demonstrated in Figure 7.1. The example is in a major mode (F major), but within it we find a harmony, B♭ D♭ F, from the parallel minor mode (iv in F minor). The phrase thus includes a mixture of harmonies from the parallel major and minor modes. With the D♭, the composer has added a "spot of color" that heightens the meaning of the poetic line.

---

[1]Chords deriving from a modal mixture are also known as *borrowed chords*—that is, chords taken from one mode for use in the other.

FIGURE 7.1

Schubert, *Die Winterreise,* D. 911,
"Das Wirtshaus"

(Here [in this churchyard] I thought, will I abide.)

All chords from the minor mode available for use as mixed-mode chords are shown in Figure 7.2. However, there are two qualifications.

1. The three triads with the added symbols V/— actually function more frequently as secondary dominants and when so used are identified with secondary dominant symbols (V/—). As a secondary dominant, each can also be found with an added minor seventh above its root (V⁷/—).

   In the symbol V/N, *N* refers to the Neapolitan chord (♭II), presented later in this chapter.

2. The chords in black notes, the v triad and most seventh chords, are seldom used singly for mixed-modal purposes but are useful in a harmonic sequence.

FIGURE 7.2   *Chords from C Minor as Used in C Major*

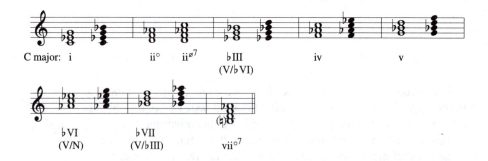

Chords borrowed from a major key for use in a parallel minor key are uncommon except for the Picardy third. In the transformation of the medieval modes through the use of *musica ficta,*[2] $\hat{7}$ in the Aeolian mode (the same as the natural or pure minor

[2]Review "Medieval Modes" in *Elementary Harmony,* fifth edition, Appendix D, page 433.

scale) was raised one half step to become a leading tone (#$\hat{7}$). This in turn necessitated raising $\hat{6}$ to #$\hat{6}$, resulting in the present melodic minor scale. Consequently, except for the tonic and the mediant, each triad constructed from the ascending form of this scale includes either #$\hat{6}$ or #$\hat{7}$ and duplicates a triad already diatonic in a major key.

ASSIGNMENT 7.1   Spell each of the chords of Figure 7.2 in any major key.

In the Workbook: Answers are given.

Although Figure 7.1 shows successive major and minor triads above the same root (B♭ D F–B♭ D♭ F), the mixture chord may be introduced independently of its major-key counterpart. Figure 7.3 shows both the ii°⁷ and the iv triads introduced by the major tonic triad, F A C to G B♭ D♭ F and to B♭ D♭ F. Note particularly the use of added dissonance with each mixture chord, a seventh at the first appearance and an accented nonharmonic tone at each of the three subsequent appearances.

FIGURE 7.3

Fauré, *Lydia*, Op. 4, No. 2

(Let your kisses, your dove-like kisses sing upon your budding lips.)

The ♭VI, like the diatonic vi, is commonly used in the progressions ♭VI–iv–V, Figure 7.4, and in the deceptive cadence, V–♭VI, Figure 7.5.

FIGURE 7.4

Brahms, *Liebeslieder Walzer,* Op. 52, No. 14

(Like the clear waves shines the moon above.)

FIGURE 7.5

Bach, "Vater unser im Himmelreich" (#267)

F: V₆/iii   iii   V/V   V₆   I   vi   ii₆   V   ♭VI
      5   5   5

Tonicization and Sequence

Figure 7.6, measures 37–38, shows the mixture chords ♭VI and ♭VII tonicized by their respective secondary dominant sevenths. Note in the V⁷/♭VI that its triad, F A C (♭III), could function either as a mode-mixture chord or as a secondary dominant; but, with a minor seventh added, it functions only as a secondary dominant.

These chords are a part of a harmonic sequence, roots up a fourth and down a third, F–B♭–G–C–A–D.

FIGURE 7.6

Chopin, Polonaise in A Major, Op. 40, No. 1

D: I   V

The minor dominant triad (v; shown in black in Figure 7.2) makes a rare appearance as a modal-mixture harmony by its placement in a harmonic sequence (Figure 7.7). Also included is the iv triad, which, like the v triad, is preceded by its secondary dominant.

The sequence may be considered to begin at the °⁷vi, considering the implied root of this chord to be D. Note also the tonal ambiguity of the first measure. The ascending chromatic bass line strongly suggests I–IV⁷–V⁷–I in D minor, but the expected D minor tonic is replaced by I₆ of B♭ major.

FIGURE 7.7

Bach, "Ach Gott und Herr" (No. 279)

Temporary Change of Mode

Sufficient use of borrowed chords in a passage can lead to the effect of a temporary change of mode, usually major to minor, or an uncertainty as to which mode is predominant. In Figure 7.8, the alternation of I and i triads has the effect of confusing the mode until the ♭VI seems to indicate a minor key, only to end in the original key of G major.

FIGURE 7.8

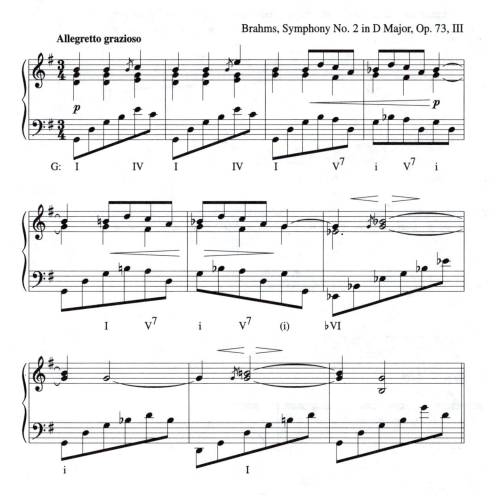

Brahms, Symphony No. 2 in D Major, Op. 73, III

The opposite change of mode, from minor to major, is far less common, though change in both directions is frequently used by Schubert. Extensive use of this device can easily be heard in the second movement of his Symphony No. 9 in C major, D. 944. In Figure 7.9, measures 10–11, a single progression in major, I–V–I, is heard between the opening and closing B minor harmony.

FIGURE 7.9

Schubert, *Die schöne Müllerin*, D. 795,
"Die liebe Farbe"

(I shall dress in green, in green willows, my love is so fond of green.)

Modulation by Change of Mode

Since the key signature of a major key and its parallel minor differ by three accidentals, use of chords from the parallel minor can conveniently and dramatically expedite
a modulation from a major key to one of its remote keys. In most cases, the new key is
closely related to the key of the borrowed chord, as shown in the next three examples.

Figure 7.10 shows modulation from F major to D♭ major. I followed by i in the
key of F makes possible an easy transition to the key of D♭ major whether the modulation is analyzed as pivot chord (F: i = D♭: iii) or as a direct modulation at the beginning of the new phrase.

Figure 7.11 shows modulation from D♭ major to E major. As in the previous example, I is altered to i at measure 67, except that i is not spelled D♭ F♭ A♭ (i) but is spelled
enharmonically as C♯ E G♯, which functions easily as the pivot, i = vi, to E major.

FIGURE 7.10

F major to
D♭ major

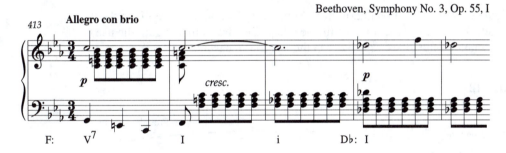

Beethoven, Symphony No. 3, Op. 55, I

FIGURE 7.11

D♭ major, i, D♭ F♭ A♭ =
E major, vi, C♯ E   G♯ (second spelling shown)

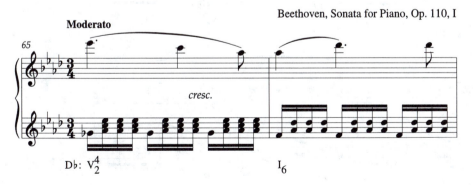

Beethoven, Sonata for Piano, Op. 110, I

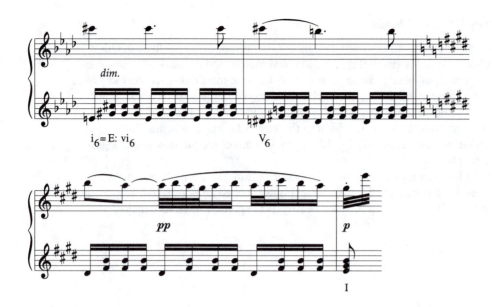

Figure 7.12 shows a modulation from B♭ major to G♭ major where ♭VI in the deceptive cadence becomes the tonic of the new key. Be sure to investigate the use of the many nonharmonic tones, especially in the last four measures.

FIGURE 7.12

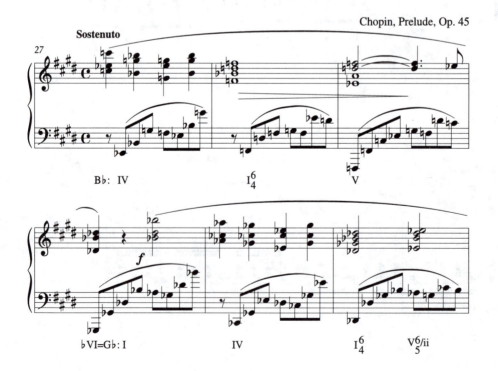

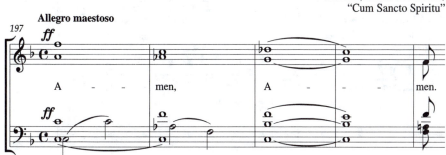

ii   V   I

ASSIGNMENT 7.2 *Harmonic analysis.*   Analyze these examples, and describe the use of mixture chords in each.

(1)

Rossini, *Messe Solennelle,*
"Cum Sancto Spiritu"

(2)

Schubert, "Litanei," D. 343

aus der Welt hin ü – ber – schei – den, al – le

(3)

Mozart, *Don Giovanni,* K. 527, Act I,
"Catalogue Aria"

del – le vec – chie fa con – qui – sta

pel pia – cer de por – le in li – sta,

(With the old women he will make his conquest, just to put them on his list. But his great passion is for young inexperienced girls.)

(4)

Schubert, "Jägers Liebeslied," D. 909

(5)

Bach, *Orgelbüchlein,*
"O Mensch, bewein dein Sünde gross"

(6)

Schubert, Sonata in A Major for Piano, D. 664, II

(7)

Massenet, *Manon,* Act I

(Yes, I believe that lovely lass is Manon, my cousin. I am Lescaut.)

(8) This excerpt displays a modulation made somewhat obscure by its notation. Here are suggestions to help with analysis:

1. Identify the key of the cadence on the dominant chord in measure 31. Refer to footnote 2 of Chapter 3 (page 73). Use the reference included there for review if necessary.

2. Spell the pivot in both keys. It will be an enharmonic spelling.

3. The movement from the pivot to the next chord is a "regular" progression, though one of the least common ones.

Brahms, *Ein deutsches Requiem,* Op. 45,
"Ye Now Are Sorrowful"

Look up-on me; ye know that for a lit - tle time

la - bour and sor - row were mine, but at the last

I have found com - - fort,

The Neapolitan Sixth Chord

The term *Neapolitan sixth* refers to a major triad built on the lowered second scale degree in either major or minor (C: D♭ F A♭). How this chord came to be named Neapolitan is not known. The inclusion of "sixth" reflects its almost exclusive use in first inversion, at least until the mid–nineteenth century, by which time use of the chord with its root in the bass had become more frequent. For analysis, the roman numeral ♭II$_6$ identifies the sonority, though an alternative symbol, N$_6$, is now generally used. When it is found with its root in the bass, the symbols N and ♭II and the term Neapolitan identify this chord.

FIGURE 7.13

C major: N (♭II)   N$_6$(♭II$_6$)   c minor: N (♭II)   N$_6$(♭II$_6$)

ASSIGNMENT 7.3   Spell the Neapolitan sixth chord in each major and minor key.

In the Workbook: Answers are given.

The Neapolitan sixth chord functions exactly as does the diatonic ii$_6$ in major or ii°$_6$ in minor, progressing easily either to tonic six-four or to the dominant. The progession N$_6$–V always includes a melodic interval of the diminished third, ♭$\hat{2}$–(♯)$\hat{7}$, as in Figure 7.15, D♭–B.

FIGURE 7.14 $N_6-I_4^6$

Schubert, Quintet in C Major, D. 956, I

FIGURE 7.15 N_6–V^7

Weber, *Der Freischütz,* Act I

In addition to the usual resolution of the N_6 to I_4^6 or V, half-step movement in the bass line, either ascending or descending, is quite common. Such resolutions are usually to the $°^7$ chord, Figure 7.16, or to a secondary dominant chord, Figure 7.17, and constitute simply a temporary delay in reaching dominant harmony.

FIGURE 7.16

Mozart, *The Magic Flute,* Act II, No. 14

FIGURE 7.17

The Neapolitan chord in root position (N or ♭II) of Figure 7.18 is approached unconventionally from the III triad. Contrary motion between the outside voices helps make this a successful progression. Other exceptional practices in measures 12–13 include a cross-relation, an augmented second, and a hidden octave, all demonstrating less dependence on common practice procedures by composers of the late nineteenth century.

This figure is a skeleton reduction of the orchestral score. The arpeggiation in measures 12–13 begins in measure 9, together with a similar arpeggiation in the viola on each second and fourth beat. These simply arpeggiate the harmonies stated in the other voices, measures 9–12, but in measure 13, the harmony is incomplete without the arpeggiation.

FIGURE 7.18

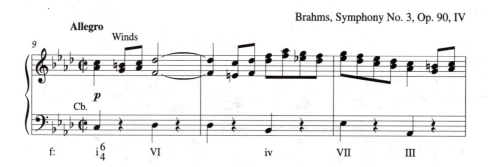

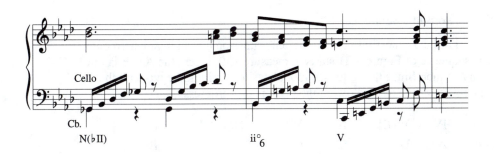

The Secondary Dominant of the Neapolitan Chord

VI in a minor key and ♭VI in a major key serve as the secondary dominant function to the Neapolitan chord, and when so used are symbolized V/N as seen in Figure 7.19.

FIGURE 7.19

Mozart, Quintet for Clarinet and Strings, K. 581, IV

     Using the principle of the common progression I–vii$^{\circ}_6$–I$_6$, a diminished triad can similarly be used between N and N$_6$ (vii$^{\circ}_6$/N). In Figure 7.20, N is preceded by its secondary dominant, the four chords constituting a short progression on the level of N.

FIGURE 7.20

Chopin, Prelude, Op. 28, No. 12

The Neapolitan Chord in a Sequence

The Neapolitan chord may substitute for the diatonic supertonic triad in any harmonic sequence. The sequence of Figure 7.21 starts at measure 130, where the A C E is i of V–i cadence in A minor. Since the sequence modulates to E minor, we will call the A minor triad the pivot, a:i = e:iv. Following the pivot is this progression:

e:	IV	V^7/III,	III,	V^7/N,	N,	V^7,	i
roots:	A	D	G	C	F	B	E

In the final measures of the excerpt, look for two more examples of V^7/N progressing to N.

FIGURE 7.21

Brahms, Quartet, Op. 51, No. 2, IV

$$i \qquad V^7 \qquad i$$

The Neapolitan as a Pivot Chord

The Neapolitan chord can be effective in modulation, acting as a function in either the old key or the new key at the pivot point. In Figure 7.22, the N_6 is spelled enharmonically to function as IV_6 in the new key, representing a change of key from five flats to six sharps. Spell the N_6 in its original key.

FIGURE 7.22

Bb minor, N_6, Cb Eb   Gb =
F# major, IV,   B   D#   F#   (second spelling shown)

Mozart, Symphony No. 39 in Eb Major, K. 543, IV

The pivot IV = N produces a modulation to a key a major third lower, enharmonically spelled here as B♭ to F♯. If the pivot chords were reversed, N = IV, what would be the key relationship and what key would be achieved from B♭ major? Look for such a modulation in Assignment 7.4 (harmonic analysis) and Assignment 7.8 (part-writing).

ASSIGNMENT 7.4 *Harmonic analysis.* Locate the Neapolitan sixth chords and explain how they are used.

(1)

(2)

Beethoven, Concerto in C Minor for
Piano and Orchestra, Op. 37, I

(3)

Beethoven, Quartet, Op. 59, No. 2, I

(4)

Bizet, *Carmen,* Act I, No. 7

Ma mè - re je la vois! _____ Oui, je re-

vois _____ mon vil - la - ge! Ô sou - ve - nirs _____ d'au - tre -

fois, _____ doux sou - ve - nirs du pa - ys! _____ Doux

(5)

Allegro non troppo ma con brio

Brahms, Symphony No. 1, Op. 68, IV

(6)

Amy Beach, *Variations on Balkan Themes,*
Op. 60, Variation 6[3]

[3]The composer published her numerous works under the name of Mrs. H.H.A. Beach (1867–1944).
Current editorial practice uses the less formal given name, unbeknownst, of course, to the composer.

(7) Included in this example are two four-measure passages that can be best analyzed as secondary tonal levels (review Figure 1.18). Within one of these is an N chord.

1. Look for a cadential progression (not an actual cadence) ending on a chord whose root is other than that of the opening measure and consider it a temporary tonic.

2. Look to see if a preceding series of chords is best analyzed in that "key."

3. Place the diagram below the measures involved. Below the line, place the chord number for the temporary tonic, and above the line, analyze the harmony as though that chord were tonic.

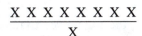

Mussorgsky, *Pictures at an Exhibition,*
"The Old Castle"

The Augmented Triad

Of the four different triads built in thirds, the augmented triad is the least used in music composition. In fact, this triad more often than not appears in a context that suggests a nonharmonic analysis rather than a harmonic one.

Looking at Figure 7.23, we see above the symbol I+ an augmented sonority. It is made up of two major thirds, D♭–F and F–A, encompassing an augmented fifth, and identified by a large roman numeral with a + sign. Play this triad alone and you will hear the characteristic sound of the augmented triad.

FIGURE 7.23

Wolf, "Auf einer Wanderung,"
(No. 15 from *Mörike-Lieder*)

But the fact that only one note of its preceding triad is changed suggests analysis simply as a tonic triad with a passing tone (A♭–A–B♭). Even in longer durations, analysis as a nonharmonic tone is more often than not the most logical choice.

The augmented triad contains two intervals not found in other triads, the augmented fifth (A5), root up to fifth, and its inversion, the diminished fourth (d4), fifth up to root. These are enharmonic with the minor sixth and the major third, respectively. Hence, the intervals of the augmented triad equally divide the octave.

FIGURE 7.24

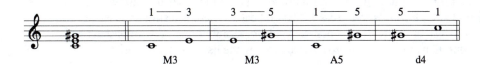

The augmented triads usually encountered are those shown in Figure 7.25.

FIGURE 7.25

ASSIGNMENT 7.5 *Chord spelling.*   Spell the I+, the IV+, and the V+ in each major key. Spell the III+ in each minor key.

In the Workbook: Answers are given.

When studying the augmented sonority in music scores, look for these features. In major:

1. The fifth of the triad is a chromatically raised tone.
2. The raised fifth moves up, usually by half step.
3. Any resolution in which the fifth ascends is possible. The usual resolutions are these:
   a. In I+ and V+, the roots may descend by fifth, such as I+–IV, or V+–I.
   b. In all three augmented triads, the root in the bass may be held over, becoming the third of the next chord, such as IV+–ii$_6$, or it may descend by third as in IV+–ii.
4. First inversions of I+ and V+ are used regularly, as in V+$_6$–I. Second inversions are rare (look for an example in the analysis assignment).

In minor: The III+ is diatonic, considering #$\hat{7}$ to be a diatonic scale degree. III+, with either root or third in the bass, generally moves as expected to VI.

The Augmented Triad in Context

In Figure 7.26, a process similar to that in Figure 7.23 is seen in measure 120, where on beat 1, the E of A C♯ E moves to E♯ of A C♯ E♯ on beat 3. There is a similar passage in the following measure. Are these augmented triads, or simply I and IV with passing tones of longer duration? Only a subjective evaluation by the listener is appropriate.

FIGURE 7.26

Bizet, *Carmen,* Act I, No. 10

In Figure 7.27, there appear to be two augmented triads in second inversion. These are of such short duration that analysis as appoggiatura chords is probably more appropriate. However, considering each as a triad reveals a harmonic sequence to be present in the first six triads. Trace the letter names of their roots to discover the root relationship in the sequence.

Observe again that chords otherwise uncommon may be viable in a harmonic sequence. Which such chord has been created by this process?

FIGURE 7.27

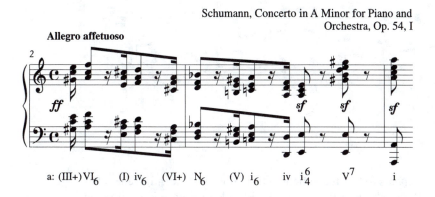

Schumann, Concerto in A Minor for Piano and Orchestra, Op. 54, I

When the augmented triad is approached and followed by a chord with a different root, its identity is more secure, though this usage is far less common. In Figure 7.28, the fifth of G♯ B♯ D✕ is seen in a strong rhythmic position. The D✕ is approached and left as a neighbor-tone figure.

FIGURE 7.28

Dvořák, Concerto for Violin in A Minor, Op. 53, III

In a minor key, the fifth of the augmented triad is at the same time the leading tone of the key, and so is usually approached and resolved accordingly. In Figure 7.29, we see the usual resolution to VI. But how do you explain the entire harmonic progression from III+ to tonic? First, observe the character of the bass line, and second, look for a harmonic sequence.

FIGURE 7.29

Bach, "Wir Christenleut" (#321)

g: II   III+₆   VI   IV₆   VII   V₆   i

Other Augmented Sonorities

When the fifth of what appears to be an augmented triad does not ascend, some other tone of the sonority is the nonharmonic tone. In the E♭ G B of Figure 7.30, it is the root of E of E G B that descends as a chromatic passing tone.

FIGURE 7.30

Grieg, "Letzter Frühling," Op. 34, No. 2

Andante

APT

G: vi   (♭VI+)   I⁶₄   V⁷   I

Also review in *Elementary Harmony,* pages 273–274, the authentic cadence in minor in which a sixth above the root of V resolves to the fifth, often mistaken as an augmented triad (for example, V in F minor: Over the chord members C–E, an A♭ resolving to G).

ASSIGNMENT 7.6 *Harmonic analysis.* Locate the augmented triads. Explain how each is used, including the name of the nonharmonic device that creates the raised fifth of the triad.

(1)

Beethoven, Sonata in D Major for Piano, Op. 28, III

(2)

Vivaldi, Concerto Grosso, Op. 3, No. 10

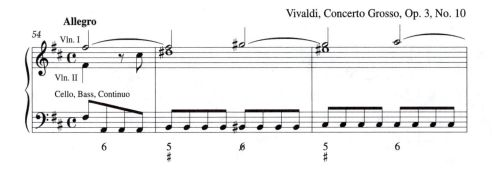

(3) How do you explain the unusual succession of roman-numeral symbols?

Bach, "O Ewigkeit, du Donnerwort" (#26)

(4) Note the simultaneous use of $\sharp\hat{4}$ and $\natural\hat{4}$ in measure 9 and $\flat\hat{7}$ and $\sharp\hat{7}$ in measure 11. How do you explain these?

Schubert, *German Dance,* D. 790, No. 5

(5) This excerpt does not show the complete orchestral score, but it does accurately represent the harmony and the principal melodic line. The augmented triad is in a position rarely seen.

Wagner, *Siegfried Idyll*

Writing Mixture Chords, the Neapolitan Sixth Chord, and Augmented Triads

Procedures for writing the chords discussed in this chapter generally do not differ from those previously studied. Be sure that altered tones are not doubled and that they resolve in the usual manner—that is, flatted tones downward and raised tones upward, except in unusual situations. Note that the altered root of a triad, when found in the bass voice, may be doubled.

In the Workbook: Assignment 7A precedes Assignment 7.7. Answers are given.

ASSIGNMENT 7.7. *Writing mixture chords.* Fill in the alto and tenor voices, and make a harmonic analysis.

In the Workbook: Assignments 7B and 7C precede Assignment 7.8. Answers are given.

ASSIGNMENT 7.8 *Part-writing exercises that include examples of all harmonies and modulations presented in this chapter.* Add alto and tenor voices, and make a harmonic analysis.

ASSIGNMENT 7.9 *Figured bass realizations.*
(a) The bass line only is given.

(b) Examples from music literature are given. Copy out these examples on three staves and write a part for keyboard based on the composer's figuration.

(1)

(2) This excerpt begins with the V/ii in G major.

Keyboard Harmony

ASSIGNMENT 7.10   Play these progressions in any key.

(a) Mixture chords. The progression is first given in a major key, followed by the same progression where borrowed chords are substituted.

I IV V I; I iv V I

I ii V I; I ii° V I

I ii⁷ V I; I iiø⁷ V I

I V vi; I V ♭VI

I vi IV V I; I ♭VI iv V I

(b) The Neapolitan sixth chord.

Major keys	Minor keys
I N$_6$ I$_4^6$ V I	i N$_6$ i$_4^6$ V i
I N$_6$ V I	i N$_6$ V i
I♭VI N$_6$ I$_4^6$ V I	i VI N$_6$ i$_4^6$ V i
I N$_6$ V$_2^4$ I$_6$ vii$_6^\circ$ I	i N$_6$ V$_2^4$ i$_6$ vii$_6^\circ$ i
I N$_6$ $^{\circ 7}$/V V I	i N$_6$ $^{\circ 7}$/V V i

(c) Augmented triads

I I+ IV V I
I V V+ I
I IV IV+ ii V i
i III+ VI iv V i

Summary

The chords discussed in this chapter serve primarily as substitutes for their unaltered counterparts and provide additional color to the musical texture.

Chords of *modal mixture* are those that are diatonic in their own key but when used in the opposite mode require accidentals to achieve the same sound. Using chords from a minor key in its parallel major key is far more common that the reverse. Transfer from major to minor is little used, since the melodic requirements of ♯$\hat{6}$ and ♯$\hat{7}$ in minor create chords that already exist in a major key. Only the tonic triad, changed to major (Picardy third), remains.

As pivots in modulations, modal-mixture chords can lead to many keys unavailable when using a pivot diatonic in both keys.

The *Neapolitan sixth chord* (N$_6$) is a major triad built on the lowered second scale degree. Though used most often in first inversion (hence the word "sixth" in its name), it is occasionally found with its root in the bass. Second inversions are rare. This chord functions identically to its diatonic counterpart, ii or ii°. It is also useful as a pivot, leading to a remotely related key.

Augmented triads are composed of two major thirds, the most common being I+, IV+, and V+ in major, and III+ in minor, the + indicating a triad larger than a major triad. The triad members equally divide the octave, so like the °7 chord, whose members also equally divide the octave, the chord has little stability. Most augmented triads follow the unaltered version of the triad with the same root. In these cases, the altered tone functions simply as a chromatic passing tone, making analysis as a true harmonic structure questionable. In its less common occurrence, following harmony with a different root, analysis as chordal structure is more secure.

8

Augmented Sixth Chords

The dramatic choral opening of Gluck's 1767 opera *Alceste*, Figure 8.1, is heard immediately after the closing notes of the overture. The emotional intensity of the text, "Lord, give us our king, our father," is heightened by a type of sonority new to our harmonic studies. This is the augmented sixth chord, so named because it includes the interval of an augmented sixth (A6), an interval a half step larger than the major sixth. In Figure 8.1, D minor, the augmented sixth interval in both instances consists of B♭ (♭$\hat{6}$)[1] in the bass and G♯ (♯$\hat{4}$) in the alto.

FIGURE 8.1

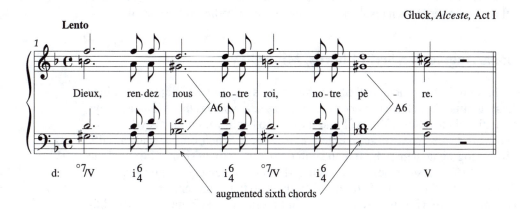

Gluck, *Alceste,* Act I

augmented sixth chords

---

[1]In this chapter, ♭$\hat{6}$ in a minor key always refers to the sixth scale step of the descending form of the minor scale.

The example in Figure 8.2 shows the simplest approach to the augmented sixth interval and is probably typical of its earliest usage. With A♭ (♭$\hat{6}$) already established in the bass, an upper voice, F, moves as a passing tone, $\hat{4}$ to ♯$\hat{4}$, creating the augmented sixth (A6) interval A♭–F♯. As the A6 interval expands to the dominant tone of the key, the entire chord (of subdominant function) moves to a dominant function, either to i$^6_4$ or to V. This linear motion in chord creation we have seen before, especially in the V^7 chord. There, the interval of the seventh was always included in the passing tone 8 7 over V until that tone was written simultaneously with V to become V^7.

FIGURE 8.2

Mozart, Piano Trio, K. 498, II

In Figure 8.1, we also find linear movement to and from the A6 interval, though in different circumstances. Here, two augmented sixth chords and two °^{7} chords alternately progress, by stepwise motion in the bass, to and from the tonic six-four chord. The final A6 of the series then resolves *each one* of the preceding sonorities to V.

The Conventional Augmented Sixth Chords, Minor Keys

Though the sound of augmented sixth chords is the same in both major and minor keys, those in minor keys have but one altered tone each, whereas those in major keys require additional alterations. You will find it easier to begin with minor keys.

There are three types of augmented sixth chords. Each one is traditionally known by a geographic name: the Italian sixth (It6), the German sixth (Gr6), and the French sixth (Fr6). These names, conceived early in the nineteenth century, quickly became standard for this group of chords and remain so to the present time.

The *Italian sixth* (It6) is a triad, usually in first inversion (Figure 8.3). In addition to the interval of the augmented sixth, it includes the doubled tonic tone, $\hat{1}$ (when there are four voices). Remember these scale-step numbers: ♭$\hat{6}$ $\hat{1}$ ♯$\hat{4}$. The two remaining chords consist of those scale steps plus one other.

Each of the augmented sixth chords is often identified by its figured bass symbol. In this case, "augmented six chord" refers specifically to the Italian sixth (figured bass "6").

FIGURE 8.3   *The Italian Sixth Chord*

The *German sixth* (Gr6) is a four-note chord (Figure 8.4). It is the same as the Italian sixth, with $\hat{3}$ added ($\flat\hat{6}$ $\hat{1}$ $\hat{3}$ $\sharp\hat{4}$). From its figured bass symbol, it is identified as an "augmented six-five chord."

FIGURE 8.4   *The German Sixth Chord*[*]

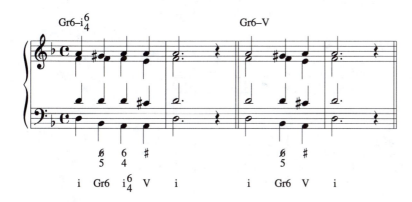

Figure 8.1 includes both an It6 and a Gr6. Can you identify them? Which one resolves to i_4^6 and which one to V?

Play by itself the Gr6 in Figure 8.4. Does it sound like a dominant seventh chord? Yes, because the interval of the augmented sixth is enharmonic with a minor seventh. Then why not write it that way? The difference is in the resolution of the two chords. The upper note of the minor seventh resolves down, as you know from

---

[*]The parallel fifths in Gr6–V are discussed on page 257.

previous study, whereas the upper note of the augmented sixth resolves up. Played separately, the intervals m7 and A6 sound identical, but in context, each demands a different resolution (Figure 8.5).

FIGURE 8.5   *A6 and m7*

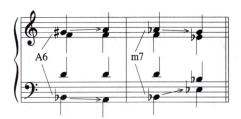

Now play by itself the It6 in Figure 8.3. With one note fewer than the Gr6, it sounds like an incomplete dominant seventh chord.

The *French sixth* (Fr6) is also a four-note chord, adding $\hat{2}$ instead of $\hat{3}$ to the Italian sixth chord ($\flat\hat{6}\ \hat{1}\ \hat{2}\ \sharp\hat{4}$). In figured bass terms, it is called an "augmented six-four-three chord." (See Figure 8.6.)

FIGURE 8.6   *The French Sixth Chord*

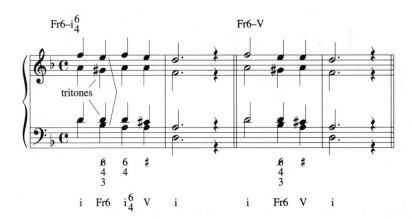

The *French sixth* is unique in that its sound resembles that of no other chord, as you can tell by playing or listening to Figure 8.6 or 8.7. In addition to its A6, it displays two tritones. In Figure 8.5, they are B♭–E and D–G♯. From Verdi's *Il Trovatore,* Figure 8.7 shows a Fr6 in a well-known aria. In the key of E minor, how is this chord spelled? Also spell the A6 interval and the two tritones.

FIGURE 8.7

Verdi, *Il Trovatore,* Act II, "Stride la vampa"

The Conventional Augmented Sixth Chords, Major Keys

All three augmented sixth chords are spelled exactly the same in parallel major and minor keys. The notation on the staff looks different, since $\hat{6}$ must be lowered to $\flat\hat{6}$ in all three chords. In the Gr6, $\hat{3}$ must also be lowered to $\flat\hat{3}$.

FIGURE 8.8   *The Augmented Sixth Chords in Major Keys*

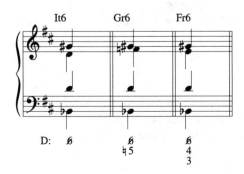

Each of the illustrations in major keys that follow includes more of compositional interest than simply preceding the augmented sixth chord with I and following it with I$^6_4$ or V, as in previous examples.

The It6 of Figure 8.9 occurs at the point where the soprano tone $\sharp\hat{4}$ (F$\sharp$ of $^\circ$/V) is already established, while it is the bass that moves down by chromatic half step to $\flat\hat{6}$. The alto, then moving in passing tones, reaches C$\natural$, the tone that added to an It6 creates a Gr6.

FIGURE 8.9

Beethoven, Sonata in A Major for Piano, Op. 101, I

A: I$_6$ $^\circ$/V   It6   I$^6_4$

In Figure 8.10, beginning in measure 52, the first bass note of each beat is a nonharmonic tone, retardation or suspension, until V^7 is reached. Because of this repeated pattern, it is obvious that B above the symbol Gr6 is not part of G$\sharp$ B D F, but a suspension in B$\flat$ D F G$\sharp$.

A leap to the bass or to the upper note of the augmented sixth interval becomes more common in music of the late Baroque and Classical periods. Figure 8.10 shows a downward leap of a diminished fifth in the upper voice.

FIGURE 8.10

Mozart, Symphony in D Major *(Prague)*, K. 504, II

D: Gr6   I$^6_4$

The Fr6 of Figure 8.11 is the culmination of the prolongation of ii^7 through four measures in reaching its cadential goal. These measures include three spellings of the ii^7 chord—F$\sharp$ A C$\sharp$ E, F$\sharp$ A$\sharp$ C$\sharp$ E, F$\sharp$ A$\sharp$ C E (Fr6) and the contrary passing tones of measure 103.

FIGURE 8.11

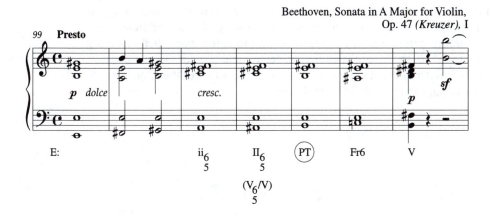

Beethoven, Sonata in A Major for Violin,
Op. 47 *(Kreuzer),* I

ASSIGNMENT 8.1 *Spelling conventional augmented sixth chords.*   Follow this procedure:

1. Spell the two tones that resolve by half step to the dominant tone of the key, $\flat\hat{6}$ as the lower tone and $\sharp\hat{4}$ as the upper tone.

   Example: In F minor or F major.   D♭ and B

2. It6, add $\hat{1}$:   D♭ F B

3. Gr6, add to the It6,
   $\hat{3}$ in minor or
   $\flat\hat{3}$ in major: D♭ F A♭ B

4. Fr6, add to the It6, $\hat{2}$:   D♭ F G B

Spell each of the augmented sixth chords in each major and minor key. Remember (1) that each set of spellings in minor is valid in the parallel major key, (2) that there are no parallel major keys for G♯, D♯, and A♯ minor, and (3) that there are no parallel minor keys for D♭, G♭, and C♭ major. These last three keys and their augmented sixth chord spellings in both modes should be included in your practice. It is suggested that you spell each chord in each key from the minor circle of fifths plus the three major keys in (3) above: *Example:*

Key	It6	Gr6	Fr6
a or A	F A D♯	F A C D♯	F A B D♯
e or E	C E A♯	C E G A♯	C E F♯ A♯

In the Workbook: Answers are given.

Alternative Spelling of the Gr6 in a Major Key

In a major key, the Gr6 includes $\flat\hat{3}$. When the Gr6 progresses to I^6_4, $\flat\hat{3}$ must progress upward (Figure 8.12a).[2] A number of composers prefer to spell this tone enharmonically as $\sharp\hat{2}$, considering the raised tone preferable to a lowered tone when resolving upward. In Figure 8.12b, the E♭ of the chord has been replaced with D♯, making such a resolution possible. There is, of course, no change in the sound of the chord, and no change in its function, so the symbol Gr6 still applies.

FIGURE 8.12

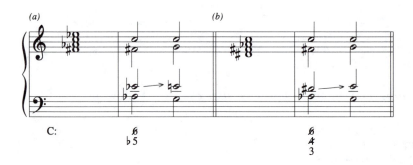

Robert Schumann, for one, preferred the alternative spelling, which we see in Figure 8.13. Appearing in measure 1 of the *lied,* it is the Gr6 in B♭ major: G♭ B♭ C♯ E instead of G♭ B♭ D♭ E.

FIGURE 8.13

Schumann, *Dichterliebe,* Op. 48, No. 12,
"Am leuchtenden Sommermorgen"

---

[2]This situation resembles that in Figure 2.26 where the seventh of °7/V progresses upward when resolving to I^6_4. The solution there was the same as here: Spell the seventh enharmonically.

In its respelling, the chord is sometimes known as a *doubly augmented six-four-three*. In Figure 8.12*b*, A♭ up to D♯ is a doubly augmented fourth. In the figured bass symbol, ♯ indicates that the diatonic tone D is to be raised one half step. This is contrary to some Baroque figured bass procedures in which ♯ is used for the single purpose of indicating an augmented fourth, even if the upper note is diatonic. There is no convenient figured bass symbol for a doubly augmented fourth.

ASSIGNMENT 8.2 *Respelling the Gr6 in major keys.*   First spell the Gr6 as in Assignment 8.1, and then spell ♭3̂ enharmonically as ♯2̂, as described in the discussion of Figure 8.12.

Use the circle of fifths in major to be sure that you have spelled the chord in all possible keys.

In the Workbook: Answers are given.

Occasionally you will encounter an It6 or a Gr6 spelled as though it were a Mm seventh chord. To the ear, there is no difference, of course. Composers use alternative spellings of any altered chord infrequently, usually when such a spelling allows easier reading of the music notation (Figure 8.14).

FIGURE 8.14

Brahms, Sonata in E Minor for Violoncello and Piano, Op. 38, I

```
C E G B♭ =
C E G A♯
```

The preceding presentation has covered the conventional uses of augmented sixth chords. Chapter 9 continues with the augmented sixth in modulation, followed by less common uses of these sonorities.

In the Workbook: Assignment 8A precedes Assignment 8.3. Answers are given.

ASSIGNMENT 8.3 *Analysis of augmented sixth chords.*   Each example includes at least one augmented sixth chord. Make a roman-numeral analysis of the entire example, noting especially the type of the augmented sixth chord, its spelling, and the method of resolution.

(1)

Mozart, *Così fan tutte,* Act I, No. 12,
"In nomini"

nè val da' bar - bar-i chie-der pie - tà.   chie - der pie-

tà   chie - der pie - tà.

(2)

Beethoven, Sonata in C Minor for Piano, Op. 13, III

(3)

Schumann, Concerto for Piano and Orchestra, Op. 54, III

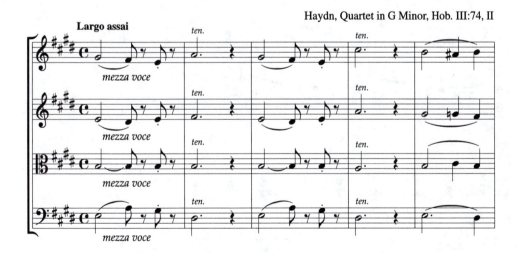

(4) Be sure to locate the modulation before describing the use of the augmented sixth chord.

Haydn, Quartet in G Minor, Hob. III:74, II

(5) This short excerpt includes several techniques discussed in earlier chapters:

    (a) Lowering one tone of a diminished seventh chord

    (b) Change of mode

    (c) Harmonic sequence

Brahms, Piano Quintet, Op. 26, I

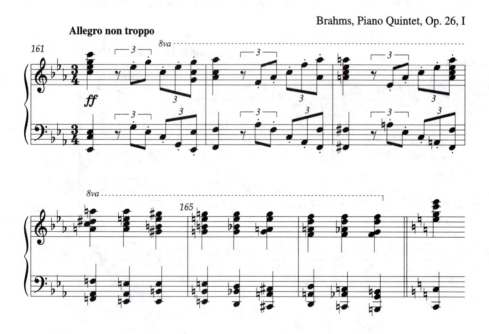

(6) In this chromatic late-nineteenth-century work, look for an augmented triad, the N6, accented passing tones, and an unusual approach to the augmented sixth chord.

Franck, Chorale No. 2 in B Minor

(7)

Chopin, Ballade No. 3, Op. 47

(8) Though the C clef and the transposing instrument make this excerpt look complex, the harmony is nonmodulating and straightforward. Watch for these interesting features:

    (a) A given note of the syncopated Violin I part may precede or follow the harmony with which it is associated.

    (b) An augmented sixth chord, two measures in duration, not complete until a nonharmonic tone resolves to one of the chord's members.

    (c) The avoidance of fifths at measure 6.

    (d) An example of the simultaneous use of $\flat\hat{7}$ and $\sharp\hat{7}$.

Brahms, Quintet for Clarinet and Strings, Op. 115, II

Writing Augmented Sixth Chords

Since each augmented sixth chord includes ♭6̂ and ♯4̂, two active tones that ordinarily resolve in contrary motion, resolution of the one or two remaining tones leaves little to choice.

Italian Sixth

Two of its three tones make up the interval of the augmented sixth, and neither of them can be doubled. Therefore, the only remaining tone is doubled, and resolved by either contrary or oblique motion (Figure 8.1, D down to C♯ and D up to E).

German Sixth

All four tones must be present, so no tone is doubled. In progressing to tonic six-four, both unaltered tones usually remain stationary (Figure 8.1, D to D and F to F).

Resolution to V in four-part harmony always results in parallel fifths (in Figure 8.4, alto F–E above the bass B♭–A). The usual solution, until the middle-to-late nineteenth century when the fifths were often allowed to stand, was to change the Gr6 to an It6 before resolving the chord. Haydn, in Figure 8.15, at the last possible moment moves F to the unaltered tone, D, of the It6. Leaving F to resolve to E would have resulted in fifths with the bass, B♭–A.

FIGURE 8.15

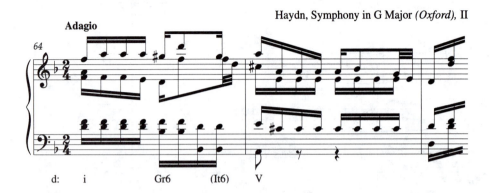

Haydn, Symphony in G Major *(Oxford)*, II

In the Beethoven example, Figure 8.16, the B♭ in the uppermost voice moves stepwise, B♭–A–G, creating a succession of augmented sixth sonorities, Gr6, Fr6, It6, the It6 resolving to V. At the rapid tempo of Figure 8.16, the moving voice will probably be heard as passing tones. But in the same passage in a slow tempo, the individual sound of each of the three augmented sixth chords is very clear. Play Figure 8.16, first in a fast tempo, then in a slow tempo with the three lower voices repeated on each beat. This succession, either as seen here or in reverse (It6, Fr6, Gr6) is quite common.

FIGURE 8.16

Beethoven, Sonata in G Minor for Cello and Piano, Op. 5, No. 2, II

Gr6 (Fr6) (It6)

French Sixth

This chord, the one with the most complex sound, displays the fewest problems in its resolution. Each unaltered tone resolves by step or by repeated tone (Figure 8.6, to tonic six-four, D–D and E–F; to V, D–C♯ and E–E).

ASSIGNMENT 8.4 *Writing augmented sixth chords.*   On the staff, write the given chord progression. Each consists only of the opening tonic triad, followed by an augmented sixth chord and a cadence.

The beginning soprano note is given as a number above the opening tonic (I) triad. Move each soprano note to the closest note of the following chord.

Use the alternative spelling for the Gr6 when marked "(alt)."

Example: **C: I It6 V I**

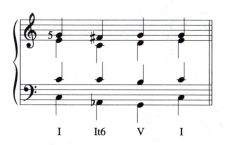

1. G: $\overset{5}{\text{I}}$ Gr6 I$^6_4$ V I
2. e: $\overset{1}{\text{i}}$ It6 V i
3. c♯: $\overset{3}{\text{i}}$ Fr6 i$^6_4$ V i
4. B♭: $\overset{1}{\text{I}}$ Fr6 V I
5. E: $\overset{5}{\text{I}}$ Gr6(alt) I$^6_4$ V I
6. d♯: $\overset{1}{\text{i}}$ It6 i$^6_4$ V i
7. D♭: $\overset{5}{\text{I}}$ It6 V I
8. F: $\overset{3}{\text{I}}$ Gr6(alt) I$^6_4$ V I

In the Workbook: Answers are given.

ASSIGNMENT 8.5 *Writing short examples of augmented sixth chords from a figured bass.*   Add inner voices and make a harmonic analysis.

ASSIGNMENT 8.6 *Extended figured bass exercises.*   Add alto and tenor voices, and make a harmonic analysis.

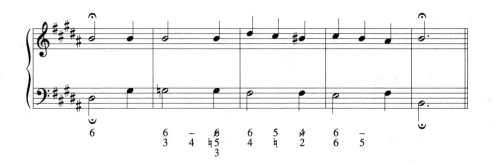

ASSIGNMENT 8.7 *Figured bass exercises.*   The bass line only is given.

ASSIGNMENT 8.8 *Melody harmonization.*   In each short melody, find a location for an augmented sixth chord. Complete the harmonization for the remaining given melody notes.

Keyboard Harmony

ASSIGNMENT 8.9 *Playing augmented sixth chords at the keyboard.*   Follow this procedure:

1. Choose a key and one of the augmented sixth chords (Figure 8.17*a*).
2. Spell the chosen augmented sixth chord (Figure 8.17*b*).
3. With the left hand, play ♭$\hat{6}$ (Figure 8.17*c*).
4. Play the remaining members of the chord in the right hand. For the Gr6 and the Fr6, simply play the remaining three tones of the chord. The It6 is a triad; double $\hat{1}$ (Figure 8.17d).

FIGURE 8.17

(a)	(b)	(c)	(d)
Choose key and chord:	Spell chord: Bb D G#	Play:	Play:
D minor, Italian sixth		l.h.	r.h. l.h.

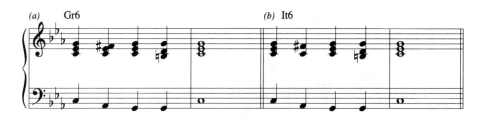

ASSIGNMENT 8.10 *Playing basic progressions.*

(*a*) Play each example from Figure 8.18 in any minor key.

(*b*) Substitute the major tonic triad for the minor tonic triad, and play the same progressions in any major key.

(*c*) Play any of the above with $\hat{1}$ or $\hat{3}$ in the soprano of the opening tonic triad.

FIGURE 8.18

ASSIGNMENT 8.11 *Playing more-advanced progressions.* For each progression, choose a soprano tone for the opening tonic triad and complete the exercise.

All the exercises listed include a Gr6. Repeat exercises, using in each a Fr6 and then an It6.

Minor keys	Major keys
i VI Gr6 i$^6_4$ V i	I bVI Gr6 I$^6_4$ V I
i VI^7 Gr6 i$^6_4$ V i	I IV$_6$ Gr6 I$^6_4$ V I
i iv$_6$ Gr6 i$^6_4$ V i	I iv$_6$ Gr6 I$^6_4$ V I
i ii$°^4_3$ Gr6 i$^6_4$ V i	I ii$^4_3$ Gr6 I$^6_4$ V I

Summary

Augmented sixth chords are so named because of the presence of the interval of an augmented sixth (A6). The interval, usually built on $\flat\hat{6}$ of the key in major or minor, is a half step larger than a M6, the upper tone being $\sharp\hat{4}$ of the key.

Chords that include the A6 interval are usually of subdominant function, progressing to i_4^6, I_4^6, or V. The A6 interval resolves by contrary motion to the dominant tone of the key ($\flat\hat{6}-\hat{5}$ and $\sharp\hat{4}-\hat{5}$). In C, the interval A♭–F♯ resolves to G–G.

Augmented sixth chords are of three varieties, all with an A6 interval in common. Each is spelled the same in parallel major and minor keys. The Italian sixth (It6) is a triad; the additional tone is $\hat{1}$ (in C: A♭ C F♯). The German sixth (Gr6) is like the It6 with an additional tone—in minor $\hat{3}$, and in major $\flat\hat{3}$ (in C minor and major: A♭ C E♭ F♯). The French sixth (Fr6) is like the It6 with the additional tone $\hat{2}$ (in C: A♭ C D F♯).

The Gr6 is enharmonic with a major-minor seventh chord. For example, C E G A♯ is enharmonic with C E G B♭. The difference in spelling is required by the difference in the resolution of the enharmonic tone. The A♯ of the Gr6 resolves upward whereas the B♭ in the chord of dominant function resolves downward.

The It6 is enharmonic with an incomplete major-minor seventh chord. The sound of the Fr6 is unlike any other sonority in the harmonic repertoire.

The writing of the Gr6 presents two problems:

1. The members of the Gr6 chord cannot resolve stepwise to V without incurring parallel fifths. However, a common solution is to progress from Gr6 to It6 before resolution. Although many other unique solutions exist, composers, especially in the middle-to-late nineteenth century, often allowed the fifths to stand.

2. The tone $\flat\hat{3}$ in the Gr6 resolves upward in the progression to tonic six-four. Some composers respell the Gr6 substituting $\sharp\hat{2}$ for $\flat\hat{3}$ to avoid allowing a lowered tone to make an upward resolution.

9

Augmented Sixth Chords: Modulation and Other Uses

Although the augmented sixth chord in its progression to the dominant in a key is the most common use of that sonority, other uses are both frequent enough and important enough to warrant our consideration.

Modulation with the German Sixth Chord

Since the sound of a German sixth chord is enharmonic with that of a major-minor seventh chord, its use as a pivot is effective and often quite dramatic. The Gr6 may be respelled as any other Mm^7 chord, or any Mm^7 chord may be respelled as a Gr6. For example, the Mm^7 C E G B♭ and the Gr6 C E G A♯ sound identical, and therefore can be effective as a pivot.

The Three Common Gr6 Pivots

Of all the possibilities, three specific pivots account for most examples of this type of modulation.

V^7 = Gr6 (Figure 9.1a and b)
Gr6 = V^7 (Figure 9.1c and d)
V^7/IV = Gr6 (Figure 9.1e and f)

The process used to accomplish these modulations may seem somewhat complex, but composers have used it to advantage in making unusual and often surprising changes of key. Figure 9.1, designed for reference only, shows how these three pivots are used. For a detailed explanation of the process, we have chosen the pivot V^7 = Gr6. Parts a and b from Figure 9.1 demonstrate how that pivot will reach several different keys. The two remaining pivots shown at c–d and at e–f function similarly.

This is the procedure.

At *a* of Figure 9.1: Modulate downward by diatonic half step from C major to B major or B minor.

1. In C major, V^7 is G B D F.
2. Spell the seventh (F) enharmonically as E♯.
    G B D E♯ is a Gr6.
3. Resolve the A6 interval, G–E♯ to the octave F♯ ($\hat{5}$ of the new key).
4. Complete the tonic six-four chord by adding the notes B and D and resolve to V–I in B minor. For the parallel key, B major, raise the D in B D F♯ to D♯.

At *b* of Figure 9.1: Modulate downward by chromatic half step from C major to C♭ major.

1. In C major, V^7 is G B D F.
2. Spell the lower three notes, G B D, enharmonically as A♭♭ C♭ E♭♭.
    A♭♭ C♭ E♭♭ F is a Gr6.
3. Resolve the A6 interval, A♭♭–F, to the octave G♭ ($\hat{5}$ of the new key).
4. Complete the tonic six-four chord by adding the notes C♭ and E♭ and resolve to V–I in C♭ major. In this instance, there is no key parallel to C♭ major in the circle of fifths.

FIGURE 9.1   *The German Sixth as a Pivot Chord*

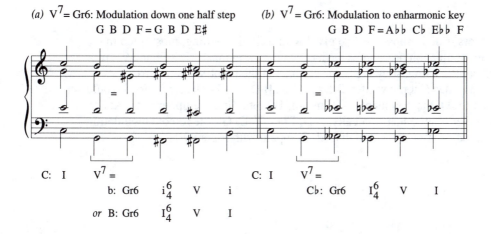

(c) Gr6 = V⁷: Modulation up one half step
Ab C Eb F♯ = Ab C Eb Gb

(d) Gr6: V⁷: Modulation to enharmonic key
Ab C Eb F♯ = G♯ B♯ D♯ F♯

C: I   Gr6 =
    Db: V⁷   I

C: I   Gr6 =
    C♯: V⁷   I
or Gr6 =
    c♯: V⁷   i

(e) V⁷/IV = Gr6: Modulation up a major third
D F♯ A C = D F♯ A B♯

(f) V⁷/IV = Gr6: Modulation to enharmonic key, up a diminished fourth
D F♯ A C = Ebb Gb Bbb C

D: I   V⁷/IV =
    F♯: Gr6   I⁶₄   V   I
or f♯: Gr6   i⁶₄   V   i

D: I   V⁷/IV =
    Gb: Gr6   I⁶₄   V   I

Composers usually show the Gr6 pivot with a single spelling, most often in the new key, as in modulation procedures we have studied previously. But Figure 9.2 provides us with a modulation showing both spellings of the pivot V⁷/IV = Gr6.

In this case, had Chopin written B D♯ F♯ A as B D♯ F♯ G×, the A6 interval would have resolved to A♯, the dominant of D♯ minor. By retaining the upper note, A, and spelling the lower tones enharmonically, B D♯ F♯ to Cb Eb Gb, the remote modulation B major to Eb major is easily accomplished. Compare with Figure 9.1*f*.

FIGURE 9.2   *V⁷/IV = Gr6*

B major, V⁷/IV, B   D♯   F♯   A =
E♭ major, Gr6,   C♭ E♭   G♭   A (both spellings shown)

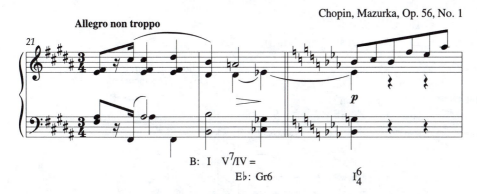

Chopin, Mazurka, Op. 56, No. 1

B: I   V⁷/IV =
Eb: Gr6   I$_4^6$

Figure 9.3 shows first the spelling of V⁷, then its enharmonic Gr6 spelling.

FIGURE 9.3   *V⁷ = Gr6*

B♭ major, V⁷,   F A C E♭ =
A minor, Gr6,   F A C D♯ (second spelling shown)

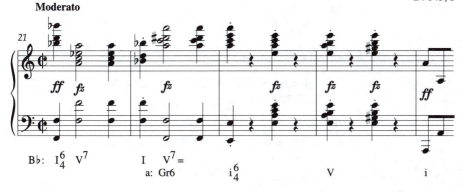

Schubert, Sonata in A Minor for Piano
D. 845, I

B♭: I$_4^6$ V⁷   I   V⁷ =
        a: Gr6   i$_4^6$ V   i

Figure 9.4 shows the less common practice of spelling the Gr6 pivot in the old key, requiring in this case the upper note, G♭ of the m⁷ interval, to resolve upward to G♮.

FIGURE 9.4 $V^7 = Gr6$

D♭ major, V⁷,   A♭ C E♭ G♭ =
C major, Gr6,   A♭ C E♭ F♯   (first spelling shown)

Berlioz, *Les Nuits d'Été,*
Op. 7, "L'Ile inconnue"

The modulation of Figure 9.5, from C up a half step to C♯ minor, is necessarily enharmonic because there is no minor key with D♭ as a tonic. (Review this same modulation in Figure 9.1*d*.)

FIGURE 9.5 $Gr6 = V^7$

C minor, Gr6,   A♭   C   E♭   F♯ =
C♯ minor, V⁷,   G♯   B♯   D♯   F♯   (second spelling shown)

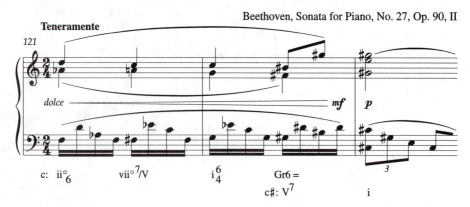

Beethoven, Sonata for Piano, No. 27, Op. 90, II

Other Uses of the Pivot Mm⁷ = Gr6

The use of any other Mm^7 chord in a Gr6 pivot is possible, though such is far less common than those just described. As an example, Figure 9.6 shows a modulation from D minor to A minor, using the pivot V^7/VI = Gr6. The pivot occurs over two beats where the spelling is mixed. If the bass line C–F is considered to be an arpeggiation in both chords, the spelling is F A C E♭ = F A C D♯.

FIGURE 9.6 $V^7/VI = Gr6$

Beethoven, Sonata for Cello and Piano, Op. 102, No. 1, I

Other Modulations Using the Gr6

You will occasionally encounter a modulation in which a Gr6 is involved but not as a pivot, two examples of which are seen in Figures 9.7 and 9.8.

In the first, Figure 9.7, the A6 interval is approached and left by contrary chromatic motion, G♭–G♮–A♭ and B♭–B♭♭–A♭ (intervals m6–A6–P8). Should you consider the B♭ minor triad at measure 82 to be tonic, the progression leads to the key of the mediant.

The initial reaction to the use of the It6 can lead one to both see and hear a modulation to D♭ major. The It6 resolves to the D♭ six-four chord followed by the °7/V and the V7/V in that key, only to lead into a V7–I cadence in the original key of G♭ major (note the alternative spelling of °7/V, F♭ spelled as E). Thus, this progression is best analyzed on the tonal level of V.

FIGURE 9.7

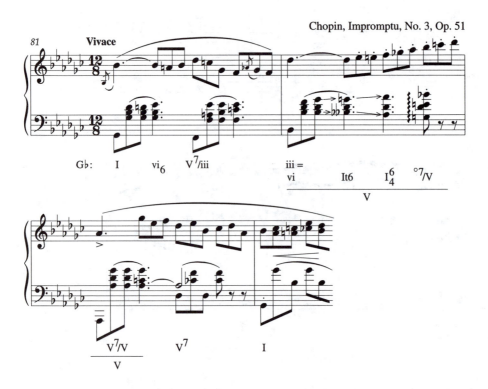

Chopin, Impromptu, No. 3, Op. 51

In the second example, Figure 9.8, the Gr6 follows the °7 chord in B major, A♯ C♯ E G, whose lowest note resolves early, A♯–A (review Chapter 2, page 46). The resulting spelling of A C♯ E G functions as a Gr6, A C♯ E F×, resolving to the dominant, G♯, of C♯ minor.

FIGURE 9.8

Haydn, Quartet in E♭ Major, Hob. III:80, II

B: I   V$^4_3$ I   vii°^{7} c♯: Gr6   i$^6_4$ V   i

Spelling the Augmented Sixth Pivot Chord

Spelling the Gr6 pivot is easy in principle, though somewhat complex with key signatures that include many accidentals. Follow these steps, as illustrated in C major, Figure 9.1*a* and *b*. Use the same procedure for the other two pivots.

A. V^7 (G B D F) = Gr6:

    1. Spell enharmonically the upper note.   F = E♯
    The three lower notes remain unchanged.   G B D

    2. Gr6 = G B D E♯. New key: B major or minor.

B. To reach the enharmonic equivalent of the new key, C♭, reverse the spellings in 1 above.

    1. The upper note remains unchanged.   F
    Spell the remaining notes enharmonically.   A♭♭ C♭ E♭♭

    2. Gr6 = A♭♭ C♭ E♭♭ F. New key: C♭ major.

In each part of Figure 9.1, the interval from the old key to the new key is indicated. Before spelling a pivot, be sure to check that the new key is in the circle of fifths. For example, V^7/IV = Gr6: If Figure 9.1*f* were in C major, a diminished fourth up would be F♭. There is no F♭ major or minor in the circle of keys, so only the keys on E can be reached as in Figure 9.1*e*.

ASSIGNMENT 9.1 *Spelling the Gr6 pivots.*   From the given major or minor key, spell each pivot in both the old key and the new keys. Name the key or keys achieved. When an achieved key has an enharmonic equivalent, spell the pivot enharmonically (in parentheses below) and name the enharmonic key(s).

    Using the example that follows, starting from any major or minor key, will ensure coverage of all the possibilities.

Example: Modulation from G major or G minor

V^7 = Gr6	D F♯ A C	= D F♯ A B♯	in F♯ major or in F♯ minor
		(E♭♭ G♭ B♭♭ C)	in G♭ major
Gr6 = V^7	E♭ G B♭ C♯	= E♭ G B♭ D♭	in A♭ major or in A♭ minor
		(D♯ F𝄪 A♯ C♯)	In G♯ minor
V^7/IV = Gr6	G B D F	= G B D E♯	in B major or in B minor
		(A♭♭ C♭ E♭♭ F)	in C♭ major

In the Workbook: Answers are given.

ASSIGNMENT 9.2 *Analysis of music excerpts that include examples of the use of the augmented sixth chord in modulation.*   Indicate the pivot by showing its function and its spelling in both keys. When the A6 chord is not the pivot, describe its contribution to the modulatory process.

(1)

Mendelssohn, Piano Trio in D Minor, Op. 49, III
(piano score only)

(2)

Mozart, Sonata in D Major for Piano, K. 284, III,
Variation VII

(3) In Part 1 of this binary form, the augmented sixth chord is not obvious, its upper note replaced in the melodic line by a lower-neighbor tone. For analysis, add an augmented sixth interval above the triad to complete the pivot chord.

Another A6 pivot is located in Part 2. Of the two pivots, one is spelled in the old key, the other in the new key.

Schubert, Waltz, D. 365, No. 14

(4) Consider the lowest voice in measure 60 and measure 65 as a repeated passing tone. These sonorities are, of course, in third inversion, the sevenths of which function as passing tones. Note that the pivot chords do not resolve directly to the dominant or to tonic six-four. Explain the activity between each pivot and its following cadence.

Mozart, Sonata for Violin and Piano, K. 454, II

(5) Here is an excerpt with a sampling of several compositional devices covered in your earlier studies and concluding with an A6 pivot modulation.

Brahms, "Wie Melodien zieht es mir," Op. 105, No. 1

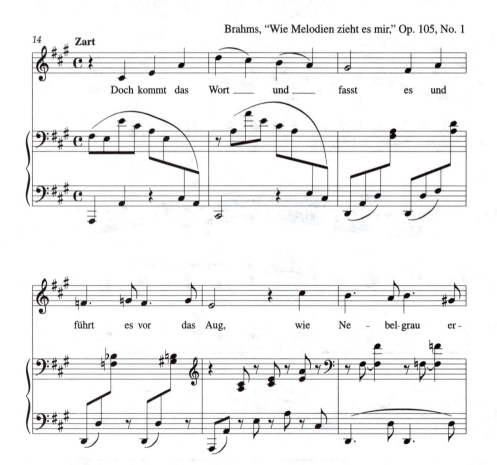

(Like sighs or like the grey mists, my thoughts vanish when words attempt to express them.)

ASSIGNMENT 9.3 *Writing modulations with the Gr6 as the pivot.*   Write in four parts the chords given and continue to a cadence in an appropriate key. The new key may be major or minor, including any available enharmonic version. For practice, spell the Gr6 in both keys.

(*a*) I V ♭VI I Gr6 = V⁷ - - -

I V vi Gr6 = V⁷ - - -

(*b*) i V i V⁷/iv = Gr6 - - -

I V I V⁷/IV = Gr6 - - -

(*c*) i iv V⁷ = Gr6 - - -

I IV V⁷ = Gr6 - - -

In the Workbook: Answers are given.

ASSIGNMENT 9.4 *Part-writing.*   Each exercise includes a Gr6 used as a pivot in a modulation. Describe its function in both keys.

Other Uses of Augmented Sixth Chords

The presentation of augmented sixth chords to this point has included those most commonly encountered. As with any other sonority, composers on occasion find other ways to use these chords to enhance the desired musical effect. These include

1. Inverted forms of the commonly used structures
2. Chords so spelled as to resolve other than to the dominant tone
3. Irregular resolution of the interval of the augmented sixth

Figure 9.9 shows in just six measures an unusually large grouping of these exceptional practices, described here as numbered in the example.

(1) *Measures 145–146:* The example begins with a conventional Gr6 and its resolution to tonic six-four.

(2) *Measure 147:* The same Gr6 is found with ♯$\hat{4}$ instead of ♭$\hat{6}$ as the lowest tone. When any augmented sixth chord is inverted, it will contain the inversion of the augmented sixth interval, the diminished third (d3). In this measure, the d3, F♯–A♭, is the inversion of the A6, A♭–F♯.

(3) *Measure 147:* As the Gr6, ♯$\hat{4}$ in the bass, is repeated, the soprano descends, creating a series of inverted Gr, Fr, and It chords, ending with only the interval d3, which resolves to a unison on $\hat{5}$.

(4) *Measure 149:* The sonority is a Fr6, but the A6 interval is ♭$\hat{3}$–♯$\hat{1}$, resolving to $\hat{2}$ (V$_4^6$).

(5) *Measure 150:* Another Fr6, but with the A6 interval ♭$\hat{2}$–$\hat{7}$, resolving to the tonic triad in root position.

FIGURE 9.9

Tchaikovsky, *Eugene Onegin,* Act I, No. 9

Hugo Wolf, in Figure 9.10, combines the two spellings of the Gr6, both built above $\hat{1}$. The C♭ of the "regular" spelling, F♭ A♭ C♭ D, and the B of the alternative spelling, F♭ A♭ B D, both resolve upward to C♮. The sonority so written gives the appearance of a triad on each staff, facilitating the reading of the score.

The augmented sixth chord is not in its usual arrangement. Describe how it relates to its preceding and following tonic triad.

FIGURE 9.10

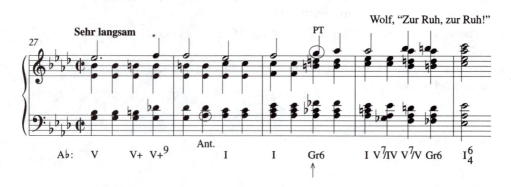

Wolf, "Zur Ruh, zur Ruh!"

*For E♭ G B D♭, see "Augmented Minor Seventh Chords," page 284. The added anticipation, F, creates the sound of a ninth chord (Chapter 10).

The construction and resolution of the Fr6 in Figure 9.11 is no different from those already studied. The chord's lowest tone, however, is $\flat\hat{7}$, and the A6 interval resolves out to $\hat{6}$, here the root of V/ii. The effect is that of a "secondary Fr6" to its chord of resolution. Should we spell the Fr6 in thirds, and thereby consider the note A as its root (A C♯ E♭ G), we see beginning at this point a progression of roots by fifth: A–D–G–C–F.

FIGURE 9.11

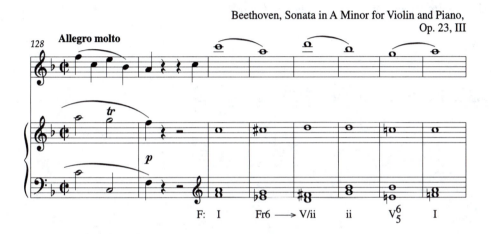

An interesting late-nineteenth-century example by César Franck, Figure 9.12, shows a Gr6 that avoids the look but not the sound of parallel chords. Spelled conventionally, all four members of the chord are approached and left by downward stepwise motion. The effect is that of three major-minor seventh chords in parallel motion. What conventional resolution of the augmented sixth has been avoided?

FIGURE 9.12

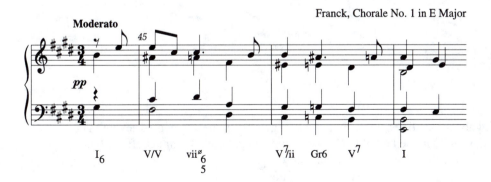

Augmented Minor Seventh Chords

These are augmented triads with an additional interval of a minor seventh above the root. Like the augmented triad, the raised fifth above the root is usually the result of the use of a chromatic passing tone. The interval between the chord's raised fifth and its seventh is a d3. Although not an augmented sixth chord, the chord members are usually arranged so that the interval of the A6 is displayed (Figure 9.13), the lower note of the interval usually found in an inner voice rather than in the lowest voice.

There chords, usually limited to the function of V^7 and V^7/IV, are only infrequently used. If desired, they can be labeled as $V + ^7$ and $V + ^7/IV$.

FIGURE 9.13

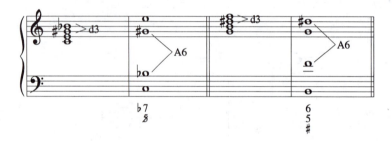

In Figure 9.14, after V^7/IV is sounded three times, its fifth is raised in the manner of a passing tone. Locate the A6 interval in the voices above the bass.

FIGURE 9.14

Mendelssohn, *Songs Without Words,* Op. 38, No. 1

E♭:   I   V⁷/IV

In a highly chromatic example by Franck, Figure 9.15, the augmented seventh is built on $\hat{6}$, E♭ G B D♭ in the key of G (VI + $^{♭7}$). Notice again the dominant effect, that of a rather unconventional secondary dominant to N_6.

FIGURE 9.15

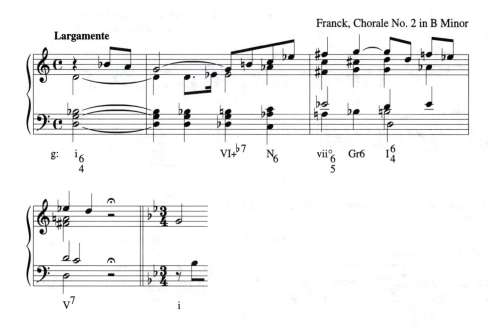

ASSIGNMENT 9.5 *Analysis of less common augmented sixth usages.* In analyzing each example, locate the harmony that includes the interval A6 or d3, and compare its use to that of the conventional augmented sixth chords.

(1)

(2)

Dvořák, Symphony No. 9 in E Minor, Op. 95
(New World), II

(3) These are the closing measures of the *chanson* by Fauré.

Fauré, "Au bord de l'Eau," Op. 8, No. 1

(4)

Strauss, *Till Eulenspiegels lustige Streiche*, "Epilog"

(5)

Franck, Symphony in D Minor, I

(6)

Beethoven, Piano Concerto No. 3, Op. 37, I

(7) The augmented sixth chords resolve to secondary dominant chords and are part of the process of modulation. Describe the modulatory process, including the function of the augmented sixth chords.

Beethoven, Quartet, Op. 18, No. 1, IV

(8) In "word painting," a composer heightens the meaning of a word or a short phrase by some musical device. In this excerpt, can you locate the word(s) and describe the device used?

Schubert, *Die Winterreise,* D. 911, "Frühlingstraum"

(And as the cocks are crowing, I rise to look without. The day is cold and dreary; the ravens are screaming aloud.)

Keyboard Harmony

ASSIGNMENT 9.6 *Playing modulations with Gr6 as the pivot, using the patterns in Assignment 9.3.*   Choose one of the patterns and its key. Before playing, spell the pivot in both keys. After playing the pivot, resolve to I_4^6 to complete the exercise.

Figure 9.16 shows examples using two of these patterns. The chord in parentheses shows the spelling of the pivot; its sound and that of the following chord are identical. Play only one chord at this point.

For the further practice, also modulate to the parallel key or to any key enharmonic with the parallel keys. For example, in Figure 9.16*a*, modulate also to A major, and in 9.16*b*, modulate also to E♭ minor and to D♯ minor.

FIGURE 9.16

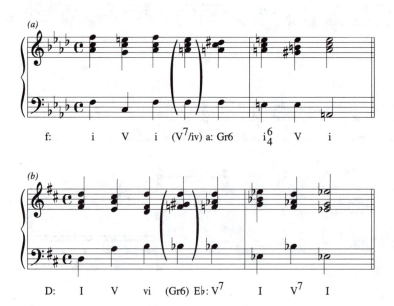

Summary

The Gr6 chord is enharmonic with the major-minor seventh chord and therefore is useful as a pivot chord in modulation. Though the Gr6 can equal any major-minor seventh chord, three such pivots are most commonly used: $V^7 = Gr6$, $Gr6 = V^7$, and $V^7/IV = Gr6$. Each will lead to parallel major and minor keys or to their enharmonic equivalents where available. Other uses of the Gr6 in modulation are possible, but occurrences are uncommon.

There is a variety of single uses of the augmented sixth chord other than those studied in Chapter 8, none of which is commonly used. These include the inversion of the augmented sixth chord, resolution to harmonies other than dominant or tonic six-four, and irregular resolution of the augmented sixth interval.

The *augmented minor seventh chord* is like the augmented triad with a minor seventh added. As in the augmented triad, its fifth is usually the result of a passing tone above a given root. It is most commonly found as V + ^{7}/IV (in C: C E G♯ B♭) or as V + ^{7} (G B D♯ F). The d3 interval is usually found inverted to an A6 in two of the voices above the root of the chord (in the C E G B♭ chord, B♭–G♯ above the root, C). For this reason, it is included with the augmented sixth chords.

10

Chords of the Ninth, the Eleventh, and the Thirteenth

The principle of chord construction by adding thirds can be continued past the triad and the seventh chord to include chords of the ninth, the eleventh, and the thirteenth (Figure 10.1). No further additions are possible, since another third duplicates the root two octaves higher.

FIGURE 10.1   *Chords Larger Than the Seventh*

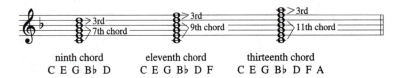

ninth chord	eleventh chord	thirteenth chord
C E G B♭ D	C E G B♭ D F	C E G B♭ D F A

Chords of the Ninth

Ninth chords of dominant and secondary dominant function are those most commonly used. Each consists of a major-minor seventh chord plus a ninth above its root. These chords are symbolized as V^9, V^9/V, and so forth. The "9" indicates that the ninth above the root is diatonic in the key in both major and minor keys. In major keys, the ninth may also be lowered a half step, $V^{\flat 9}$, $V^{\flat 9}/V$, and so forth. These sonorities are shown in Figure 10.2.

The ninth chords ii^9, iv^9, and IV^9 are occasionally seen, but any others are quite uncommon, except in sequences.

FIGURE 10.2   *Chords of the Ninth*

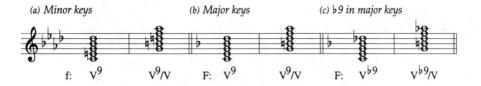

ASSIGNMENT 10.1   Spell the chords of Figure 10.2 in each major and minor key.

In the Workbook: Answers are given.

In the Workbook: Do Assignment 10A. Answers are given.

The ninth chord contains two dissonances, a ninth and a seventh above the root of the chord. These are treated in the same manner as already described for the seventh of a seventh chord; that is, each of these tones is introduced as a nonharmonic-tone figure (passing tone, upper neighbor, suspension, or appoggiatura from below) and then resolves downward as in Figure 10.3. Note that in four-part writing, there is an omitted note, usually the fifth or, infrequently, the third.

FIGURE 10.3   *Resolution of the Ninth*

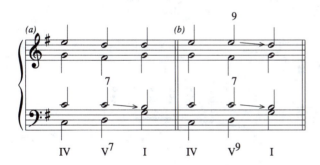

The most important aspect of the ninth chord is the treatment of the ninth itself. Our discussion of these chords will be based on the differences in the approach to and the resolution of the dissonant interval of the ninth. The following list will locate a ninth chord built on a particular root.

Major keys	**Minor keys**
V^9, Figures 10.13, 10.14	V^9, Figures 10.5, 10.6
$V^{\flat9}$, Figure 10.17	iv^9, Figure 10.7
$V^{\flat9}$/ii, Figure 10.17	IV^9, Figure 10.8
V^9/iii, Figure 10.17	
V^9/IV, Figure 10.11	
V^9/V, Figures 10.10, 10.15	
ii^9, Figure 10.9	

Ninth Chords in Which the Ninth Resolves before a Change of Root

Often, a chord contains both the seventh and the ninth above the root with only the ninth resolving above that root. This early resolution is identical to the early resolution described in the discussion of the diminished seventh chord (review page 46). Thus, such a ninth can usually be considered simply a nonharmonic tone in the seventh chord.

In the Verdi aria, Figure 10.4, six of the measures include an accented nonharmonic tone on the first beat. In three instances, these tones are a ninth above their respective roots. But because each "ninth" resolves over its root, the aural effect as a nonharmonic tone is no different from that in the other three instances, where the nonharmonic tone is not a ninth.

Were these unquestionably ninth chords, the lot would constitute three different ninth chords, as indicated.

FIGURE 10.4

Verdi, *Il Trovatore*, Act IV, No. 19

However, when such a ninth is held or repeated, a stronger feeling for an independent ninth chord may result. In Figure 10.5, measure 280, six repetitions of the ninth precede its resolution to V^7. The ninth, C, could easily be considered an implied and extended suspension from the C of the previous chord. But the sudden change of register, its preceding beat of silence, and its repetitions all strengthen analysis as a true ninth chord.

This excerpt is preceded by two successive diminished seventh chords, A♯ C♯ E G and D♯ F♯ A C, successfully dissipating any sense of key. Since E minor is the goal of the passage, the second $^{\circ 7}$ chord appears to be the ct$^\circ$ of VI followed by the first inversion of N^7(!) leading to the V–i close of a highly dramatic passage.

FIGURE 10.5

Beethoven, Symphony No. 3, Op. 55, I

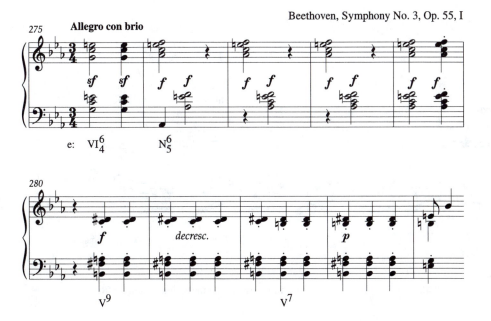

Ninth Chords in Which the Ninth Resolves Simultaneously with the Chord Change

Analysis of a sonority as a ninth chord is more secure when the ninth resolves together with a change of harmony. The examples following show a variety of approaches to the ninth: upper neighbor (Figures 10.7 and 10.9), suspension (Figure 10.8), appoggiatura (Figure 10.10), and passing tone (Figure 10.11).

In our first example, Figure 10.6, the V^9 is extended over two beats. Preceded by rests, it shows no note of approach, but in the cadence, the ninth resolves conventionally.

FIGURE 10.6

V^9

Beethoven, Sonata for Violoncello and Piano, Op.5, No. 2, III

The following two figures demonstrate the iv^9 and IV^9 in minor keys, the difference in the triad determined by the direction of the sixth scale step. Note also the double suspension to introduce the ninth and seventh of the IV^9.

FIGURE 10.7

iv^9

Domenico Scarlatti, Sonata, K. 1[1]

---

[1]K., when used with a work by Domenico Scarlatti, refers to the numbering system by Ralph Kirkpatrick.

FIGURE 10.8

IV^9, minor key

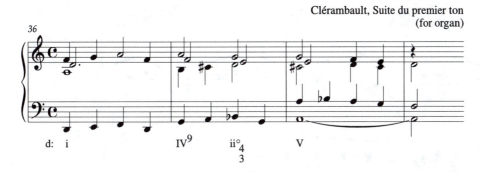

Clérambault, Suite du premier ton
(for organ)

d: i IV^9 $ii°{}^4_3$ V

The ii^9 of Figure 10.9, though nondominant, acts as a kind of embellishing chord to the dominant triad.

FIGURE 10.9

Poco andante

Grieg, "In der Heimat"

F♯:   V ii^9 V

The ninth chords in Figures 10.10 and 10.11 are examples of this sonority serving as secondary dominants, V^9/V and V^9/IV. In the Chopin example, all the harmony is found over an "interrupted" pedal.

FIGURE 10.10

Tchaikovsky, *The Nutcracker,* Overture

Allegro giusto

pp

B♭: V^9/V V

FIGURE 10.11

Chopin, Nocturne, Op. 72, No. 1

Ninth Chords in Which the Ninth and the Seventh Are Arpeggiated

The ninth may be resolved by leap to the seventh, 9–7, Figure 10.12*a*, or through a passing tone to the seventh, 9–8–7, Figure 10.12*b*.

FIGURE 10.12

Figures 10.13 and 10.14 illustrate the leap 9–7. The ninth chord of the latter figure is shown in first inversion, a comparatively rare occurrence.

FIGURE 10.13

FIGURE 10.14

In Figure 10.12*b*, we saw the pattern 9–8–7 above the root. In Figure 10.15, we see the same pattern accompanied in thirds, 7–6–5. The appoggiatura chord over V is itself preceded by a chordlike cluster that includes harmonic and nonharmonic tones. Try to trace each of these through the appoggiatura chord to the C♯ major cadence chord.

FIGURE 10.15

Irregular Resolution of the Ninth

Assuming the usual resolution of the ninth to be down by step, resolutions are occasionally found in which the ninth proceeds in some other way. In Figure 10.16, the ninth, D, resolves up by step. The use of this chord in third inversion is quite rare.

FIGURE 10.16

Ninth Chords in Sequence

When found in sequence, ninth chords and seventh chords are usually found alternately. Use of sequence allows the presence of ninth chords not ordinarily encountered, such as the V♭9/ii and the V9/iii seen in Figure 10.17.

FIGURE 10.17

Tchaikovsky, *Romeo and Juliet*

Eleventh and Thirteenth Chords

Chords of the eleventh containing a ninth and chords of the thirteenth containing a ninth or an eleventh are comparatively rare. When an eleventh is present without a ninth, or a thirteenth without a ninth or an eleventh, the sonority will usually prove to consist only of a simple nonharmonic tone over the bass tone (Figure 10.18*a* and *b*).

A sonority can more accurately be called an eleventh chord when the ninth is also present, or called a thirteenth chord when either the ninth or the eleventh is present (Figure 10.18*c* and *d*). But even when a sonority is more positively identifiable as an eleventh or a thirteenth chord, the dissonances in each almost invariably resolve while the root of the chord is being held (early resolution), so that at the time of a change of root, only a more simple sonority, seventh or ninth, remains. Under these circumstances, it is difficult to assume the existence of any eleventh or thirteenth chord, when the simpler analysis of seventh or ninth chord plus dissonance is available.

FIGURE 10.18   *Sonorities That Include an Eleventh or a Thirteenth*

Assuming, however, the existence of these chords, we can examine their properties. In any chord that includes an eleventh above the bass, the third will be omitted, since the resolution of the eleventh is to the third of the chord (Figure 10.18 *a, c, d*). What is the letter name of the omitted third in Figures 10.19 and 10.20?

The chord identified as V^{11} in Figure 10.19 is obviously an appoggiatura chord resolving to V^7. Yet its repetition and insistence certainly provide the aural sensation of an eleventh chord in its own right.

FIGURE 10.19

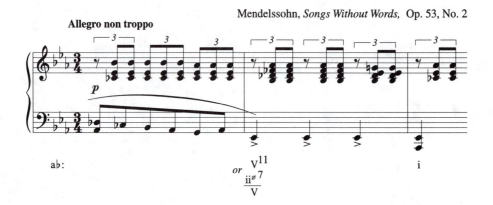

Mendelssohn, *Songs Without Words,* Op. 53, No. 2

The eleventh of the chord in Figure 10.20, measure 451, is doubled. The upper eleventh skips down to the fifth to begin the long chromatic line. The lower sustained eleventh eventually resolves early but is sustained long enough to be considered successful in creating the effect of an eleventh chord.

The "ninth" of (V^9/V) in measure 452 is created solely by the coincidence of C$\sharp$ in the chromatic melodic line occurring on a strong beat over V^7.

FIGURE 10.20

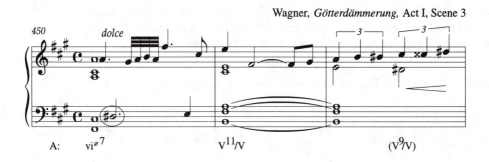

Wagner, *Götterdämmerung,* Act I, Scene 3

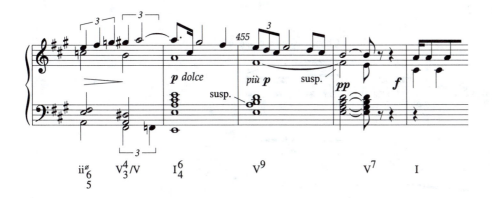

Figure 10.21 demonstrates each of the chords of the ninth, the eleventh, and the thirteenth. Note these features:

1. All three are introduced as unprepared appoggiaturas.
2. All show early resolution to the next sonority.
3. The ninth of the first V^9 does not resolve, since the pattern of its measure is repeated sequentially in the next measure.
4. The V^{13} includes a ninth in its structure. Upon the resolution of the thirteenth, the V^9 remains.
5. The ninth of V^9 is repeated an octave higher and resolves into tonic six-four.

FIGURE 10.21

All these intervals—the seventh, the ninth, the eleventh, and the thirteenth—sound above the root C♯ in Figure 10.22. But it should be obvious that this cluster constitutes a IV^7 over the arpeggiated V^7. The seventh and the ninth are held over (though not sustained) as a long double suspension into the final tonic triad. The eleventh, F♯, resolves to E♯ of V^7, and the thirteenth, A♯, is suspended into the V^7.

The chord of resolution (beat 3) first appears to be IV, but its B and D♯ mark the end of the double suspension begun at the start of the measure.

FIGURE 10.22

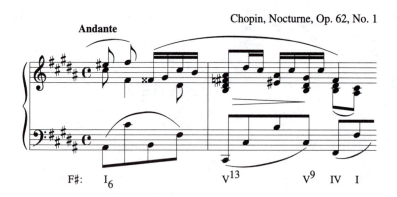

ASSIGNMENT 10.2 *Harmonic analysis.*   Each of these excerpts includes one or more examples of the use of the ninth above its root. They range from obvious nonharmonic-tone devices to more complex structures. Determine the function of the ninth and explain its approach and resolution as part of your analysis of the entire example.

(1)

(2)

Chopin, Mazurka, Op. 56, No. 3

(3)

Rossini, *Petite Messe Solennelle*

(4)

Wagner, *Die Walküre,* Act I, Scene 3

(5)

Brahms, Romanze, Op. 118, No. 5

(6)

Franck, *Symphonic Variations*

(7)

Mozart, Sonata in E♭ Major for Violin and Piano, K. 380, II

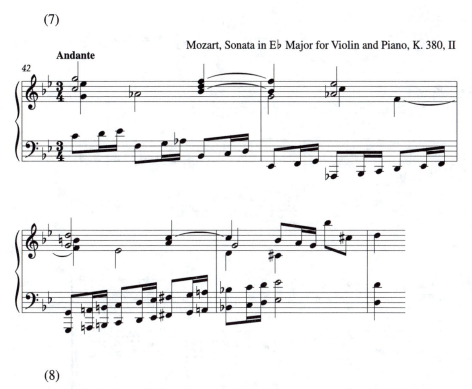

(8)

Schubert, Quartet in D Minor
(Death and the Maiden), D. 810, "Scherzo"

Writing Ninth Chords

The ninth of the ninth chord is usually introduced in the manner of a nonharmonic tone. It usually resolves down, either stepwise or by skip to the seventh of the chord, and is introduced in one of four ways.

1. As a passing-tone figure—See Figure 10.11.
2. As a suspension—See Figures 10.8 and 10.15.
3. As a neighboring tone—See Figures 10.7, 10.9, and 10.14.
4. As an appoggiatura, with skip from below—See Figures 10.10 and 10.13.

Some attention must be given to placement of chord members in the vertical structure.

1. The ninth of the chord is most often found in the soprano (highest) voice. This is particularly true in ninth chords other than V^9.
2. The ninth is found at the interval of at least a ninth (rather than a second) above the root of the chord.
3. When the ninth is not the highest note, the third of the chord is almost invariably lower than the ninth (see Figure 10.6).
4. Examples of the chord with a note other than the root in the bass are uncommon (see Figure 10.14, third in bass, and Figure 10.16, seventh in bass).

ASSIGNMENT 10.3 *Writing ninth chords.*   These may be done for practice in four-voice chorale style, as illustrated in Figure 10.23, and in keyboard style, using Figure 10.24 as an example.

FIGURE 10.23

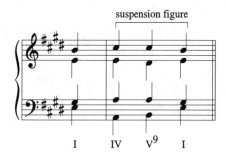

Write the following progressions in keys as assigned or self-chosen. The number in parentheses indicates the soprano position of the opening tonic triad. The ninth is to be in the soprano in each example. Introduce and resolve the ninth by the non-harmonic pattern indicated.

The ninth introduced as a suspension

(5) I IV V^9 I   (5) i iv V^9 i

(3) I vi ii^9 V^7 I   (5) i iv^9 V^7 i

(3) I vi V^9/V V I   (5) i IV^9 V^7 i

(3) I ♭VI $V^{♭9}$/V V I

(5) I iv $V^{♭9}$ V I

The ninth introduced as a passing tone

(1) I V V⁹ I   (3) i V⁹/iv iv V i

(3) I V⁹/IV IV V I

The ninth introduced as a neighbor tone

(5) I V⁹ I   (5) i V⁹ i

The ninth introduced as an appoggiatura

(1) I vi ii⁹ V I   (3) i iv⁹ V⁷ i

(3) I I₆ V⁹/V V I   (3) i i₆ V⁹/V V i

In the Workbook: Answers are given.

The Ninth Chord in the Harmonic Sequence

In the keyboard harmony section following, Figures 10.24–10.27 show a selection from the possible harmonic sequences using ninth chords with the popular root movement down a fifth and up a fourth (review Figure 10.17). These are written in "keyboard style"—that is, with three notes in the right hand and one in the left. Where secondary dominant ninth chords are used, the principal roman numeral indicates the scale-step number of the root, such as II⁹, with its secondary dominant symbol, V⁹/V, found immediately below. The purpose is to facilitate locating the left-hand note in keyboard performance (the root of V⁹/V or II⁹ is $\hat{2}$).

In studying these examples, note these characteristics:

1. Ninth chords alternate with seventh chords.
2. The fifth of the ninth chord is usually omitted.
3. In minor, $\flat\hat{7}$ and $\flat\hat{6}$ are always used, except in cadential harmony.
4. A diatonic ninth chord whose triad is minor can be altered to become a secondary dominant ninth by raising its third. (In Figure 10.25, ii⁹ becomes II⁹ (V⁹/V): F A♭ C E♭ G becomes F A C E♭ G.)
5. In the secondary dominant ninth chord, a diatonic ninth that ordinarily resolves by whole step can be lowered as a ♭9. (In Figure 10.25, VI♭9 becomes V♭9/ii: C E♭ G B♭ D becomes C E G B♭ D♭.) In some instances, lowering the ninth also requires lowering the seventh to avoid a d3 between the ninth and the seventh. (In Figure 10.25, I⁹ becomes V♭9/IV: E♭ G B♭ D F becomes E♭ G B♭ D♭ F♭.)

ASSIGNMENT 10.4 *Writing the harmonic sequence using ninth chords.*   After you have gained experience in playing the keyboard exercises, write out similar harmonic sequences in keys as assigned or self-chosen. Try writing secondary dominant ninth chords with either diatonic or lowered ninths.

Keyboard Harmony

ASSIGNMENT 10.5 *Playing at the keyboard the progressions listed in Assignment 10.3.* These may be played with three notes in the right hand and one in the left. Omit the fifth in each ninth chord.

ASSIGNMENT 10.6 Play the harmonic sequences of Figures 10.24–10.27 in keys as assigned.

1. Play sequences in major keys, Figure 10.24.
2. Play the same sequences but with ninth chords altered to become secondary dominant ninths. Figure 10.25 shows one possibility.
3. Play sequences in minor keys, Figure 10.26. Remember, always use $\flat\hat{7}$ and $\flat\hat{6}$ except at the cadence.
4. Add alterations as in item 2 above and as shown in Figure 10.27.

FIGURE 10.24   *Diatonic Harmonic Sequences, Major Keys*

FIGURE 10.25   *Sequence Including Altered Chords, Major Keys*

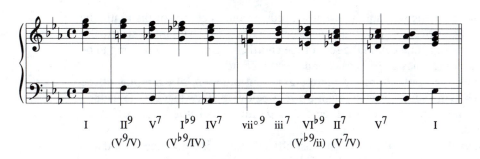

FIGURE 10.26   *Diatonic Sequences, Minor Keys*

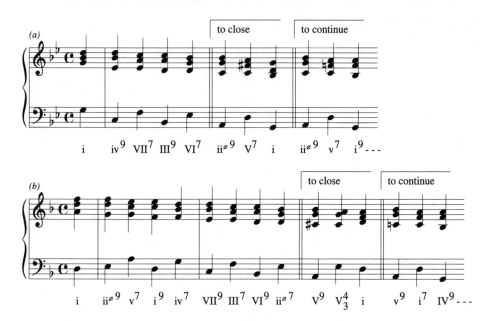

FIGURE 10.27   *Sequence Including Altered Chords, Minor Keys*

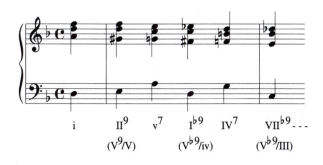

Summary

Adding thirds above the seventh of seventh chords produces chords of the ninth, the eleventh, and the thirteenth. In actual practice, these three dissonant intervals usually resolve to a harmonic tone before the root of the chord changes, thereby proving to be simple nonharmonic tones above a triad or a seventh chord.

Only with the ninth chord are there significant numbers of examples of the dissonance resolving simultaneously with the root below it. But whatever the method of resolution, the preparation of all three dissonant intervals is the same as that for seventh chords.

The interval of the ninth, although most often diatonic, is sometimes found as a lowered tone—for example, as either D or D♭ above the C major-minor seventh chord. Ninth chords are found mostly above dominant, supertonic, and subdominant roots. However, in the harmonic sequence, they may appear above any other root, usually alternating with seventh chords.

11

Chords and Progressions in Special Situations

Our study of the harmonic resources of the eighteenth and nineteenth centuries is virtually complete, having covered those structures and progressions most likely to be encountered. But there still remains a large store of materials "not likely to be encountered," from which examples will unexpectedly appear in a music score. We will inspect a few such examples.

A second section of this chapter will demonstrate how some intricate and fascinating harmonic successions have been produced through the combined use of two or more individual compositional devices, such as harmonic sequence and change of mode.

Some Less Common Chord Structures

Nowhere in our study have we encountered in a major key a major triad built on ♭$\hat{7}$. Yet one appears in Figure 11.1 in the progression ii–♭VII–V/V. Note how smoothly Haydn slips into the ♭VII, G B D, as though it were VI to the preceding B D F♯ triad, and then slips back to A major by a chromatic alteration of the soprano line.

FIGURE 11.1   *♭VII in major*

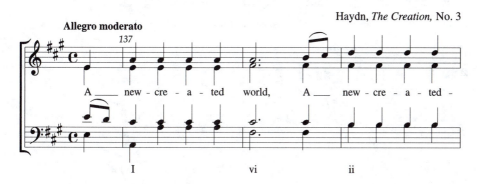

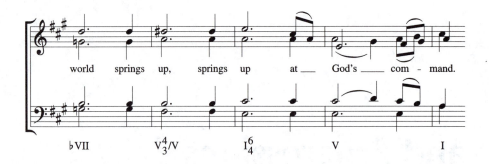

Usually, the complete common harmonic sequence, roots up a fourth and down a fifth, starts with the triads IV–vii°–iii - - - -. But in E major of Figure 11.2, the sequence begins with the secondary dominant, A♯ C× E♯ G♯, tonicizing the vii (minor) triad, D♯ F♯ A♯, a chord that is most rare under any other circumstance. The rest of the sequence is completely predictable.

FIGURE 11.2   *vii (Minor Triad) in Major*

A chromatic bass line (moving by half step) will often create one or more chords that are not to be found elsewhere. One of the best-known examples of the descending chromatic bass line, this one of ten measures' duration, is Chopin's Prelude in E Minor, the first part of which is shown as Figure 11.3. It should first be recognized that the right-hand "melody" is probably a pedal point on B, with an upper neighbor, in measures 1–4, and on A until measure 8. The beginning harmony and that of the cadences is clear:

e: i _____ V^7/iv _____ iv _____ V iv V iv V ___ i

measure   1   4   9   10   11   12   13

Between those points, the common harmonic succession shown above is controlled by the chromatic bass line and where that is static, as in measures 4–5, by the chromatically descending inner voice. No chord-by-chord analysis can be meaningful in progressions such as these.

FIGURE 11.3

Chopin, Prelude in E Minor, Op. 28, No. 4

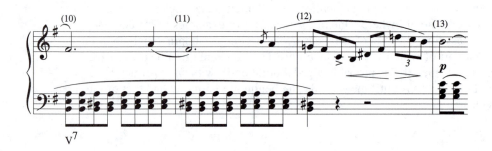

Complex Harmonic Progressions

The simultaneous use of two or more conventional compositional devices, listed below, or even two varieties of the same device, will often produce sonorities and types of harmonic succession not otherwise ordinarily encountered. The illustrative examples will be based on combinations from

1. Harmonic sequence
2. First inversions in series
3. Secondary tonal levels
4. Change of mode
5. Enharmonic spellings
6. Chromatic lines

1. Sequence and Change of Mode

Figure 11.4 presents a relatively easy example of this combination. Figure 11.6 is a much more complex example. The music of Figure 11.4 begins and ends in C major and displays the common harmonic sequence roots up a fourth and down a fifth. The sequence is altered by change of mode immediately after the opening tonic triad when its root is held over as a suspension, over which is the Neapolitan triad, forming a N_2^4 chord. The change of mode continues to the V–I cadence and includes a $v^{\varnothing 7}$ chord, rarely seen elsewhere. In this example, the lower clef is the left-hand part for the piano. The omitted right-hand part consists of arpeggiation of the chords shown.

FIGURE 11.4

Mozart, Concerto for Piano and Orchestra, K. 503, I

The excerpt from the Brahms Trio, Figure 11.6, includes harmonic sequence, change of mode, enharmonicism, and one new feature, the whole-tone scale.

To aid our study of the complexity of this sequence, we will consider the two diminished seventh chords as incomplete dominant ninth chords (review Figure 2.14). Addition of the "missing root" to each of these results in the chord spellings (D) F♯ A C E♭ and (B♭) D F A♭ C♭. Their implied roots, D and B♭, are marked with an * in the analysis below Figure 11.6.

Our excerpt begins with the half cadence iv–V in G minor. The sequence begins in measure 110 with the implied root, D, and moves down a fifth and up a third, shown in Figure 11.5. But note that each movement by third is a minor third, made possible in measure 113 by the change of mode, E♭–e♭.

Note also that for three measures beginning in measure 113, the triad's root is found on beat 1, above which is its tonicizing chord, held over from the previous beat. The first of these shows the upper three notes, F A♭ C♭, of the previous °7/vi over E♭, the root of vi. Examine the following measures for a continuation of this process.

FIGURE 11.5   *Root Movement of Figure 11.6*

FIGURE 11.6

Change of mode occurs at measure 112 where the repetition of °⁷/VI is altered to °⁷/vi. Thus, it is possible to consider the following chords as V⁷/iii–iii in G major, though we have retained symbols for G minor. More important at this point is that this change of mode has made it possible for the soprano to describe a descending *whole-tone scale,* a scale made up entirely of whole steps, here A♭ (G♯) F♯ E D C B♭.[1]

---

[1]The use of the whole-tone scale is discussed in more detail in Chapter 13 in connection with the music of Debussy.

FIGURE 11.7   *Whole-Tone Scale Line*

whole-tone scale

How should we consider this line? Did Brahms write the harmony to accommo-date the scale line, or was the scale line the result of the chosen harmony? Most likely, Brahms worked within the possibilities offered by the chosen root movement of the sequence, but there is no way to know that with certainty.

2. An "Interlocking" Sequence

This sequence features the alternation of two different root-movement patterns—in this case, roots up a second, down a fifth, and roots up a fourth and down a fifth. Fig-ure 11.8 shows in C major the bass line of such a movement in which the last triad of each sequential pattern is considered the tonic of that pattern. The result is a series of tonal levels resulting from an alternating series of pivots, i = ii and I = IV.

FIGURE 11.8   *"Interlocking" Root Movement*

iv   V   i = ii   V   I = IV   V   I = ii *etc.*

Taken from a work in C♯ major, our excerpt (Figure 11.10), begins in A♯ minor and ends in F♯ major. (If you find these keys too challenging, play and analyze in A minor–F major by deleting all ♯'s, lowering each ✕ to ♯ and each ♮ to ♭.) To help sim-plify this complex passage, we will use a secondary tonal analysis.

In Figure 11.9*a*, the letters above the roman numerals are chord roots, and the letters below the line are the roots of each temporary tonic. The sequence begins with iv–V–i on a level of e♯; i (e♯) equals ii of ii–V–i on the level of d♯; i (d♯) equals iv of iv–V–i on the level of a♯; and so forth. Then in Figure 11.9*b*, we see the relationship of the temporary tonics (pitch names below the lines) and observe that they constitute a simple harmonic sequence, roots down a second and up a fifth. The succession of seven roots from a♯ to f♯ makes possible a modulation to the mediant, a♯ minor to F♯ major.

FIGURE 11.9

(a)

Measure	29	30	31		31	32	33		33	34	35		35	36	37	
Chord root	a#	E#	a#		a#	B#	e#		e#	A#	d#		d#	E#	a#	
Analysis	i	V	i	=	iv	V	i	=	ii	V	i	=	iv	V	i	=
Root of I (i)	a#					e#				d#				a#		

37	38	39		39	40	41		41	42	43		43	44	45		45	46	47
a#	D#	G#		G#	A#	d#		d#	G#	C#		C#	D#	g#		g#	C#	F#
ii	V	I	=	IV	V	i	=	ii	V	I	=	IV	V	I	=	ii	V	I
	G#				d#				C#				g#				F#	

(b)

e# 2 ↓ d# 5 ↑ a# 2 ↓ G# 5 ↑ d# 2 ↓ c# 5 ↑ g# 2 ↓ F#

FIGURE 11.10

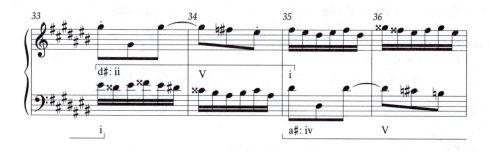

Bach, *Well-Tempered Clavier,* Vol. 1,
Prelude in C# Major

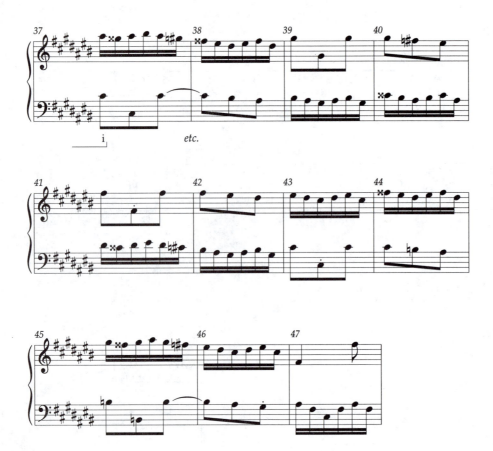

This sequence covers sixteen measures, longer than most, though the last three measures are modified somewhat. How dull might this be were the melodic materials presented repeatedly in the same relationship! But variety is assured in these ways:

1. First, note that in measure 30, the G✗ could have resolved up to A♯ and then down an octave to A♯. With that minor change, measure 30 would have the same pattern as measure 31. We could then say that measures 31–32 and 33–34 constitute a sequence.

2. At measure 35, music for right hand and left hand exchange locations. At this point, measures 35–38 are a sequence of the previous four measures (1, above) and at the same time include the two-measure statement 35–36 and its sequence, 37–38.

3. Measures 39–42 are like 31–34 at a different pitch level.

4. At measure 43, the exchange of parts occurs again. The lower voice, 43–46, continues like the upper voice of 39–42, while the upper voice at 44 continues with previous motives, both leading to the cadence at 47.

It is obvious that this excerpt displays a most imaginative and carefully considered use of sequence, in both its harmonic and its melodic elements.

3. Secondary Tonal Levels, Change of Mode, and Successive First Inversions

Mozart's String Quartet in C, K. 465, is often dubbed the "Dissonant Quartet" because of the seemingly complex harmony of its first fourteen measures (Figure 11.11). The passage opens with the single tone C and cadences at measure 14 in C major. However, the first complete chord is A♭ major. Were we to attempt a chord-by-chord analysis in either C major or A♭ major, only a meaningless series of roman numerals would result, giving no idea of the functions of the sound.

Rather than identifying the first chord immediately, we should, as usual, look for the first cadence. It is an imperfect authentic cadence, D–G$_6$, over a pedal tone, B, at measure 4. Relating the harmony that precedes the G$_6$ reveals that the series begins on N$_6$ and proceeds to its cadence on the tonal level of V (G B D) using a common harmonic progression.

$$\frac{N_6 - ii^{\varnothing 6}_{5} - V^4_2 - I_6 - V - I_6}{V_6}$$

The next cadence, also imperfect authentic, is on F$_6$ at measure 8. On a tonal level of F, measures 5–8 display the same harmonic progression as in measures 1–4. At measure 9, F$_6$ is followed by f$_6$ and then by a succession of first inversions. Thus, we can see that with the inclusion of the cadence chords at measures 4 (G$_6$) and 8 (F$_6$), the entire passage is based on a series of first inversions: G$_6$, F$_6$, (f$_6$) E♭$_6$, d$^{\circ}_6$, c$_6$, a scalewise progression from the dominant to the final C major cadence.

The analysis now achieved allows us to identify the function of the single note, C, that opens measure 1 and the interval B♭–D♭ that opens measure 5. B♭ and D♭ obviously imply B♭ D♭ F, iv of the following cadence. Thus, we can assume the single C of measure 1 represents not only the tonic of C major but also IV (F A C) of its following cadence.

FIGURE 11.11

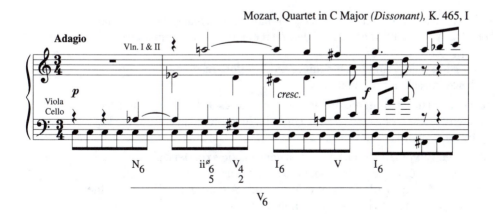

Mozart, Quartet in C Major *(Dissonant)*, K. 465, I

The extensive use of mixed modes creates a continual vacillation between major and minor tonality. Also included are these additional examples of chromaticism:

1. The progression N_6–$ii^{\varnothing 7}$ implies the minor mode before reaching the major tonic cadence in each use of tonal levels.

2. Four successive chords from the minor mode, measures 9–12, occur immediately before the final V–I cadence. Scale lines include accidentals from the keys implied by these chords.

3. Several melodic chromatic usages add to the chromatic experience.
   a. Measures 2 and 6 include intentional cross-relations (A♭–A in measure 2).
   b. In measure 11, the violin's F♯ and the viola's A♭ momentarily create the sound of a French sixth in a less common inversion.
   c. In measures 11–13, there are several chromatic scale-line passages. At the cadence, the six notes of the bass line between G and C sound at successive half-step intervals.

Altogether, this fascinating excerpt shows how otherwise commonly used chords and progressions can be so imaginatively arranged that even after repeated hearings, the passage still gives the impression of complex dissonance and chromaticism without sacrificing logical and traditional harmonic procedures. All the features we have enumerated create a saturated chromatic experience that is in direct contrast not only to the rest of the quartet's first movement but also to Mozart's style in general.

ASSIGNMENT 11.1 *Harmonic analysis.*   Each of these excerpts includes one or more features discussed in this chapter. Make a harmonic analysis, including written commentary where necessary concerning multiple uses of analytical devices.

(1)

Chopin, Mazurka, Op. 24, No. 4

(2)

Mozart, Symphony No. 40 in G Minor, K. 550, II

(3)

Carl Heinrich Graun (1704–1759), *Der Tod Jesu,* No. 2

(4) Look for further examples of the bracketed motive.

Bach, *Well-Tempered Clavier*, Vol. I,
Fugue No. 4

(5)

Brahms, *Romanzen aus Magelone,* Op. 33,
"Treue Liebe dauert lange"

treu - - es ___ Blut.
loy - - *al* ___ *heart.*

Und   wie   Ne - bel
Like   *a*   *cloud*   *then*

(6) The next excerpt includes most of the development section of the sonata. It includes two principal analytical problems, the first up to measure 112, and the second from measure 112 to the end.

Here are some suggestions to aid in the analysis.

Measures 104–109: Included are harmonic sequences of two measures and four measures. How do the lengths of the melodic sequences compare with these?

Measures 112ff: Look for the rhythmic repetition of the treble-clef notation of measure 112 to locate the beginning of each repetition.

Measure 113, and similar situations later: You see B D F A♭ in the right hand and F A♭ C in the left hand. Are two chords sounding simultaneously, or is there a pedal point involved? Either solution is possible.

Measures 124–133: Compare the root movement of measures 124–129 with that of measures 129–133. (Consider the last chord of the first group to overlap as the first chord of the second group.) Though the two groups of root movements are not identical, there is a marked relationship between these groups (use enharmonic spellings if necessary).

Beethoven, Sonata in C Major for Piano, Op. 53, I

12

The Close of the Nineteenth Century— The Beginning of New Directions

At the turn of the nineteenth to the twentieth century, it was obvious that the authority of the traditional practices of the previous three centuries was rapidly declining and that newer concepts of music making were coming to the fore. The result was the emergence in the twentieth century of music entirely unlike that of previous centuries.

In this chapter, we will investigate the evolution of some of the practices responsible in large part for the revolutionary changes to come. In such a study, as in the study of twentieth-century music itself, it is necessary to bear in mind the the principal concepts of traditional music—first to better understand the process of change, and second, to serve as a standard of comparison between the old and the new. For these reasons, we will open this chapter with a concise review of the concepts in harmony that we have learned over the duration of this course of study.

Review of Traditional Harmony

1. *Tonality.* In every composition, there is one tone that assumes more importance than the others, and to which the others are related. This phenomenon is emphasized by the almost exclusive use of the V–I progression (authentic cadence) at the close of a composition and its liberal use elsewhere.

2. *Scale systems.* Tonality in the common practice period is expressed through two scale systems, major and minor, other scale systems of earlier times having fallen into disuse.

3. *Keys.* Each major and minor scale can be found on fifteen different pitch locations, called keys. These keys are systematized in two circles of fifths, one for major and one for minor.

4. *Chords.* Music of the common practice period is based largely upon the use of chords. A chord is defined as a simultaneous sounding of pitches spelled, usually, in major and minor thirds, the lowest note of these thirds being considered the root. Not all possible chord constructions in thirds were regularly used.

5. *Inversion.* A chord retains its identity whether or not the root is found as the lowest sounding voice.

6. *Chord succession.* The progression of one chord to another is based upon the movements of their roots, root movement by descending fifth being the most common. Certain progressions tended to become much more widely used than others, and not all possible root relationships within a key were regularly used. In general, any chord progression is one of a series that ultimately leads to a cadence, usually on the tonic of the key.

7. *Nonharmonic tones.* Tones not belonging to a chord may sound simultaneously with a chord structure. Such a dissonance must always be introduced and resolved in certain established ways.

8. *Melody.* Melodic lines are so constructed that each tone will be part of a chord or an acceptable nonharmonic tone to that chord. A succession of melodic tones will usually imply a conventional chord succession.

9. *Rhythm.* Rhythmic patterns are usually organized into metric units of two, three, or four beats, the primary accent falling on the first beat of any metrical group. Any other accent in any melodic line is a syncopation against the primary accent.

10. *Harmonic rhythm.* The rhythmic pattern created by the frequency of chord change conforms to the metric structures described in the preceding paragraph.

These, greatly generalized, are the basic concepts underlying the composition of music in the common practice period. Exceptions, though numerically quite frequent, actually represent only a very small percentage of the total output of the composers of the period. But this is not to imply that compositional techniques were stagnant and that no change in musical expression took place during this period of almost three hundred years. In any art form, in any science, in any institution, in life itself, change, for better or for worse, is the only constant known to human endeavor. The limitations listed above were subject to the attacks and inroads of change for the entire course of the historical period, so that by the end of the nineteenth century, no further change could take place within the style without destroying the style itself. True to predictable pressures of change, that is exactly what happened.

Of the basic concepts listed above, those concerning the sense of major and minor tonality bore the brunt of the early forces of change. The importance of the tonic was particularly subject to challenge. Composers, bound for centuries by the restrictions of a key and its closest relationships, now were breaking those bonds with a number of devices to postpone or to avoid achieving the harmonic goal and to lessen the influence of the tonic as the guiding tone of the composition. Although we have already encountered such devices in the music of earlier composers, including the deceptive cadence, successive diminished seventh chords, direct modulations to remote keys, and less common root movements, the number and frequency of such evasive practices increased dramatically in the waning years of the nineteenth century. We will examine several such practices in this chapter.

Triads in Chromatic Third Relationship

Two diatonic triads with roots a third apart have two tones in common—for example, C E G and E G B, or F A♭ C and D♭ F A♭. When one of the triads is altered to produce a major or minor triad, but with the same letter names or their enharmonic equivalents, a *chromatic third* relationship results. Figure 12.1 shows the triad spellings in a chromatic third relationship with the triad C E G. Note that the root relationship includes the augmented second and the diminished fourth, both enharmonic with the interval of a third, as in C E G–D♯ F♯ A♯, the latter enharmonic with E♭ G♭ B♭.

FIGURE 12.1

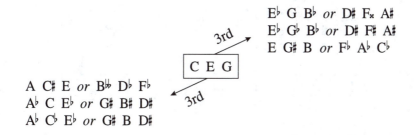

ASSIGNMENT 12.1 *Spelling chromatic third relationships.*   Choose any major or minor triad. Using Figure 12.1 as a guide, spell the triads in a chromatic third relationship to the chosen triad.

In the Workbook: Answers are given.

The use of this relationship is not original to the late nineteenth century. The music of Figure 12.2, a madrigal for five voices, is from the late sixteenth century. A short period of extraordinary harmonic experimentation preceded the establishment of the conventional standards of the common practice period.

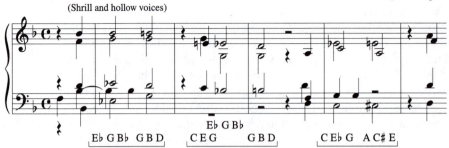

Luzzasco Luzzaschi, *Quivi sospiri*

Our next example shows in D minor the relationship A C♯ E–F A C. The F A C triad then alternates with its dominant to produce a series, I–V⁷–I–V⁷- -, the last V⁷ of which is left unresolved as it moves to the V⁷ of the original key. For this reason, we identify this progression as a secondary tonal progression on the level of ♭III.

The chord on the first beat of measures 16 and 18 might be considered a dominant eleventh. However, the interval B♭–D appears more likely to be nonharmonic to F A C. A similar effect is created in measure 25, where the interval F–A is nonharmonic but the addition of C♯ results in the sound of an augmented triad.

FIGURE 12.3

Schubert, Sonata in A Major for Piano, D. 959, III

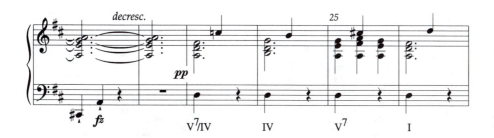

In music of the late nineteenth century, root movement by chromatic thirds is often used to create frequent changes of key, to cause delay in reaching the tonic, or to obscure the progress of the harmonic movement leading to the ultimate tonic cadence. This type of root movement is used in Figure 12.4 to mark off four separate phrases in as many keys, each in a chromatic third relationship: B♭ D F♯ B♭. The pitch names of these keys describe an augmented triad, B♭ D F♯ (G♭). Three of the phrases begin and end on their respective tonics, making the chromatic third relationship easy to see. The first phrase ends on the dominant of B♭, but it too is in a third relationship to the first triad of the second phrase, F A C–D F♯ A.

At this late date in the nineteenth century, the strictness in the application of conventional part-writing procedures is considerably relaxed in the music of many composers. In this example, note (1) the consistent use of parallel fifths and (2) the lack of resolution of the altered tones G♭ in measures 1 and 2 and B♭ in measures 5 and 7.

As evidence of the changing times, compare the freedom seen in this excerpt with any work of Wolf's contemporary Brahms, whose music on the whole still adheres to conventional practices.

FIGURE 12.4

A harmonic sequence, roots up a chromatic third and down a fourth, is seen in Figure 12.5 *a.* Above the staff, letter names indicate the root of each chord and brackets indicate locations of the chromatic thirds. We have considered each of the weak-beat intervening triads to be "appoggiatura triads," first because each has the same basic spelling as the following triad and, second, because the aural effect is strongly that of harmonic movement from strong beat to strong beat.

The sequence lasts through the ♭VI of measure 51, after which the root movement to measure 52 consists of two ascending thirds. Note that after the ♭VI, the harmonic progression is conventional, in spite of its complex appearance.

A♭ C♭ G♭ B♭♭ F♭

I – ♭III – ♭VII – ♭II – ♭VI – to I

None of these is identified with V/– symbols, since none expresses a secondary dominant relationship.

In Figure 12.5*b,* the chord symbols should clarify the harmonic movement and the accompanying chord spellings. The symbols V/– and N$_6$ are not used because the harmonic sounds do not reflect these functions. The striking enharmonically mixed spellings of several chords result from the bringing together of several simultaneous vocal lines, each written for ease in reading.

FIGURE 12.5

(a)

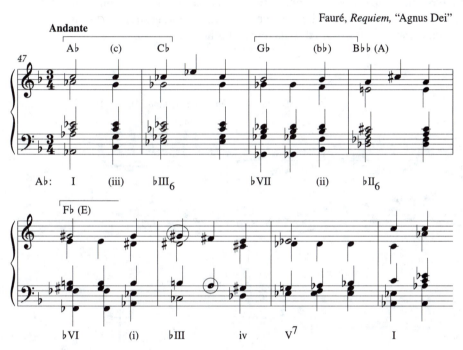

Fauré, *Requiem,* "Agnus Dei"

(b)

```
        I    |  ♭III  |  ♭VII  |   ♭II   |  ♭VI   |   (i)   |
     A♭ C E♭ | C♭ E♭ G♭ | G♭ B♭ D♭ | B♭♭ D♭ F♭ | F♭ A♭ C♭ | A♭ C♭ E♭ |
                                     | A  C♯ E  | E  G♯ B  | G♯ B D♯ |

      |  ♭III  |   iv   |   V⁷    |    I    |
      | C♭ E♭ G♭ | D♭ F♭ A♭ | E♭ G B♭ D♭ | A♭ C E♭ |
      | B  D♯ F♯ | C♯ E G♯ |
```

Root Movement by Tritone

In the conventional harmonic progressions already studied, root movement by tritone has occurred infrequently. The progression N_6–V (C: D♭ to G) is one example. Approaching a diminished sonority such as IV–vii° is common, but when the diminished triad is considered an incomplete seventh chord (B D F as an incomplete G B D F), no tritone movement exists.

Any other root movement by tritone has been uncommon and, when found, usually for some special situation. The example, Figure 12.6, by Berlioz was written in 1820. The tritone relationship serves a purpose other than as a functional member of root movements. Here it is an antiphonal exchange between two orchestral groups as indicated, an ear-catching device still used to the present time.[1]

FIGURE 12.6

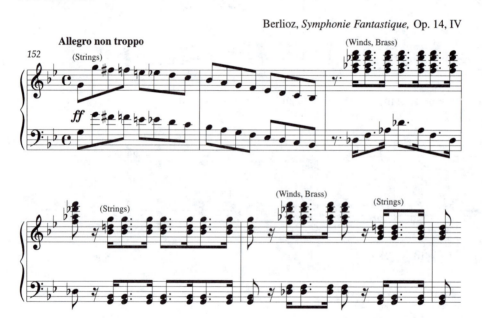

Berlioz, *Symphonie Fantastique,* Op. 14, IV

When used as a part of harmonic progression, the root movement by tritone will usually cause a sudden change in key orientation. The short eight-measure passage of Figure 12.7*a* includes three such root movements, as bracketed. Two of these, in measures 10–13, are part of a harmonic sequence, roots down a tritone and up a fourth (C–G♭–C♭–F). The other tritone movement, E♭–A in measures 14–15, precedes two seventh chords in a chromatic third relationship leading to a conventional authentic cadence.

---

[1]Review *Elementary Harmony,* page 234, for an excerpt from Rimsky-Korsakov's *Scheherazade* in which a sustained tritone implies the alternating functions of an augmented fourth and a diminished fifth.

Figure 12.7*b* reduces the eight measures to block chords. When you play this succession, it will probably sound meaningless. Now play or listen to the composition. You should be impressed by what Duparc[2] has done with this unusual basic material.

FIGURE 12.7

Duparc, "Extase"

[2]Henri Duparc, 1848–1933, composed only fourteen songs and very few other works during the years 1868–84. In 1884, he suffered a mental breakdown that made further work impossible but did not affect his memory of past accomplishments. His *chansons* still form an important part of the standard vocal repertoire.

Evasion of Tonic

We have seen that the function of any given sonority tends to lead it to another given sonority, continuing in a pattern in which all those sonorities gravitate toward the tonic of the key. When these common harmonic functions are used exclusively in music composition, the results often become boring and tiresome unless handled masterfully, as in Figure 12.8, from one of Mozart's earliest sonatas. In this excerpt the tonic appears eight times in nine measures. (The figure does not imply that this music is typical of Mozart's writing. Rather, it illustrates the practice of frequent return to tonic common to music of the early harmonic period.)

FIGURE 12.8

Mozart, Sonata for Piano, K. 284, II

In contrast, Schumann, in Figure 12.9, avoids the opening tonic harmony until the close of the excerpt in measure 15. A single tonicization of IV at measure 10 is the only other expression of a dominant–tonic relationship. The processes of elongation are worth your study; only material you have already studied is included.

FIGURE 12.9

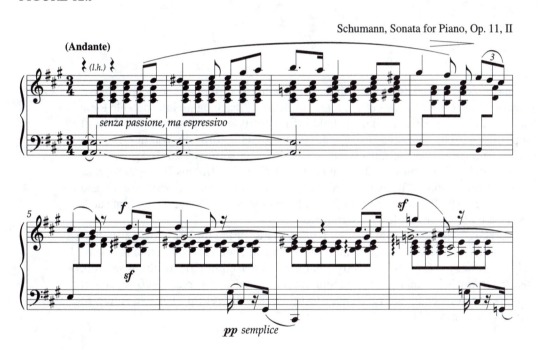

Schumann, Sonata for Piano, Op. 11, II

Examples by two late-nineteenth-century composers, Brahms and Wagner, show two extremes in the avoidance of the tonic. In Brahms, reaching an indisputable tonic triad of the opening key, E minor, is held off for thirty-two measures, just short of completing a thirty-five measure A section of a ternary form. In Wagner, tonic is avoided repeatedly after the sounding of a series of as few as two chords.

Figure 12.10*a* shows the first ten measures from the Brahms Intermezzo; *b* of the same figure begins at measure 31 to show the first tonic chord at measure 32, and the transition to the B section in E major. Between measures 10 and 32 are hints at A minor and F minor, never clearly established.

Although the bass line in the first few measures of the intermezzo clearly indicates E minor, at each point where there should be an E minor triad, Brahms deceptively introduces C E G, establishing a pattern to be used in most of the A section, whether the key is E minor or an excursion into some other key area. The B section of the work includes expected references to tonic, and the return of A is a return to avoided tonic harmonies.

FIGURE 12.10

Brahms, Intermezzo, Op. 119, No. 2

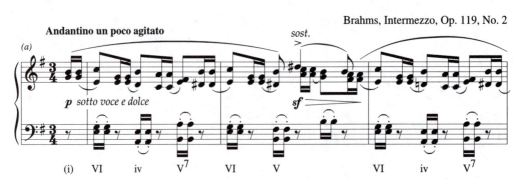

As was the preceding Brahms example, Figure 12.10, the following excerpt from Wagner is made up of recognizable common harmonic progressions. In these passages, however, as few as two successive chords will imply a tonic without actually reaching the tonic; they will be followed by similar short progressions on successive tonic levels.

At least eleven keys are implied in these twenty-seven measures. All can be explained through the use either of actual chromatic third relationships or of pairs of triads in which a chromatic third relationship can be implied. The eight measures, 842–849, provide examples of each type of relationship.

These eight measures are made up of two groups of four measures, the second a sequence of the first. Here are the first four measures shown as triad spellings:

$$
\begin{array}{ccccc}
& A\flat\ C\ E\flat & E\flat\ G\ B\flat\ D\flat & C\flat\ E\flat\ G\flat & B\flat\ D\ F \\
A\flat: & \text{I} & \text{V}^7 & e\flat: \quad \text{VI} & \text{V}
\end{array}
$$

Observe first that the aural impression is that each pair of triads suggests a half cadence in its respective key, even though it is not usual to attempt the establishment of a key with these few sonorities. But assuming the actuality of two different keys, how did we get from one to the other? The answer lies in the chromatic third relationship, E♭ G B♭ and C♭ E♭ G♭. It is this procedure that is found throughout this excerpt.

Observe next that since the second four measures are a sequence of the first four, we should expect no new problems—but there is one.

$$\begin{array}{cccc}
\text{C♭ E♭ G♭} & \text{G♭ B♭ D♭ F♭} & \text{D F♯ A} & \text{C♯ E♯ G♯} \\
\text{C:} \quad \text{I} & \text{V}^7 & \text{f♯:} \quad \text{VI} & \text{V}
\end{array}$$

We are suddenly thrown from a flat key to a sharp key through the chromatic third relationship G♭ B♭ D♭–D F♯ A. Remember that this relationship can also be achieved through the enharmonic spelling of either triad. So if we respell G♭ B♭ D♭ as F♯ A♯ C♯, the relationship to D F♯ A is clear.

Finally, how did we get from the first to the second four-measure group? Certainly, the pair B♭ D F and C♭ E♭ G♭ is not an example of chromatic thirds. We might consider, in measure 845, that had V, B♭ D F, resolved to its tonic, E♭ G B♭, there would be a chromatic third relationship between E♭ G B♭ and C♭ E♭ G♭. If this explanation seems too contrived, analysis as a direct modulation is certainly satisfactory.

In Assignment 12.2 (page 357), you will be asked to locate the remainder of the chromatic third relationships by measure number and by the spelling of the two participating triads.

In Figure 12.11, we have indicated another possible way of considering this music. There are two lines of analysis below the music. The upper line is a conventional roman-numeral analysis, including key names. In most cases, these key names are implied because of the limited number of triads involved. An arrow in this upper line indicates the location of a direct modulation. In the lower line, letter names of chromatic half steps between two triads are connected by an arrow to show a chromatic modulation.

FIGURE 12.11

Wagner, *Tristan und Isolde,*
Act II, Scene 2

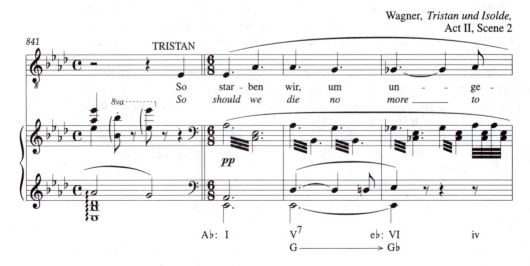

*The progression of the nonharmonic tone G to G♭ may be considered the chromatic half step modulatory link.

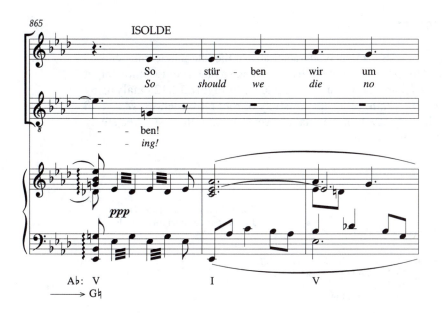

In addition to the processes of change of implied key, the following procedures are of interest:

1.

	Intervals of root movement	Intervals between actual or implied tonics
5th	6	2
3rd	7	7
2nd	10	1
Tritone	0	1

These figures show dramatically the departure from the use of the perfect fifth (fourth) as the principal interval between roots or tonics.

2. In root movements of a second, as in measures 845–846, parallel motion is avoided by placing the second of the two chords in second inversion, creating contrary motion between the outside voices.

It should be noted that *Tristan und Isolde*, finished in 1859, is not late-nineteenth-century music, but in spite of its early appearance, it is generally considered to represent the spirit and goals of the later progressive nineteenth-century composers. Certainly it represents the ultimate accomplishment in avoiding tonic while at the same time operating within the tonal system of the common practice period.

Unconventional Root Movement

Although chords built in thirds remained characteristic of the late nineteenth century, movements from chord to chord continually became freer, so that a composition might contain more exceptions than traditional progressions. In Figure 12.12, analysis by roman numeral yields no meaningful results. A study of root movements reveals root movement by fifth to be only seven of the total of twenty-two; of the rest, three are by chromatic third and three are by tritone.

FIGURE 12.12

Fauré, *La bonne chanson,* Op. 61,
"J'allais par des chemins perfides"

Indeterminate Tonic Implication

Figure 12.13, although appearing much simpler than several of the previous examples, is far more forward looking. Whereas the examples of Brahms and Wagner demonstrate techniques that have reached their ultimate development, this short song by Mussorgsky includes features that anticipate styles of twentieth-century composition.

1. The key signature of two sharps, with the first and last notes on D, strongly implies D major. There is, however, only one implication of dominant harmony of that key, the incomplete chord on A in measure 7. Other indications of a tonal center on D are (a) the pedal tone on D (measures 9–10), ending with an augmented sixth chord in a less common inversion, resolving to a D minor triad, and (b) two suggestions in the bass line of subdominant–tonic cadences, measures 2–3 and the final cadence.

2. Many of the progressions are strongly associated with B♭ major. There is only one dominant of this key, but its resolution is delayed through an F A C♯ triad (measures 5–7).

3. The modal inflection, E♮, in the implied key of B♭ is reminiscent of the Lydian mode (measures 3–4 and 6).

4. The vocal line doubled in the piano line, over a series of first inversions (measure 9) describes a unique scale line, E♭–D–C–B–B♭–A♭. All but one of those melody tones are also the triad roots, E♭–D–c–b–c⁷–A♭, a progression resembling nothing from the conventional practices of functional harmony.

5. The work as a whole vacillates between the tonic centers of D and B♭, the two summed up in the final B♭ triad. The bass line of the last four measures implies a strong root progression in D, whereas the final right-hand chord at the same time implies B♭. This is a rather remarkable instance of a single consonant triad implying two different tonal areas.

FIGURE 12.13

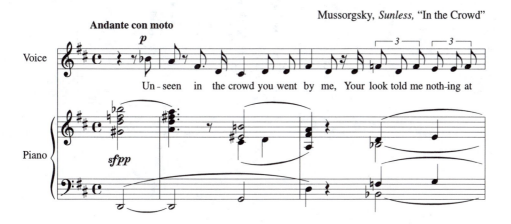

Mussorgsky, *Sunless,* "In the Crowd"

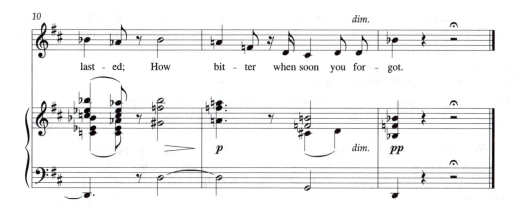

With the works of Wagner, Brahms, Wolf, and others of the late nineteenth century, the common practice period came to a historical close. But contemporary with them were young composers such as Claude Debussy, with new, fresh concepts of music composition, whose procedures will be covered beginning in the next chapter.

Even so, music based on the principles and techniques of the common practice period lived on in many composers, their musical styles often incorporating many of the newer ideas. Composers relying heavily on the old common practice principles are often known as "post-Romantic" composers. Among these are many famous names, including Mahler, de Falla, Rachmaninoff, Sibelius, and Richard Strauss. A group of songs by Strauss for voice and orchestra, now usually titled *Four Last Songs,* written in 1948, is probably the final major composition strongly tied to the romantic tradition.

Through the entire duration of the twentieth century, the principles of the common practice continued to be heard in new music other than that of the "serious" composers. Among such types of music are commercial music for television and films, popular music such as "country and western" (but excluding jazz and rock-and-roll), and educational, religious, and military music. For the foreseeable future, knowledge of both the traditional and the twentieth-century concepts of music composition is required of the professional musician.

ASSIGNMENT 12.2 *Harmonic analysis.*   From Figure 12.11, locate examples of chromatic third relationships. Indicate the location by measure number and spell each of the two triads involved.

	Measure number	Triad spellings
1.	_____	_____ - _____
2.	_____	_____ - _____
3.	_____	_____ - _____
4.	_____	_____ - _____
5.	_____	_____ - _____
6.	_____	_____ - _____
7.	_____	_____ - _____

Look for short harmonic passages where the key, if not firmly established, is at least implied. In progressing from one such passage to another, try to discover the link between the two. Two hints:

1. Look for chromatic third relationships.

2. Specifically, at one point the vocal line leaps up a perfect fourth. The upper note assumes the function of tonic, in spite of the preceding material.

ASSIGNMENT 12.3 *Harmonic analysis.* Analyze the following excerpts, particularly for the devices described in this chapter. Use roman-numeral symbols where helpful; otherwise, describe in prose or verbally the principles governing the harmonic movement.

(1) The first excerpt is the piano reduction of the orchestral accompaniment to a very florid solo piano passage. At each asterisk, a two-measure repetition occurs in the original score.

Liszt, Concerto No. 2 for Piano

(2)

Franck, Prelude, Chorale, and Fugue for Piano, "Chorale"

(3)

Wagner, *Tristan und Isolde,* Act III, Scene 2

flücht'-ges Weh'n! _____ Muss sie nun
fleet - ing breath! _____ Must she now

g: i   V

(4) The initial aural impression of this music is that of repetition of each measure on a different pitch level. These ideas will help clarify the differences:

1. Examine the bass lines of the first four measures. Are they alike or different?

2. Which two measures are identical harmonically (though at different pitch locations)?

3. Look for harmonic sequence.

4. Look for chromatic thirds.

5. List each chord root occurring on beat 1 (measures 707–710). Compare your results with Figure 12.4.

Wagner, *Die Walküre,* Act III, Scene 3
"Magic Fire Music"

ASSIGNMENT 12.4   Each bass note is the root of a major triad. Write in the three upper voices, continuing from those given. Use contrary motion between soprano and bass where possible.

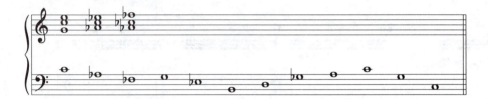

ASSIGNMENT 12.5   Continue this sequence for about eight more chords. Roots move down a M3 and up a m3 (or enharmonically, down a d4 and up an A2, as needed). Use major or minor triads, as seem suitable.

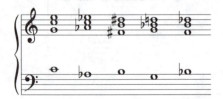

ASSIGNMENT 12.6   Continue this sequence, roots down a tritone, up a fourth. Conclude the sequence upon reaching the F♯ major triad.

ASSIGNMENT 12.7

(*a*) The following passage is based on the progression I–V (or i–V) with the V progressing to the next triad by chromatic third, up or down. Continue this progression, bringing it to an authentic cadence several measures later.

(*b*) Using this same passage, write a different conclusion by changing the direction of the root movement of the third at some point.

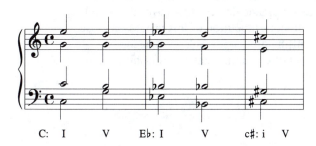

C: I   V   Eb: I   V   c#: i   V

ASSIGNMENT 12.8   The following passage is that of Assignment 12.7 with non-harmonic tones added. Complete this example in a similar manner. Then, rewrite your solution(s) to Assignment 12.7*b* in this manner.

Summary

In the latter half of the nineteenth century, rapid changes within the major-minor tonal system were taking place, eventually leading to new concepts of music composition in the twentieth century. These changes are of particular significance:

1. The increased use of root movements by intervals other than the perfect fifth, including movement by third in a chromatic relationship and by the tritone, thereby greatly reducing the traditional preponderance of root movement by perfect fifth.

2. The increased use of harmonic progressions in which traditional chords resolved in ways contrary to traditional practice.

3. Delaying the arrival at the V–I cadence by various means, including deceptive resolutions (V–vi, V–V/IV, among others), the liberal use of secondary dominant harmonies, and diminished seventh chords, especially in succession. These devices also created and prolonged each of successive temporary key areas, thereby extending the temporal distance between the opening and final tonic harmony.

4. The short-term evasion of tonic accomplished by allowing the harmonic progression (often as few as two chords) to imply movement to a tonic, but at the point of resolution evading the tonic by chromatic devices that move the sound into a new tonal area. The effect of continuous repetition of this process at close temporal intervals is that of constant shifting of recognizable but unachieved tonal areas, with the resulting aural effect of wandering key relationships and a vague sense of tonality.

13

Debussy and Impressionism

Based on the date of his birth, study of the music of Debussy (1862–1918) could well have been incorporated in the previous chapter. However, the thirty-six years of his mature creative activity, beginning about 1882, are divided almost exactly by the year 1900, and the nature of his creative accomplishments in breaking with nineteenth-century traditions demands that he be considered the first of the "modern" twentieth-century composers.

Impressionism

Debussy's compositional style is usually termed "impressionism," a word borrowed from a school of French painters of that time, including Monet, Pissarro, and Renoir. The paintings of the impressionists avoid emphasis on the geometric or specific relationships of their subject matter; important is that elusive, subjective feeling aroused in a mere momentary glimpse of the scene being portrayed. Consequently, the artist may be primarily concerned with the interplay of light and reflection, of shadow and haze, and the many other elements one often disregards when viewing a scene objectively.

Though Debussy himself denied that he was an "impressionist," his contemporaries felt that he achieved in music the characteristics of the impressionist paintings. In expressing a mood or conjuring up an atmosphere, Debussy follows the precept of Beethoven, who described his own *Pastoral* Symphony (the sixth) as "more expression of feeling than tone-painting." Debussy's compositional style was accomplished in part through the introduction of an amazing number of new compositional practices, and in part through his rejection of many of the conventional devices of his early contemporaries Brahms, Wagner, and others.

Tonality and Cadence Structure

There is no break with tonality in the music of Debussy. A key feeling is maintained, though it is often vague and, at times, missing for short periods by devices to be presented shortly (but never by the traditional series of diminished seventh chords). Frequent use of long pedal points on the tonic against more or less unrelated progressions (in the traditional sense) in the upper voices maintains tonal stability, as in Figures 13.4 and 13.9 and much the same as in the Mussorgsky example, Figure 12.13.

Cadences are rarely simple V–I or IV–I progressions. When such cadences occur, they are usually camouflaged to diffuse the traditional cadential effect, as in the final cadence of Debussy's first known work, "Nuit d'étoiles," Figure 13.1, written when he was fourteen.

Observe the positive V–I of the cadential bass tones against which is sounded V^7–iv–I+ preceding the final tonic.

FIGURE 13.1

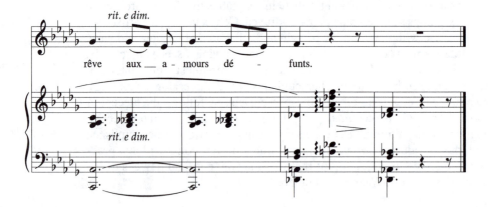

A clearly stated V–I, when used, never includes a preceding tonic six-four; its effect is diffused by some other closing progression. In the popular "Clair de lune," the "final" V–I, Figure 13.2*a*, is followed by seven measures using only I, iii, and ♭III$_6$, Figure 13.2*b* (showing the last five measures only). Although the bass line of the final two chords is dominant to tonic, the dominant tone is the third of the ♭III triad.

Where have you seen this progression, I–iii–♭III₆, before? Review Figure 12.5, written several years earlier than "Clair de lune."

FIGURE 13.2

Debussy, *Suite bergamasque,* "Clair de lune"

The Whole-Tone Scale

Debussy made extensive use of scales other than major and minor, both for use in melodic lines and as a basis for chord construction. One, the *whole-tone scale,* equally divides the octave into six whole steps (Figure 13.3).

The whole-tone scale is like other music devices that equally divide the octave—the diminished seventh chord and the augmented triad. These impart no sense of major or minor tonality, either when found harmonically as chords in succession or when found melodically as four or more notes of the scale in succession.

Use of this scale before Debussy is not unknown, but in those cases, its use was justified by conventional accompanying progressions so manipulated as to produce the scale. (Review the example by Brahms, Figure 11.6.) In Debussy's music, the whole-tone scale is a principal compositional device.

FIGURE 13.3   *Whole-Tone Scale*

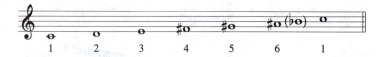

Spelling this scale requires that any one pair of adjacent tones be at the interval of the diminished third (d3). In Figure 13.3, that interval is A♯–C. If the major second above A♯ were used, this C scale would end on B♯. If the B♭ shown in parentheses were used, the d3 would be G♯–B♭. Another way to spell the scale might be C D F♭ G♭ A♭ B♭ C (D–F♭ = d3). When choosing a d3, avoid double sharps and double flats.

Debussy's "Voiles" makes extensive use of the scale shown in Figure 13.3. For example:

1. The entire ascending scale starting on F♯ is seen in Figure 13.4*a*, the last measure of the work, where Debussy has chosen to locate the diminished third from G♯ to B♭.

2. The entire descending scale, Figure 13.4*b*, is written in thirds. The upper voice begins on G♯. When the lower octave is reached, the enharmonic A♭ is used, followed immediately with the diminished third A♭–F♯.

3. Two of the descending harmonic thirds in the fourth measure are written as diminished fourths (F♯–B♭ = F♯–A♯, E♭–A♭ = E–G♯).

4. In the bass clef, the melodic line in octaves uses the same scale formation and serves as a counter-melody to the descending thirds above it.

FIGURE 13.4

Debussy, *Préludes,* Book I, No. 2, "Voiles"

Transposition of the scale is possible, but only at the interval of the minor second, C♯ D♯ E♯ G A B C♯ or its enharmonic equivalent on D♭. Transposing up another minor second produces the scale of Figure 13.3, but starting on D.

The bass line of Figure 13.5 demonstrates the transposed melodic scale, though it lacks one note, G. All notes are included in the harmonic passage in the treble clef.

From either scale, only two triads spelled in thirds are possible; both are augmented. From Figure 13.3, they are C E G♯ and D F♯ A♯. In the treble clef of Figure 13.5, they are E♭ G B and F A C♯. All, of course, are available in enharmonic spellings.

FIGURE 13.5

Debussy, *Pelléas et Mélisande,* Act IV, Scene 2

In Figure 13.6, chords located at each group of doubly dotted eighth notes are derived from the scale on D♭. These are nontertian chords spelled D♭ E♭ A and C♭ D♭ G. The missing note of the scale, F, is prominently stated in the vocal line. The more traditional chords in thirty-second notes function as appoggiatura chords, each made up of tones "nonharmonic" to its following chord.

FIGURE 13.6

Debussy, *Trois ballades de François Villon,*
"Ballade de Villon à s'ayme"

The Pentatonic Scale

The *pentatonic* (five-tone) scale probably derives from primitive times; it is common in emerging folk cultures and in the prevailing music of many nonwestern cultures, music of considerable interest to Debussy. The scale is made up of the interval succession M2–M2–m3–M2–m3, an easy example of which is found on the black notes of the keyboard, Figure 13.7*a*. The grouping of three notes and two notes, or vice versa, is characteristic of any spelling, such as  A B C♯, F♯ G♯ and E♭ F, A♭ B♭ C.

The complete scale starting on G♭ is seen in the small thirty-second notes of Figure 13.7*b*. All the remaining notes are also from this scale, including the harmonic intervals in the bass clef and an additional complete scale in the treble clef.

FIGURE 13.7   *Pentatonic Scale*

Debussy, *Préludes,* Book I, No. 2, "Voiles"

The Medieval Modes[1]

Used infrequently since about 1650, modes other than major and minor became part of the Debussy style. Their use is not always obvious; complete compositions are not based on a given mode. Rather, one or more modes may be hinted at in melodic fragments or in short harmonic progressions. In Figure 13.8, measure 67, the D♯ of the melodic line E–D♯–C♯ over the A major triad suggests the Lydian mode. Note also the harmonic progressions in chromatic thirds, F♯ A C♯ to D F A in measure 66, and A C♯ E to C E♭ G in measures 67–68.

FIGURE 13.8

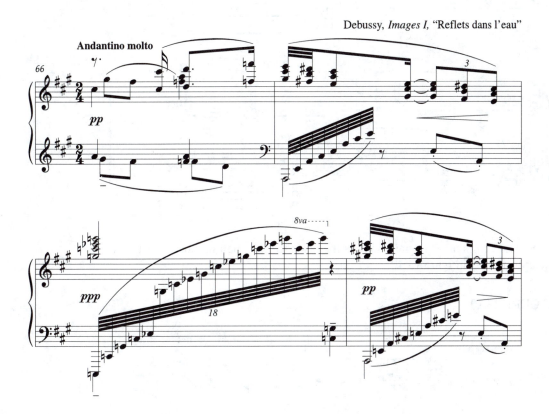

Debussy, *Images I,* "Reflets dans l'eau"

The descending Dorian scale, G♯ F♯ E♯ D♯ C♯ B A♯ G♯, is obvious in measures 72–74 of Figure 13.9.

---

[1]Review *Elementary Harmony,* Appendix D, "The Medieval Modes."

FIGURE 13.9

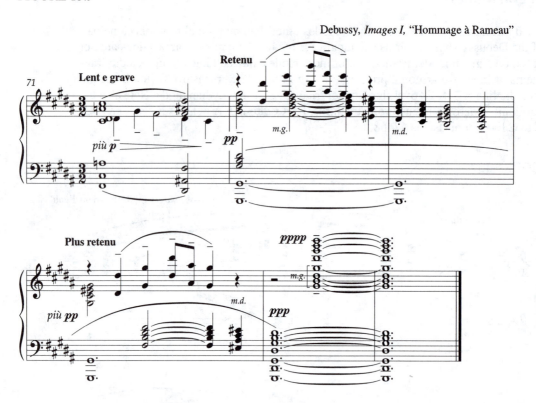

Debussy, *Images I,* "Hommage à Rameau"

The complete Phrygian mode is the basis for the opening phrase of the string quartet shown in Figure 13.10.

FIGURE 13.10

Debussy, Quartet for Strings, I

Chords and Harmonic Progressions

Traditional chords built in thirds are commonly used, and these include all varieties from the triad through thirteenth chords. At the same time, a wide variety of original sonorities, common in later music, first appear in the works of Debussy. In either case, conventional root movement is almost nonexistent, the few exceptions being passages of two to four chords. Chord types and methods of progression are so inextricably intertwined in most cases that they will be discussed simultaneously.

Conventional Chords

Figure 13.11 shows a passage consisting of triads, and these with conventional contrary motion between the outer parts. Yet the progression itself, I–iii–ii–I–♭VII–IV–iii–ii–I, is most unconventional in common practice terms. Note also the cadence treatment: The last two bass notes imply V–I during the arpeggiation of the supertonic triad (compare with Figure 13.1).

FIGURE 13.11

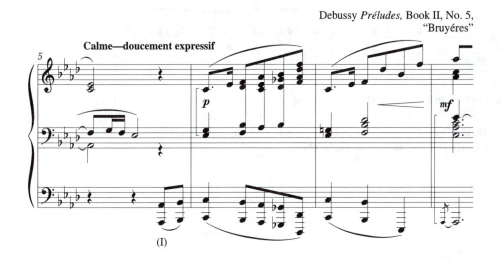

Debussy *Préludes,* Book II, No. 5, "Bruyéres"

Still more unconventional is the use of the simple triads and seventh chords in extended parallelism, sometimes called "planing," as in Figures 13.12 and 13.13. In addition, note the use of progression by chromatic thirds—all of Figure 13.12 and the first measure of Figure 13.13. Also, review Figure 13.5 as an example of parallel augmented triads.

FIGURE 13.12

Debussy, *Préludes,* Book I, No. 4,
"Les sons et les parfums tournent dans l'air du soir"

FIGURE 13.13

Debussy, *Pour le piano,* "Sarabande"

Parallelism is not limited to single types of chords in succession, as Figure 13.14 shows. Further study of Debussy's music will show many different patterns of parallel motion, including uses of triads or larger chords in any inversion, or two sets of parallel chords in contrary motion to each other.

FIGURE 13.14

Debussy, *Pelléas et Mélisande,*
Act III, Scene I

Quartal and Quintal Harmony; Added-Tone Chords

In addition to tertian harmony (chords built in thirds), the use of quartal harmony (chords built in fourths) and quintal harmony (chords built in fifths) is common in Debussy's works. Figure 13.15, for example, shows two chords in quartal harmony, B E A D and D G C F, both with octave doubling in the upper voice.

FIGURE 13.15

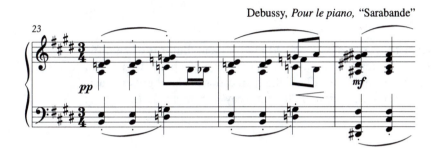

Debussy, *Pour le piano,* "Sarabande"

Quintal harmony is shown on the bass staff of Figure 13.16*b* with the chords G D A and A E B. But there is another possible explanation of these sonorities. Chords in a similar passage in the first measure of the Prélude (Figure 13.16*a*) do not include the upper tones (A and B) of the quintal chords, leading to the conclusion that these may be *added tones* to the original progression. This use of fifths, however, is important as a precedent for its extensive use in the music of later composers.

FIGURE 13.16

Debussy, *Préludes,* Book I, No. 10,
"La cathédrale engloutie"

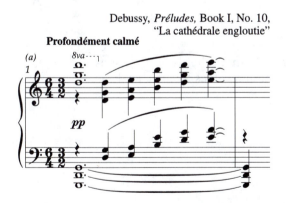

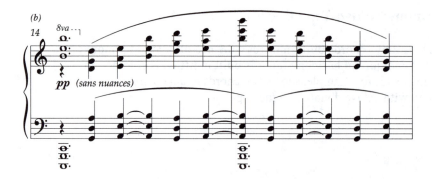

Triads with *added sixths* (example: C E G A) are frequent, but it is often difficult to determine if the chord is really a first inversion of a seventh chord. There is no doubt about the chord A C♯ E F♯ in Figure 13.17, the final cadence chord giving musical expression to the composer's indication of "fading away" (*en se perdant*).[2]

FIGURE 13.17

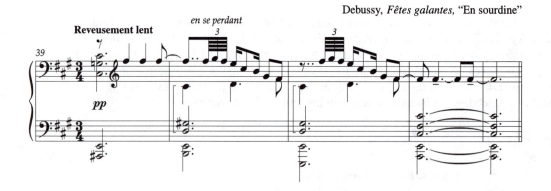

Debussy, *Fêtes galantes,* "En sourdine"

All the chords of Figure 13.18 are either added-note chords or inversions of seventh chords in parallel motion. Since no seventh resolves as such, analysis as added-note chords is plausible.

[2]An oft-quoted example of an early use of this cadence is in the conclusion of Mahler's *Das Lied von der Erde* (1908), where it is held for seventeen measures to emphasize the effect of the vocal soloist's final word, "ewig" ("forever"). Debussy applied the same cadence eleven years earlier.

FIGURE 13.18

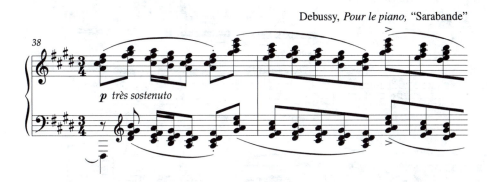

Debussy, *Pour le piano*, "Sarabande"

Tritones and Augmented Fifths

These intervals from earliest times have been considered unstable, and their use has therefore been severely restricted.[3] The increased use of these intervals by Wagner is carried still further in the music of Debussy, where examination of almost any excerpt will demonstrate the greater frequency of their use and the ultimate freedom in their movement, now without the requirement of a specific kind of resolution. Typical is the type of passage in Figure 13.19, where most of the chords contain tritones or augmented intervals.

The harmonic sequence at measure 180, roots up a minor third and down a minor second starting on G, is followed in measure 181 by the same sequence a major second higher—a sequence of a sequence!

FIGURE 13.19

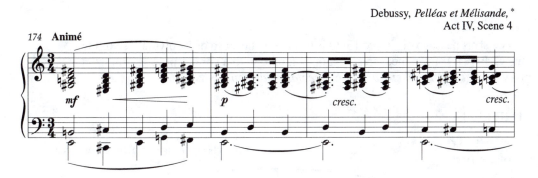

Debussy, *Pelléas et Mélisande,* *
Act IV, Scene 4

*The vocal line is omitted.

[3]Review the article "The Devil in Music" in *Elementary Harmony,* page 232. A melodic example from Debussy's *Prelude to the Afternoon of a Faun* is included.

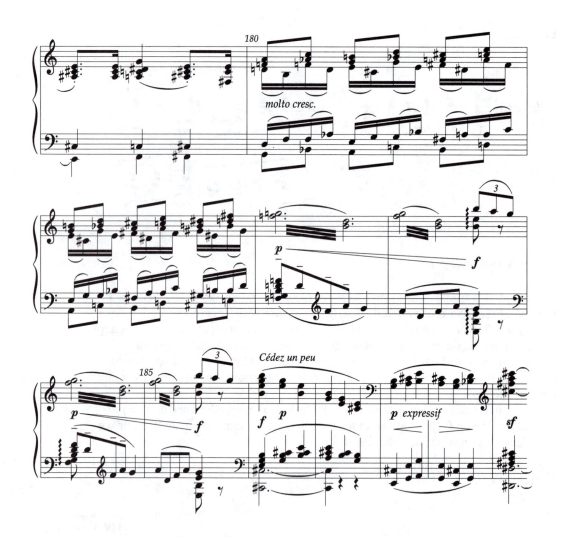

The short passage of Figure 13.20 is of interest because of its pivotal use of the tritone C–F♯ = B♯–F♯ in measures 55–56. Compare with a similar progression from Rimsky-Korsakov's *Scheherazade* in *Elementary Harmony*, page 234.

FIGURE 13.20

Debussy, *Images I,* "Reflets dans l'eau"

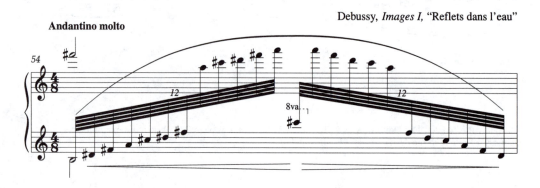

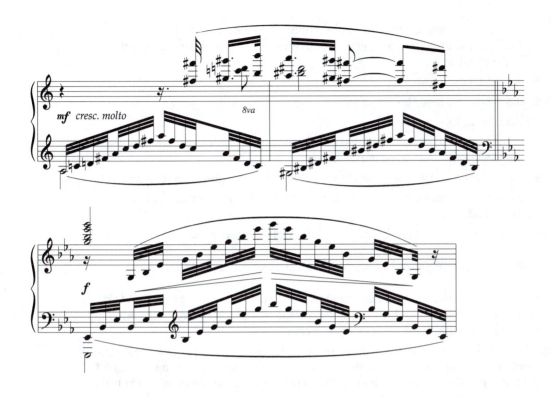

The foregoing examples are far from being a complete survey of Debussy's innovations in melody and harmony, and we have not even mentioned rhythm. Though of considerable interest for his varieties of rhythmic expression, these are probably best considered an extension of previous practices rather than a glimpse of what is yet to come. But all three aspects are worthy of further investigation to discover Debussy's many unique compositional practices. The *Préludes*, Books I and II, are excellent for additional study because they are easily available in a single compact volume of about 100 pages.

Suggestions for Analysis

The following list includes the novel features of Debussy's style. Use it to assist you in your beginning efforts in analysis. Be on the lookout for still other possibilities. (A complete list derived from all Debussy's compositions would be lengthy and impractical.) Also note any traditional practices and how they relate to Debussy's innovative practices, and how any of these practices used in combination relate to one another.

Obviously, most analysis must be descriptive; roman-numeral symbols will only occasionally be useful.

1. Whole-tone scales and chords.
2. Pentatonic scales and chords.
3. Modal scales and chords.

4. Chords containing tritones (sevenths, ninths, elevenths, and thirteenths). Describe the resolution or nonresolution of each tritone and the movements of the chord roots.

5. Added-tone chords.

6. Root movement by chromatic thirds.

7. Parallelism (planing)

8. Other traditional or nontraditional chord progressions. For the latter, describe the nature of the harmonic movement.

9. Quartal and quintal chords, and any other chords built other than in thirds.

10. Nonharmonic tones, prepared or unprepared, in relation to either traditional or nontraditional harmonic sonorities.

11. Cadences: How do they resemble or differ from traditional cadences?

An analysis of Figure 13.17 might include the following observations.

Measure 39: Although the notes arranged in thirds spell the ninth chord, F♯ A♯ C♯ E G, the aural effect of the F♯ in the treble clef is that of unprepared nonharmonic tone, the remaining notes constituting a °7 chord.

Measure 40: Although with the addition of thirds this sonority might be called a thirteenth chord, the aural effect is that of two nonharmonic tones in the treble clef, held over from the previous measure, the F♯ resolving as a suspension (but note the dissonant preparation) and the C♯ resolving as a retardation over E G♯ B D. The two dissonances are dissonant with each other (P4), a nontraditional use of multiple nonharmonic tones.

The °7 resolves conventionally to V$^4_3$ (note the rising resolution of the seventh, G♮ to G♯). With the addition of F♯, the harmony could be a ninth chord, or the note an unprepared suspension to E. The remaining note, C♯, held over from the previous measure, is a retardation to D, marking the beginning of the melodic line C♯ D F♯ C♯ D F♯.

Two accented appoggiaturas, approached and left in the same direction, appear in the uppermost lines. C♯, though on a weak sixteenth note, is accented by virtue of the syncopation. G♯, though actually a chord tone, sounds in retrospect like an appoggiatura where, in its repetition in measure 41, it immediately precedes the long-held final F♯.

Measure 41: The root of V^7 appears in the bass, anticipating a conventional authentic cadence.

Measure 41: The cadence is traditional except for the added sixth in the melody.

ASSIGNMENT 13.1 Make a complete analysis of the following examples.

(1)

Debussy, *Pour le piano,* "Prélude"

(2)

Debussy, *Chansons de Bilitis,*
"Le tombeau des Naïades"

Mais rest- ons i - ci,   où   est leur tom -

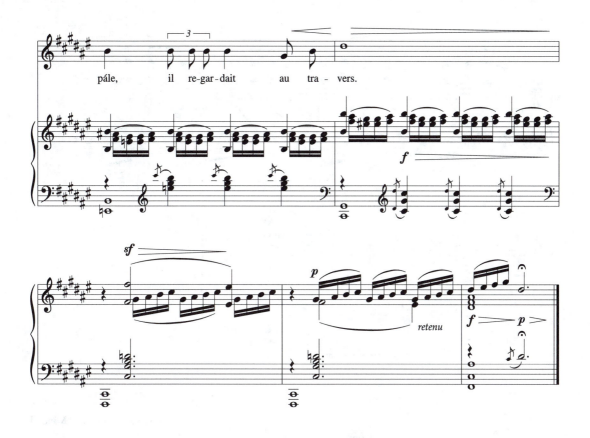

(3)

Debussy, *Préludes,* Book I, No. 6
"Des pas sur la neige"

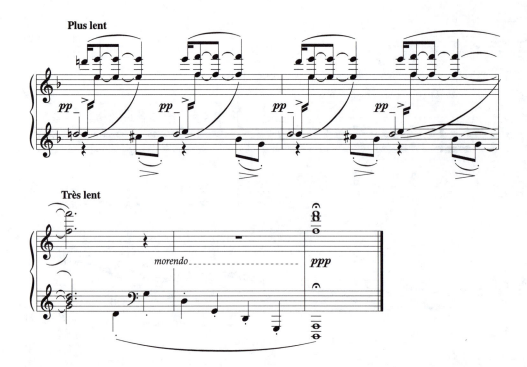

(4)

Debussy, Quartet in G Minor, I

As you might imagine, the musical ideas and accomplishments of Debussy had great influence on other composers of his time. Following are excerpts from the works of two such composers. As you study this music, try to pick out those features reminiscent of Debussy's practices while at the same time looking for any compositional practices that relate to the pre-Debussy period or that appear to utilize even newer ideas or procedures.

(5) This composition is an early work of Nadia Boulanger (1887–1979). Although successful as a composer, she became better known as a teacher in theory studies: harmony, orchestration, and counterpoint. Her students included such well-known composers as Aaron Copland, Roy Harris, Elliott Carter, Virgil Thomson, and Walter Piston.

Nadia Boulanger, "Avec mes sens, avec mon coeur" (1910)

(6) Maurice Ravel (1875–1937) was the younger of the two most important impressionist composers. The work presented here is a tribute to the Baroque composer François Couperin (1668–1733). Figure 6.13 is an excerpt from another such tribute, one by Grieg to Ludvig Holberg (1658–1754), a Norwegian author and a contemporary of Couperin. Both works use a device common to Baroque music. Compare Figure 6.13 with measures 25–29 below to discover this device, and describe the difference in its use.

Ravel, *Le tombeau de Couperin,*
"Rigaudon"

Summary

The examples of this chapter cannot presume to be anything but a small sampling of the multitude of devices used by Debussy in creating a startlingly new and refreshing style of writing. Debussy's impressionism cannot be defined as the use of any single device or any combination of devices. Each composition is created through its own unique combination of chosen elements, the total effect of which must be heard as well as analyzed for complete comprehension.

Debussy's style, although revolutionary, did not set a precedent for twentieth-century composition, but his influence was most profound on certain other early-twentieth-century composers—Ravel, Delius, and Scriabin, to name a few. Debussy's all-important contribution was his ability to break with the traditions of the previous three centuries, proving that a new direction in music, like that of the early seventeenth century,[4] was possible again in the early twentieth century.

[4] Review the article "The Theory of Inversion" in *Elementary Harmony,* page 196.

14

After Debussy: An Introduction to Twentieth-Century Music

The success of the musical practices of Debussy effectively marked the end of the common practice period. No longer constrained by former limitations, composers searched for new modes of musical expression, resulting in a wide diversity of musical styles and the technical means to achieve their creative efforts. These processes, both evolutionary and revolutionary, continue to the present day and, grouped as a whole, are not explainable by any single theoretical principle. Thus, without the controls experienced in common practice styles, such as common root movements and standard use of nonharmonic tones, music of the twentieth century can be considered only on the basis of each individual composer's practice.

The manner of analyzing twentieth-century music, then, is similar to the manner in which we investigated the music of Debussy. We look both for features that differ from those used in the common practice period and for features that are the same as, or modified from, those of that period. For example, a composer's use of pitch combinations may be highly original but at the same time expressed in traditional rhythmic patterns and metrical units. Looking back at the example by Fauré, Figure 12.5, we see a highly unconventional harmonic progression combined with a rhythmic and metrical pattern that could have occurred any time in the common practice period.

Analysis of twentieth-century music can be simplified to some extent by recognizing four major groups of compositional practices.

1. *New approaches to traditional material.* This category includes music produced through evolutionary processes: extensions and modifications of earlier practices, such as chords built with intervals other than thirds, scale patterns other than the major and minor modes, new varieties of rhythmic groupings, and many others included in later discussions.

2. *Original systems.* Music based on new systems of melodic, harmonic, or rhythmic organizations, such as the "dodecaphonic" ("twelve-tone") method and its derivations.

3. *New sound sources.* Music based on the sources for production of sound never before available, such as the synthesizer and the computer.

4. *New performance practices.* Music based on improvisation and aleatoric devices, transferring from the composer to the performer much of the responsibility in the compositional process.

Discussions of theoretical developments and processes within each of these groupings will imply neither that a particular composer's style is based solely on those described nor that they are used only by that composer. A composer's musical style still, as in previous eras, depends upon the choice of theoretical materials and the relative frequency of their use. There are many examples of music that include features from two or more of these categories, the choice itself being a component of that composer's unique writing style.

Many examples of twentieth-century music are fully comprehensible only when heard as written by the composer. In contrast, we can reduce the score of a Mozart symphony to a score for piano, or for most any combination of instruments, and still recognize its harmonic, melodic, and rhythmic elements and the interplay among those features. Looking ahead to Figure 15.20, measure 1, we find three instruments, each playing its own arpeggiated triad (B♭ D♭ [F], C E G, and E G♯ B) simultaneously with the others and in the same general range. Performance on the piano produces a muddy mixture of dissonances, whereas performance as indicated in the score—each instrument, with its own unique timbre, playing its own triad—allows each triad to be set off clearly from the others, with a considerable lessening of the dissonant effect. All examples written for combinations of orchestral instruments should be heard as originally conceived; if they are heard in a piano reduction, the listener must exercise enough imagination to reproduce mentally the composer's intentions.

Finally, it should be understood that adequate coverage of a subject as vast as that of twentieth-century music can be accomplished only by a volume or volumes dedicated to that subject alone. The diversity and the quantity of compositional experimentation allow us to cover only some of the more important highlights in the limited space available in a text such as this.

Our discussion will take us through the mid-decades of the twentieth century, concluding, at the end of Chapter 16, with a few comments concerning on-going developments late in the century and observations on the state of music in the century as a whole. For further study, here is a selection from the multitude of books on the subject.

ANTOKOLETZ, ELLIOTT, *Twentieth-Century Music*. Upper Saddle River, N.J.: Prentice Hall, 1992.

AUSTIN, WILLIAM W., *Music in the 20th Century*. New York: W. W. Norton, 1966.

BRINDLE, REGINALD SMITH, *The New Music Since 1945* (2nd ed.). New York: Oxford University Press, 1987.

COPE, DAVID H., *New Directions in Music* (2nd ed.). Dubuque, Iowa: Wm. C. Brown, 1976.

DALLIN, LEON, *Techniques of Twentieth-Century Composition* (5th ed.). Dubuque, Iowa: Wm. C. Brown, 1988.

DeLone, Richard, *Aspects of Twentieth-Century Music.* Upper Saddle River, N.J.: Prentice Hall, 1975.

Forte, Alan, *The Structure of Atonal Music.* New Haven: Yale University Press, 1973.

Griffith, Paul, *Modern Music and After* (2nd ed.). New York: Oxford University Press, 1987.

————, *Modern Music Since 1945.* London: J. M. Dent & Sons, Ltd., 1981.

Hansen, Peter, *An Introduction to Twentieth-Century Music* (4th ed.). Boston: Allyn & Bacon, 1978.

Machlis, Joseph, *Introduction to Twentieth-Century Music* (2nd ed.). New York: W. W. Norton, 1979.

Marquis, G. Welton, *Twentieth-Century Music Idioms.* Upper Saddle River, N.J.: Prentice Hall, 1980.

Martin, William, and Drossin, Julius, *Music of the Twentieth Century.* Upper Saddle River, N.J.: Prentice Hall, 1980.

Morgan, Robert, *Twentieth-Century Music.* New York: W. W. Norton, 1991.

Perle, George, *Serial Composition and Atonality* (6th ed.). Berkeley and Los Angeles: University of California Press, 1991.

Persichetti, Vincent, *Twentieth-Century Harmony.* New York: W. W. Norton, 1961.

Read, Gardner, *Modern Rhythmic Notation.* Bloomington: University of Indiana Press, 1978.

Reti, Rudolph, *Tonality in Modern Music.* Westport, Conn.: Greenwood Press, 1958.

Salzman, Eric, *Twentieth-Century Music: An Introduction* (3rd ed.). Upper Saddle River, N.J.: Prentice Hall, 1988.

Simms, Bryan, *Music of the Twentieth Century: Style and Structure.* New York: Schirmer Books, 1996.

Slonimsky, Nicolas, *Music Since 1900.* New York: Scribner's, 1971.

Stone, Kurt, *Music Notation in the Twentieth Century.* New York: McGraw-Hill, 1980.

Stuckenschmidt, H. H., *Twentieth-Century Music.* New York: McGraw-Hill, 1969.

Ulehla, Ludmilla, *Contemporary Harmony.* New York: Macmillan, 1966.

15

Twentieth-Century Music:
Melody, Rhythm,
and Harmony

This chapter will be concerned with compositional practices from the first of the four groups described on pages 398–399. The music ranges from styles only slightly removed from the common practice period to those remote enough to make any relationship difficult to ascertain. Yet all do show compositional procedures derived, however tenuously, from practices of the past, in contrast to the material of the next chapter, in which composers strive for new and unique basic concepts in music composition.

Melody

Modal derivations. After three centuries of almost total dependence upon two scale formations, major and minor, one obvious option for change was a return to the modal scales of pre-seventeenth-century music. But in twentieth-century usage, a mode is usually merely suggested, rather than featured in melodic writing.

In the work of which Figure 15.1 is an excerpt, the theme is a hymn in the Phrygian mode by Thomas Tallis (1505–1585).[1] Development of this theme shows fragmentary influence of the Phrygian and other modes. Measures 78–81 of the solo viola are clearly Phrygian on E. Changing F to F♯ in measure 82 creates a Dorian mode on E. The final C♯ of the solo becomes the third of A major, progressing in that key to the $\frac{3}{4}$ signature, where the mode is Aeolian on E.

---

[1]The complete hymn in four voices can be seen in Ottman, *Music for Sight Singing,* fourth edition (1996), number 1040.

FIGURE 15.1

Vaughan Williams, *Fantasia on a Theme by Thomas Tallis*

The scale of Figure 15.2 seems to have two implications. The vocal line, with its tonic implication of G, displays the Dorian scale G A Bb C D E F G, whereas the accompaniment, with its tonic implication of Bb, uses the same scale tones for the Lydian mode Bb C D E F G A Bb. Observe the use of "relative modes." Just as Bb major and G minor are relative keys, so Bb Lydian and G Dorian are related.

FIGURE 15.2

Britten, *Seven Sonnets of Michelangelo,* Op. 22,
"Sonetto LV"

Simultaneous use of two modes is shown in Figure 15.3, the melody based on the Lydian mode on F against the major-mode accompaniment in D♭. This procedure is known as *bimodality*.

FIGURE 15.3

Milhaud, *Trois Poèmes de Jean Cocteau,*
"Fête de Bordeaux"

Nontonal Melodic Lines

Twentieth-century melodic writing often is not based on any traditional scale constructions or any system of keys and their traditional relationships. It is in this sense that the term *nontonal melodic lines* is used. The melody of Figure 15.4 implies no particular continuous scale form, and only a vague relationship to a key or keys. The first twelve notes include all twelve notes of the chromatic scale,[2] and included therein are melodic outlines of the G minor and E♭ minor triads. The notes within each of the next three brackets may suggest the indicated but questionable key, perhaps because of conditioned traditional hearing. For example, under C (?), the note B followed by C may imply leading tone to tonic in C, and the C itself implies the same to the following note D♭. The pentatonic passage interrupts any feeling for key until the strong repeated D♭'s accompanied by a descending G♭ major scale, all ending with a cadence chord incorporating all the notes of the pentatonic scale (C D E G A).

---

[2]This twelve-tone series is not used as a "tone row" or in the "twelve-tone technique," discussed in Chapter 16.

FIGURE 15.4

Hindemith, Symphonie, *Mathis der Maler,* III

Many melodic lines cannot be described in terms of specific devices used, such as the triads and the whole-tone scale of Figure 15.4. Superficially, the melody of Figure 15.5 looks quite traditional and, in fact, begins with three measures clearly in A major. From this point on, key implications change rapidly until the return of the melody's first note, E, by means of a descending minor scale.

In the composer's score, this melody, played by violin 1, is found in canon at the unison, the second voice beginning at measure 187 played by violin 2. Both voices are doubled an octave lower by viola and cello. No specific harmonic support is offered in the remaining orchestration.

FIGURE 15.5

William Schuman, *American Festival Overture*

Melodic doubling was common in earlier centuries, but it was limited to octave sonority doubling (review page 138) and doubling in thirds and sixths, the varying sizes of these intervals, major and minor, determined by the key of the passage. Twentieth-century practice allows doubling at any interval. Figure 15.6 shows doubling at the constant interval of the major sixth. Since the lower line does not have to conform to the "key" of the upper line, several cross-relations result, such as F#–F♮, first and third notes.

FIGURE 15.6

Bartók, Concerto for Orchestra, II,
"Giuoco delle coppie"

© Copyright 1946 by Hawkes & Son (London) Ltd. Copyright Renewed. Reprinted by permission of Boosey & Hawkes, Inc.

Included in the same movement are these additional passages displaying melodies doubled at various intervals:

1. Minor thirds at rehearsal number 33
2. Minor sevenths at rehearsal number 45
3. Perfect fifths at rehearsal number 60
4. Major seconds at rehearsal number 90

Meter and Rhythm

Meter and rhythm as used in earlier centuries still play an important role in twentieth-century music. The regularly recurring accents and measure lengths so typical of the common practice period are still found in much of the music written since 1900, as shown in some of the previous examples, such as Figures 15.2, 15.3, and 15.6. Of the three principal elements of music—melody, harmony, and rhythm—characteristics of nineteenth-century rhythm have been retained in the twentieth century to a much greater extent than those of melody or harmony.

Syncopation

A marked increase in the use of syncopation often gives the impression of a radical change in rhythmic practices. But if we define syncopation as the accenting of beats or parts of beats other than those of the regularly recurring accent, these being heard against a regular metric pattern, either sounded or implied, then at least in principle there is no change in style brought about by syncopation, except in degree. Increase in frequency is accompanied by more irregularity in the placement of syncopated notes to create rhythmic patterns not typical of the nineteenth century. The well-known example from Stravinsky, Figure 15.7, demonstrates an early and still-exciting instance. The accents, however, being heard against an implied regular duple simple meter, still constitute syncopation in the accepted nineteenth-century meaning of the term.

FIGURE 15.7

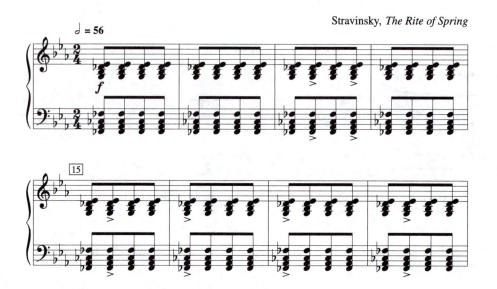

Stravinsky, *The Rite of Spring*

Successive Meter Changes

More significant, twentieth-century composers have often returned to principles of rhythmic and metric structures commonly found in sixteenth-century music composition.[3] The rhythm of the music of that era, particularly vocal music, often seems extremely free and even unregulated by standards of the common practice period. Figure 15.8*a* is the first part of a song by John Dowland, shown exactly as written by the composer (except for the > marks).

To ascertain the location of the accents, it becomes necessary to locate the accents in the poem. Then, by adding bar lines and time signatures as needed, we find we have a composition of changing meters. The four notes after the quarter rest, for example, prove to be in $\frac{6}{8}$ meter in modern notation rather than syncopation in $\frac{3}{4}$ meter (Figure 15.8*b*).

[3]Review the article "Another Metrical Concept" in *Elementary Harmony*, page 343.

FIGURE 15.8

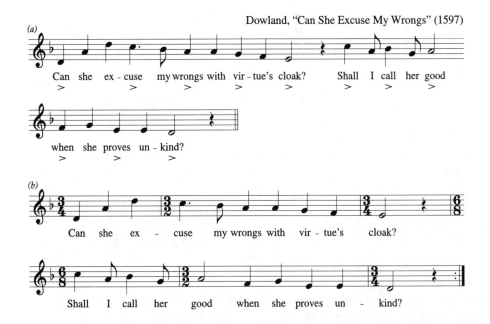

Twentieth-century music makes extensive use of this irregular metric structure and is notated usually in one of two ways. In the first way, a single time signature precedes regularly recurring bar lines, and the actual metrical accents are to be determined by the performer. Scansion of the text of Figure 15.9*a* determines the metrical interpretation shown in Figure 15.9*b*.

FIGURE 15.9

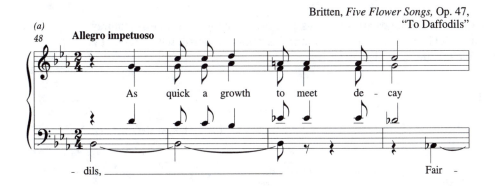

For an example in instrumental music comparable to the Britten example above, review the excerpt from Bartók's Quartet No. 4 in *Elementary Harmony,* page 346. The rhythmic accents of that excerpt, as shown in the pattern, Figure 15.10, are determined not by the $\frac{4}{4}$ signature but by the *sf* markings at irregular metric intervals.

FIGURE 15.10

Second, the meter changes are shown as successive changes in time signatures, as seen in Figure 15.11, particularly important in instrumental music where no text is available to guide the interpretation.

FIGURE 15.11

New Meter Signatures

Meter signatures rarely or never used in earlier periods abound in twentieth-century music. Besides the numerators 5 and 7 used earlier to some degree, we now find numerators from 1 through 21, used over a variety of denominators.

Alternating meters, written as $\frac{3}{4}\frac{2}{4}$ or as $\frac{3}{4} + \frac{2}{4}$, can occasionally be found in the nineteenth century. These, along with meters indicating irregular groupings within the measure, such as

$$\frac{3}{8} + \frac{2}{8} + \frac{3}{8}$$

are again common in the twentieth century, and fractional meters such as $\frac{4}{4}^{1/2}$ or $\frac{3}{8}^{2/3}$ are sometimes seen.[4]

Polymeter

The use of two or more meters simultaneously (*polymeter*) is seen only rarely in traditional music. An exceptional example is found in Act I of Mozart's *Don Giovanni,* where three orchestras play in the meters of $\frac{3}{8}$, $\frac{2}{4}$, and $\frac{3}{4}$ simultaneously and the aural effect of $\frac{9}{8}$ is produced by the use of triplets in $\frac{3}{4}$ in the horns.

For Brahms, the *hemiola* (review *Elementary Harmony,* fifth edition, page 389) was a favorite device, especially when written against the usual $\frac{6}{8}$ meter. In Figure 15.12, the phrasing in the piano score, measures 112–113, produces the aural effect of $\frac{3}{4}$, in contrast to the $\frac{6}{8}$ of the vocal line. In measure 114, the left hand returns to $\frac{6}{8}$, and in measure 115, all parts are in $\frac{6}{8}$.

---

[4]See Gardner Read, *Music Notation,* 2nd ed. (Boston: Allyn & Bacon, 1969), pages 159–163, for a listing of fifty-three different time signatures (other than the common ones) and compositions in which they are used.

FIGURE 15.12

Brahms, "Von ewiger Liebe," Op. 43, No. 1

The excerpt from Stravinsky, Figure 15.13, shows five rhythmic patterns sounding simultaneously.

FIGURE 15.13

Stravinsky, *The Rite of Spring*[5]

In the piccolo parts, the prominence of the alternating octave leaps creates the effect of a downbeat at those points, the composite of the two voices creating a $\frac{3}{8}$ meter.

FIGURE 15.14

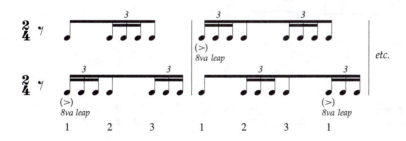

[5]This is not the complete score. Instruments duplicating these patterns have been omitted.

The oboe part in $\frac{2}{4}$ is accented on each second beat; the English horn, also in $\frac{2}{4}$, plays steady eighth notes; and the viola sounds as $\frac{6}{8}$, created by two triplets per measure. The melodic configuration of the cello and bass parts contributes to a composite $\frac{3}{4}$ meter. The same $\frac{3}{4}$ effect can be created by starting on any eighth note.

FIGURE 15.15

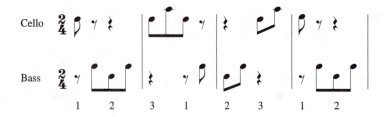

Jazz Patterns

The success of jazz in popular music has had its impact on a number of composers other than jazz specialists. Although one all-important aspect of jazz, that of improvisation, cannot be utilized in a composition in which definite pitch and duration values for all notes are given, another characteristic, its rhythm, can be easily transferred to concert music, as in the well-known works of George Gershwin—*Rhapsody in Blue* and *An American in Paris*. In Figure 15.16, measure 10, note the groups of three notes in a measure where metrical groups of four are implied, and in measures 11–14, accents alternating between offbeat eighth notes and metrical strong beats. In Figure 15.17, polyrhythm is created by the $\frac{3}{8}$ meter of the treble staff against the meter of the bass staff, which could be that of the time signature, but more likely a $\frac{3}{4}$ meter with the downbeat on any chosen note.

FIGURE 15.16

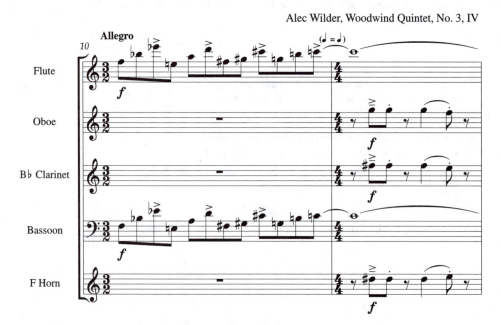

Alec Wilder, Woodwind Quintet, No. 3, IV

FIGURE 15.17

©1926 Editions Max Eschig. Used By Permission. Sole Agent U.S.A. Theodore Presser Company.

Harmony

The twentieth-century uses of tones in vertical combinations are so varied and numerous as to defy any system of classification. In the reaction against the consistent use by earlier composers of chords built in thirds, multitudes of new chordal combinations, some already seen in the music of Debussy, were conceived during the twentieth century. The triad and other chords built in thirds have not been discarded entirely, however, as seen in Figures 15.18–15.22.

Traditional Chord Types

Modal melodies are often harmonized with chords of traditional construction, the chord type on any scale step dependent upon the mode being used. In the Mixolydian melody of Figure 15.18, the lowered seventh scale degree requires the use of v (minor) and ♭VII. The composer also uses ♭III, probably to avoid the diminished triad, iii° (G B♭ D♭), required by the mode.

FIGURE 15.18

After a quick glance, one might assume that Figure 15.19 is a simple passage in D major. But investigation shows the subtle introduction of a number of sonorities and procedures unexplainable in terms of conventional practices.

A contributing factor is the long-held internal pedal on pitch D. Without the D, would measure 2, beat 3, be V$^4_2$? Do the outside voices of measure 3 constitute parallel octaves? In measure 4, is the C# in the bass a seventh approached by leap from above? And if it is a seventh, shouldn't it resolve as the bass of IV$_6$? Continue this line of questioning with measures 5–8 to discover other new uses of seemingly conventional sonorities and procedures.

FIGURE 15.19

Shostakovich, *Twenty-four Preludes and Fugues,* Op. 87,
Prelude No. 5

Superimposed Triads

Superimposed triadic lines as in Figure 15.20 can create a highly dissonant effect. It is this example we cited on page 399 in advising that passages such as these should not be judged as they sound at the piano, but as originally scored.

FIGURE 15.20

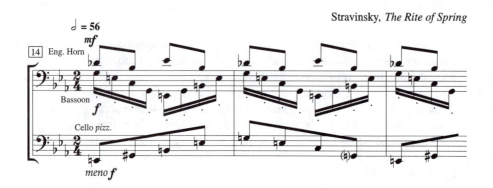

Stravinsky, *The Rite of Spring*

In Figure 15.21, simple triads are seen in contrary motion. An added complexity is the use of two sets of ascending parallel six-four chords, the upper set the same as the lower set, but one beat later. At measure 118, the two contrasting lines change directions and swap the characteristics of measures 2–3.

The visual impression of Figure 15.22 is that of a harmonic sequence. It is that, but with features somewhat more complex than the simple root movement of traditional harmony.

The strong beats of each measure are alternately consonant and dissonant. The bass movement down by fourths is, of course, the conventional sequence down a fourth and up a fifth, so traditionally you might expect B D♯ F♯ on beat 2. If the bass note on the second beat of each measure implies a triad, then superimposed triads are implied. If not, what is the construction of each dissonant chord? Is a single construction used consistently, or is there a variety?

FIGURE 15.21

Milhaud, *L'Orestie d'Eschyle,* III
"Les Euménides"

FIGURE 15.22

Janáček, *M'ša Glagolskaja*

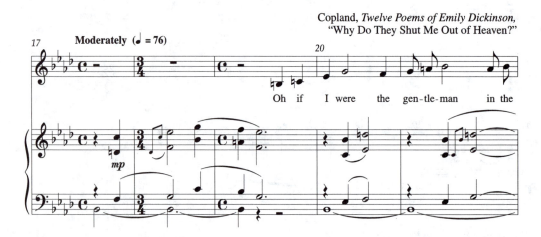

Other Chord Types

Both seventh chords and chords built in sevenths occur in Figure 15.23. Disregarding the pedal B♭, the first chord is a seventh chord, D F (A) C, and the second a chord built with sevenths, from the lowest note up, G F E♭. Both types appear in parallel motion, the seventh chords either in root position or in first inversion. Note in measures 21–23 a series of four parallel traditional seventh chords followed by four chords built with superimposed sevenths.

    This excerpt is also an example of *pandiatonicism*, music based on traditional diatonic scales and making use of both traditional chords (though not in functional progression) and original types of chords. Measures 17–23 use only members of the B♭ major scale, changing to the use of the G major at measure 24. This technique was a reaction against what many composers thought to be an excess of chromaticism, especially that of the "twelve-tone" composers discussed in the next chapter.

FIGURE 15.23

Copland, *Twelve Poems of Emily Dickinson,*
"Why Do They Shut Me Out of Heaven?"

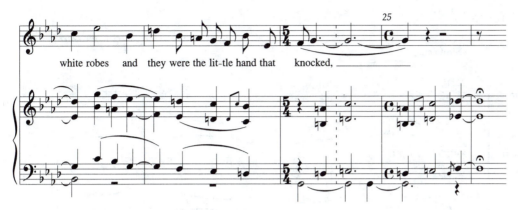

white robes   and   they were the lit-tle hand that   knocked, _____

The music from which Figure 15.24 is an excerpt is remarkable for the variety of chord types, all used in parallelism, and for the fact that it was written so early, in 1906. In the upper three staves of measure 1, we find superimposed augmented triads, D F♯ B♭ and E G♯ C, the six pitches constituting a whole-tone scale. A series of five such triads in parallel motion leads to chords built in fourths at measure 3, the first one spelled B♭ D♯ G♯ C♯ F♯ B. At measure six, the vertical structures are built on the interlocking intervals of the tritone and the perfect fifth. The first chord, built above the bass F♯ (G♭), is

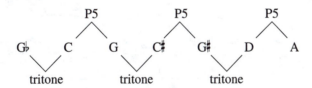

Each of these types is sounded in parallel motion until the next type is stated.

FIGURE 15.24

Ives, *Central Park in the Dark*

During the course of this background (Figure 15.24) played by the strings, other instruments play various tunes above it, as sounds heard from a distance in the night air. The most remarkable superimposition is that of a ragtime piano marked *allegro,* Figure 15.25, against the *molto adagio* of the strings, the latter informed to stop anywhere in that chordal sequence when the piano and other instruments come to their final chord!

FIGURE 15.25

Ives, *Central Park in the Dark*

Methods for juxtaposing notes to create vertical sonorities vary widely and are limited only by the imagination of the composer. In Figure 15.26, the chord at each * is a combination of seconds and thirds. The completed chord in measure 1 uses the same five pitches in both the treble clef and the bass clef, though the spacing between notes is different. The same is true of each of the remaining two similar sonorities. These chords, spelled beginning with C, are

Measure 91: C D♯ E G A♭
Measure 95: C E F G♯ B
Measure 96: C E♭ G A♭ B

FIGURE 15.26

Carter, Sonata for Flute, Oboe, Cello, and Harpsichord

An additional harmonic sonority, called a *cluster,* consists of three or more consecutive tones sounding simultaneously. Figure 15.27 shows alternating three-note clusters, A B C♯ and B♭ C D, used as a harmonic device.

FIGURE 15.27

Bartók, Quartet No. 4, IV

From these examples it can be seen that the construction of dissonant vertical sonorities need not be haphazard. Careful examination and study of even a seemingly forbidding score will usually reveal the thought processes of the composer and the logic behind the choice of sonorities.

Analysis

The procedures we have used in analyzing the examples of this chapter should be applied to the assignments in analysis. Consider the elements of melody, rhythm, and harmony as you look for the following:

1. Features resembling or related to traditional aspects of these elements
2. Features not characteristic of earlier centuries
3. Combinations of traditional and novel elements
4. Systematic approaches, particularly repetition and sequence, whether identical or varied
5. Devices used consistently, even if not in regular patterns, in establishing the style of the music

Study of formal structures should be included when the excerpt is sufficiently complete for this purpose. See the author's *Music for Sight Singing,* fourth edition, chapter 20 for complete or extended sections of twentieth-century melodies. In addition, several anthologies offer a good variety of music for analysis, including these three:

BURKHART, CHARLES, *Anthology for Musical Analysis* (4th ed.). New York: Holt, Rinehart & Winston, 1968.
WENNERSTROM, MARY, *Anthology of Musical Structure and Style*. Upper Saddle River, N.J.: Prentice Hall, 1983.
———, *Anthology of Twentieth-Century Music*. Upper Saddle River, N.J.: Prentice Hall, 1969.

ASSIGNMENT 15.1 *Analysis.*   Make use of the five suggestions just presented. Application of these to measures 1–4 of excerpt (1) below could result in these findings:

1. The syncopation, though simple, reflects a jazz influence.
2. The meter is regular, suggesting a dance form.
3. The harmony is i | V | V | i, though in the bass clef, the second beat of measure 1 is V, and the second beat of measure 2 is i, resulting in the simultaneous use of tonic and dominant harmony.
4. The tonic triad includes both a major and a minor third, as does the dominant triad of measure 3. The latter is the same as the simultaneous use of V and v in traditional harmony and is probably the precedent for the same construction in the tonic triad.
5. The seventh chords in third inversion, measure 3, move in parallel motion.
6. The tonic cadence chord contains not only $\sharp\hat{3}$ and $\flat\hat{3}$ but also the added sixth, $\sharp\hat{6}$.
7. The tonic cadence chord is approached by parallel motion in the outside voices.
8. The form of measures 1–4 is a simple phrase.

(1)

Milhaud, *Saudades do Brasil,*
VIII, "Tijuca"

(2) First, sing the melody. Then, describe the scale formation and locate any tones foreign to that formation.

Vaughan Williams, "The Sons of Light"

(3)

Hindemith, *Ludus Tonalis,* "Interludium"
preceding "Fuga quinta in E"

(4)

Honegger, Concertino
(two-piano version)

(5) This excerpt is a fine exercise in rhythmic reading, since the part for castagnetta is constant throughout. Start as easily as possible, with one or more persons reading the highest line (Flute I) and the lowest line (Castagnetta). Practice against the castagnetta with any other single line above it. Finally, combine two or more lines against the castagnetta.

Stravinsky, *Agon*, "Bransle Gay"

(6)

Barber, *Hermit Songs,* Op. 29, "The Praises of God"

Suggested Writing Activities

Study of the literature of music is always enhanced through the experience of writing original music, as we have done throughout the course. This continues to be true for twentieth-century music, but our approach must be somewhat different. The century was one of experimentation and produced a diversity of styles that cannot yet be linked to a common basic principle. Therefore part-writing, harmonizing melodies, or realizing bass lines will not suffice as a basis for writing projects.

Instead, your own experimentation is the best way to participate in the writing experience. Following is a list of suggestions, based on the music examples of Chapters 13 and 15. Different ideas but of a similar nature should occur to you as you study these examples and other repertoire of the twentieth-century literature.

1. (*a*) Choose one of the medieval modes. Write a melody of 8–16 measures based on this mode, experimenting both with smooth traditional lines and with non-traditional procedures such as wide leaps and use of tritones. (*b*) Harmonize the melodies with triads based on the chosen mode. An occasional altered triad may be used, as in Figure 15.18.

2. Write a melody of 8–16 measures, using modal inflections, but derived from more than one mode. Use Figure 15.1 and accompanying discussion as a guide.

3. Experiment with bitonality by setting your melodies to accompaniments in either major or minor keys. Refer to Figure 15.3.

4. Using a poem from Assignment 5.3 (page 168), or one of your choice, write a melody using a conventional time signature and regular measure lengths, but with an irregular metrical pattern, as in Figures 15.8 and 15.9. Note: Poetic lines that appear to be in a single meter with regularly recurring accents can actually be accommodated with several meters. Review Figures 5.29–5.36.

5. Write melodies without texts, but with alternating meters or with changing meter signatures. Review Figure 15.11.

6. Write melodies as above, using the whole-tone scale or the pentatonic scale in part.

7. Write parallel triads in root position, using (*a*) all diatonic triads, (*b*) diatonic and altered triads mixed, or (*c*) triads in chromatic thirds. Write melodic lines that can be accommodated by one of these types of triad successions.

8. Write successive parallel seventh chords or added-tone chords. Find examples in Chapter 13.

9. Experiment with triads and/or larger chords in contrary motion, as in Figure 15.21.

10. Devise an original system of chord construction and a system for the chordal progression, as in Figures 15.21–15.24.

Summary

The object of this chapter has been to show that in much of twentieth-century writing, dependence on the concepts of earlier centuries is usually obvious, or at least discernible upon investigation. At the same time, the music examples have shown that in spite of traceable evolutionary features, the systems used and the styles of writing produced have been so numerous and so varied as to preclude, at least for the present, an all-encompassing method of description or analysis.

16

Serial Composition and Later Twentieth-Century Practices

Extended use of chromaticism in the late nineteenth century, especially in music such as *Tristan und Isolde,* imposed severe restrictions on further developments within the major-minor tonal system. Hence, we have seen in the preceding chapters (13–15) examples of the many attempts to generate new and effective styles of music composition. Not included in the previous chapter was the work of Arnold Schoenberg (1874–1951), who, among others, ultimately developed a new systematic approach to music composition, one that exerted significant influence on music of the twentieth century.

Schoenberg's early compositions, such as the *Gurre-Lieder* from the years 1900–1901, demonstrates as in Figure 16.1 still another effort to avoid conventional harmonic successions and cadences. (Compare with Wagner, Figure 12.11, and Fauré, Figure 12.12.)

What we see is a scale-line succession of conventional major-minor seventh chords leading to a root movement of a diminished fourth, B to E♭ (major), followed by E♭ minor and ending with a cadence on E major. The succession of chord roots resembles no earlier harmonic pattern, nor is there any resemblance to a conventional cadence. Conventional movement by perfect fifth is notably missing. The several simultaneous melodic lines with their profusion of nonharmonic tones serve further to obscure any sense of conventional harmonic movement.

FIGURE 16.1

Schoenberg, *Gurrelieder,* Part III
(piano transcription by Alban Berg)

Used by permission of Belmont Music Publishers, Pacific Palisades, CA 90272.

Such music as this seems to express the composer's frustration in his attempt to stretch even further the boundaries of tonal music and at the same time produce original music. Realizing the futility of continuing in this style, Schoenberg set as his next goal to devise a way or ways to release music from its dependence on the limitations in effect for the preceding three centuries.

Principally, these limitations were, first, the role of tonic as the pitch to which all other pitches were subservient and, second, a system of harmonic structures in which the individual members usually moved along an established path to the music's close on the tonic tone. As we shall see, Schoenberg's solution included the concept that all twelve tones of the chromatic scale are of equal importance. This concept eliminated the supremacy of the tonic and allowed the use of many new harmonic structures that would be considered extreme dissonances in conventional harmonic practice.

Early progress toward Schoenberg's goal is shown in Figure 16.2. The chords played by the right hand are mixed tertian and quartal. The melody in the left hand, which is a melodic sequence and could, by itself, be harmonized traditionally, actually has little harmonic relationship to the harmonic progression in the upper staff. The startling V+ I progression closing the first phrase demonstrates the continuing strong influence of traditional writing, as does the tonic triad with its added sixth (C E G A) as the final cadential harmony.

FIGURE 16.2

Schoenberg, "In diesen Wintertagen," Op. 14, No. 2

Used by permission of Belmont Music Publishers, Pacific Palisades, CA 90272.

Atonality

Beginning in 1908, Schoenberg achieved the goal of complete or near-complete divorcement from a tonic tone, resulting in music that is known as *atonal* (lacking tonality in the traditional sense). In Figure 16.3*a*, the *contrived scale* (designed or created by the composer) in the cello line, measures 1–2, includes all twelve tones of the chromatic scale. We have numbered these twelve as though they were a *tone row*, described on page 441. However, the four unnumbered notes of measure 2 are repetitions of previous notes, not characteristic of tone-row usage. (Enharmonic pitch names are considered repetitions.) All voices are written in the same manner, including another scalar passage in measures 3–4.

Calculating vertical structures on each beat of the instrumental parts shows only four intervallic combinations even faintly reminiscent of traditional chords: (1) measure 1, beat 3, B F♯ A; (2) measure 3, beat 2, G D; (3) measure 4, beat 3, B♭ C E; and (4) measure 4, beat 4, G D. The final cadence, Figure 16.3*b*, is completely lacking in any traditional harmonic sense, the vertical sonority consisting of notes spaced as E A C, F D♯, and B, or spelled consecutively, C D♯ E F A B.

FIGURE 16.3

Schoenberg, *Pierrot Lunaire,* Op. 21, "Madonna"

(*a*) Opening measures

(b) Final cadence

Used by permission of Belmont Music Publishers, Pacific Palisades, CA 90272.

The vocal line demonstrates a notation devised by Schenberg to express a unique singing style. The stem of the note includes an "x"(♪), indicating the approximate pitch of a *spoken* word. The text is a recitation, its method of performance known as *Sprechstimme.*

Twelve-Tone Systems

Having achieved an atonal style, Schoenberg worked for nine years (1914–1923) developing a system for atonal composition, much as traditional music had a system for tonal writing. The result is described in Schoenberg's own words as a "method of composing with twelve tones which are related only one with another," but it is more popularly known by the terms "twelve-tone system," "twelve-tone technique," "serialism,"[1] and "dodecaphonic writing." Atonal composition was first demonstrated in 1923 in Schoenberg's *Five Piano Pieces,* Op. 23, and *Serenade,* Op. 24 (for seven instruments and voice). Its theoretical basis is a predetermined "row" (or "series" or "set") consisting of the twelve notes of the chromatic scale. All twelve tones must be used before any note of the row may be repeated, so it is impossible that any pitch can assume the role of tonic. The row itself constitutes the basic organizing principle of a composition, rather than, as in the past, a harmonic progression leading to a tonic.

---

[1]The term *serialism* refers here only to serialism of pitches, but it was later applied to other factors, such as rhythmic patterns, dynamics, and tempi. See Figure 16.18 and its discussion.

The Twelve-Tone Row

The concept of the row can be illustrated by its first complete use in Schoenberg's Op. 23.[2] In Figure 16.4*a*, the first twelve notes in the treble clef display the row. (The numbering 0 through 11 is explained immediately following.) This row includes each of the twelve tones of the chromatic scale. Figure 16.4*b* shows this row with all the notes within the range of an octave.

FIGURE 16.4

Schoenberg, *Fünf Klavierstücke,* Op. 23, No. 5, "Walzer"

Reprinted by Permission of G. Schirmer, Inc. on behalf of Edition Wilhelm Hansen.

[2]The previous movements display row technique but not with all twelve tones.

(b)   Row for Op. 23, No. 5

0   1   2   3   4   5   6   7   8   9   10   11

Identifying the Members of the Row

1. *Pitch class.* A pitch class includes all enharmonic names for a given pitch. For example, E♯, F, and G♭♭ all sound identical and therefore constitute a pitch class. The term, of comparatively recent origin, is more suited to the analysis and description of twelve-tone writing than are conventional terms, since in this style of writing, sharps and flats do not imply resolution or indicate tendencies of melodic movement. The use of pitch-class terminology in other applications of music analysis is becoming more common.

2. *Order numbers* simply indicate the location of a given pitch class in the row, derived by numbering successively from 0 to 11 each pitch in the row, as in Figure 16.4*b*. In the early period of twelve-tone writing, pitches were numbered 1 through 12 but were changed to facilitate analysis, as will be seen below in the use of pitch-class numbers.

3. A *pitch-class (pc) number* indicates the distance in half steps above 0, the first note of the row. If the row were the chromatic scale beginning on C♯, the pitch-class numbers would be

C♯	D	D♯	E	F	F♯	G	G♯	A	A♯	B	C
0	1	2	3	4	5	6	7	8	9	10	11

The row in Figure 16.4*b* also begins on C♯. Its fourth note, G, for example, is pc 6 because it is six half steps above C♯.

C♯	A	B	G	A♭	F♯	A♯	D	E	E♭	C	F
0	8	10	6	7	5	9	1	3	2	11	4

Using the Row

1. A row is devised by the composer and is used as the basis for the composition, just as mode and key were chosen in traditional composition. The concept of the row and its musical implications may occur simultaneously, similar to simultaneous concepts of theme, mode, and key in traditional music.

2. Any note of the row may appear in any octave. For example, the first two notes of the row, 0 and 1, in Figure 16.4*b* are a major third, but in the composition, Figure 16.4*a*, they are a minor sixth. The principle of the invertibility of an interval continues to apply in this new compositional technique.

3. No note of the row may be repeated (except for immediate repetition with no intervening notes) until all other tones of the row are sounded. Occasional other exceptions include repetition of a short melodic figure, or an ostinato, often in fifths. As the system developed over the years, composers relaxed these severe restrictions, allowing further exceptions for musical reasons. This, of course, is

no different from what we have learned in working with traditional music: Regular procedures predominate but are relaxed when an exception is a better choice.

4. A row may utilize any rhythmic pattern or patterns during the course of the composition.

5. A row does not necessarily coincide with a theme or a motive. Either may end during the course of a row, the next theme or motive starting with one of the remaining notes of the row.

6. The row may be used harmonically as well as melodically. The row of Figure 16.5*a* supplies both the melody and the underlying harmonic structures in Figure 16.5*b*. In succeeding measures, violin 1 continues with the remaining notes of the row, 6–11.

FIGURE 16.5

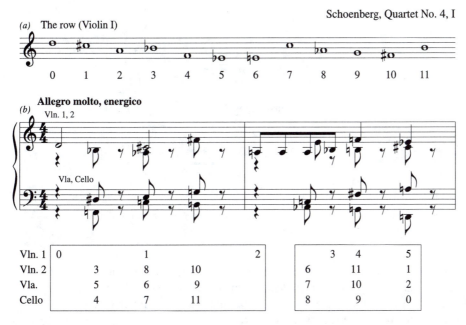

Schoenberg, Quartet No. 4, I

In this example, the chords are derived by dividing the row into four units: 0 1 2, 3 4 5, 6 7 8, and 9 10 11. The units are so chosen that they combine with the row in the violin 1 part to produce four consecutive complete rows.

7. The prime row (P) may be varied in these three ways:

   a. *Inversion* (I). Each note of the row proceeds by the same interval but in the opposite direction. The first three notes of the row in Figure 16.5, D down to C♯ down to A, are found as D up to E♭ up to G in inversion. The complete row in inversion is shown in Figure 16.6*a*.

   b. *Retrograde* (R). The P row is presented backwards, starting with its last note and ending with its first note. Reading the row, Figure 16.5*a*, from right to left produces the series of pitches shown in Figure 16.6*b*.

c. *Retrograde Inversion* (RI). The I row is found in retrograde. Reading the I row backwards produces the RI row. The row RI in Figure 16.6*c* is divided between two instruments and transposed up one half step, as found in the Quartet. Transposition will be explained in the next section. The same passage untransposed is also shown.

FIGURE 16.6

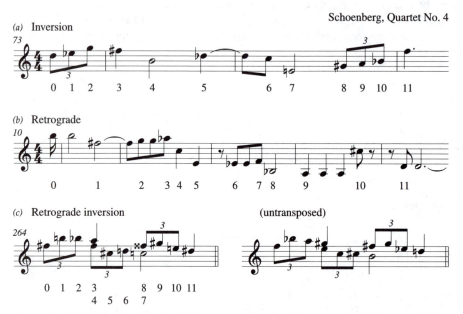

Schoenberg, Quartet No. 4

8. All transpositions of each of the forms of the row are conveniently displayed using a *matrix*. The matrix in Figure 16.7 shows the twelve transpositions each of the prime row, the inversion, the retrograde, and the retrograde inversion, a total of forty-eight rows. Here is how it is constructed.
   a. Write the letter names of the prime row in a horizontal line.
   b. Using the first letter name of the prime row, write downward (vertically) the row in inversion. In Figure 16.7, the first three notes of the uppermost horizontal line (P^0) are a half step down and a major third down (D C♯ A). The first three notes of the first vertical line are a half step up and major third up (D E♭ G).
   c. Use the letter name of each first note in the vertical line as the first note of a prime row. In Figure 16.7, the first two vertical notes are D and E♭. Since E♭ is a half step higher than D, write the second horizontal line, each note a half step higher than the first horizontal line. Continue this process, using each note in the vertical line as the first note of a transposed prime row. Remember that any spelling from a given pitch class may be used at any time. For example, an interval three half steps above E♭ can be either F♯ or G♭.
   d. Identify each row.

P = *prime row.* The first P row is identified as P^0. Each succeeding prime row is identified by the number of half steps between its first letter name and the first letter name of P^0. In Figure 16.7, the second horizontal row starts with E♭, one half step above D; therefore, the row is P^1. The third horizontal row starts with G, five half steps above D; therefore the row is P^5. Calculate the remaining rows in the same manner.

I = *inversion.* The I row is read from top to bottom. The first vertical row is the I^0 form of the row. The vertical row beginning on E is I^2 because it is two half steps above D. Number each I row.

R = *retrograde.* The retrograde row is read horizontally from right to left. The superscript for each member of the R line is the same as that for the P line; for example, D is both P^0 and R^0; E is both P^2 and R^2; and so forth.

Figure 16.6*b* shows a retrograde row. It begins on B^9, nine half steps above the D of P^0. Note that this row read backwards is the P^0 row.

RI = *retrograde inversion.* This row is read from the bottom up. I and RI share the same superscript numbers, I^0 and RI^0, I^4 and RI^4, and so forth. Figure 16.6*c* is an example of an RI row; but it is *not* RI^0. This is a transposed row. Its first note, F♯, is one half step above the first note, F, of RI^0. Therefore the row is RI^1, as seen in the matrix. You can check this further by reading the notation of Figure 16.6*c* from its last note, D♯, to its first note, and comparing the result with row I^1. (Remember that D♯ in the figure is in the same pitch class as E♭, shown as the first note of I^1 in the matrix.)

Figure 16.6*c* also shows the same passage written in the RI^0 row, of which RI^1 is the transposition.

FIGURE 16.7   *Matrix for Schoenberg's Fourth Quartet, First Movement*

	I^0	I^{11}	I^7	I^8	I^3	I^1	I^2	I^{10}	I^6	I^5	I^4	I^9	
P^0	D	C♯	A	B♭	F	E♭	E	C	A♭	G	F♯	B	R^0
P^1	E♭	D	B♭	B	F♯	E	F	D♭	A	A♭	G	C	R^1
P^5	G	F♯	D	E♭	B♭	A♭	A	F	D♭	C	B	E	R^5
P^4	F♯	F	D♭	D	A	G	G♯	E	C	B	B♭	E♭	R^4
P^9	B	B♭	G♭	G	D	C	C♯	A	F	E	E♭	A♭	R^9
P^{11}	C♯	C	A♭	A	E	D	D♯	B	G	F♯	F	B♭	R^{11}
P^{10}	C	B	G	A♭	E♭	D♭	D	B♭	G♭	F	E	A	R^{10}
P^2	E	E♭	B	C	G	F	F♯	D	B♭	A	A♭	D♭	R^2
P^6	G♯	G	E♭	E	B	A	B♭	G♭	D	D♭	C	F	R^6
P^7	A	A♭	E	F	C	B♭	B	G	E♭	D	C♯	F♯	R^7
P^8	B♭	A	F	F♯	C♯	B	C	A♭	E	E♭	D	G	R^8
P^3	F	E	C	C♯	G♯	F♯	G	E♭	B	B♭	A	D	R^3
	RI^0	RI^{11}	RI^7	RI^8	RI^3	RI^1	RI^2	RI^{10}	RI^6	RI^5	RI^4	RI^9	

Figure 16.8 is another example from the Fourth Quartet, this one divided between the viola and the first violin. First determine the form of the row by checking each C♯ (the first note) around the perimeter of the matrix. The C♯ below I^{11} provides the row shown in the music. It is called I^{11} because its first note, C♯, is eleven half steps above the first note, D, of I^0.

FIGURE 16.8

In the Workbook: Do Assignments 16A and 16B. Answers are given.

ASSIGNMENT 16.1   Complete the row analysis of Figure 16.4.

1. Figure 16.4 begins in a manner similar to Figure 16.5*b* in which the lower voice provides chords to the melody in the upper voice. The first notes of the bass clef show order numbers 5–11, after which D♭ (C♯) opens a P^0 row. In measure 5, the tied order number 4 proceeds to 5 in the treble clef.

   The completion of this row in measure 6 occurs simultaneously with the opening of another version of the same row, in turn followed by one additional presentation of the row.

2. Indicate the order numbers of the notes in measures 5–6.

3. In measure 7, a complete row begins on G♭. What is its order number? Continue the order numbers through 11, at which point order number 0 will appear, leading to the completion of the twelve-tone row.

4. When 0 appears in measure 8, it will begin a new overlapping row. Trace this row through to 11. The last note in the bass will be left over. Had the next measures been shown, what would be its probable function?

ASSIGNMENT 16.2   Analyze the material between the editorial dashed diagonal lines in this additional excerpt from the work in Figure 16.4*a*. The row shown as Figure 16.4*b* may be used to assist in the analysis. All rows are P^0 except one, which is either I^0, R^0, or RI^0.

You may also wish to investigate the rows beginning in measure 106. This passage shows that the row technique can be used with more freedom than shown in previous assigned materials. Look for these deviations from straightforward usage:

1. Measure 106. C♯ and A are used as members of two different rows, one incomplete.
2. A row covering two staves and including a repetition of a group of tones.
3. From measure 110, one complete and several partial rows.

Schoenberg, *Fünf Klavierstücke,* Op. 23, No. 5, "Walzer"

ASSIGNMENT 16.3   Using the matrix, Figure 16.7, identify these rows from the first movement of Schoenberg's Quartet No. 4. Find each row in the matrix that starts with the same letter name as the row. For example, the first note of the first excerpt, F, is the first note of the rows P^3, I^3, R^6, and RI^0. Compare each complete row in the matrix with the row in the music example.

1. Measures 95–98, cello

2. Measures 120–121, violin 1 and viola

3. Measures 34–37, viola and cello

4. Measures 155–156

ASSIGNMENT 16.4   Analyze this excerpt from Schoenberg's Fourth Quartet. It contains six complete rows, including all forms, some in transposition. Identify each from the matrix, Figure 16.7. In the first measure, the violin 1 and violin 2 parts together make up the row.

A given composition is usually not made up entirely of complete tone rows. After the initial statement of the row, development of ideas derived from that row is a common compositional practice. Figure 16.9 shows the composer using three-note groups (sets) from various rows in the matrix, several identified by row member, and below the notes, the order numbers from that row. The first three notes in the cello part, D♯ E G♯, are found in the row R^8. Their order numbers, 2 3 4, are shown as E♭ E A♭ in the matrix:

B♭ A F F♯ C♯ B C A♭ E E♭ D G ⟵——— R^8

4 3 2

Several of the bracketed three-note sets in Figure 16.9 have been left unidentified. Supply the row number for each and the order numbers from that row. In these sets, only one row is different from those already identified.

FIGURE 16.9

Schoenberg, Quartet No. 4

Copyright ©1939 (Renewed) by G. Schirmer, Inc. International Copyright Secured. All Rights
Reserved. Used by Permission.

ASSIGNMENT 16.5   As its title indicates, this short but complete work is concerned only with melodic lines, using straightforward examples of the P^0 row and transpositions of each of the P, R, I, and RI rows. Members of the rows sometimes move from one staff to another, providing several crossings of the three melodic lines.

Look for these contrapuntal features:

1. Stretto: the theme against itself, the second voice starting shortly after the first, as in measures 1–2
2. Themes in simultaneous contrary motion
3. Stretto in contrary motion

The beginning of a row can be easily identified by the M7 interval, order numbers 0 and 1 of the row; the final members of the row can be identified by the P5 interval, order numbers 10 and 11.

Dallapiccola, *Quaderno Musicale di Annalibera*, No. 3,
"Contrapunctus Primus"

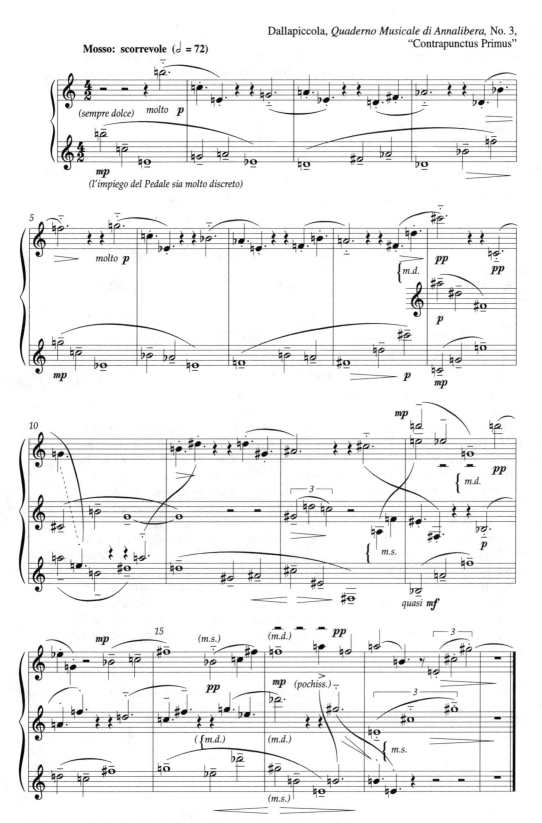

Three-Note Sets

The Concerto for Nine Instruments by Anton Webern (1883–1945), a student of
Schoenberg's, is based on a row divisible into four three-note sections, called sets or
cells.

FIGURE 16.10

Row: Webern, *Concerto for Nine Instruments*

To understand the following procedures, first construct a matrix for the row in
Figure 16.10.

In this row, each set includes a minor second and a major third, each in a different
configuration.

Set 1	half step down, major third up	B B♭ D
Set 2	major third up, half step down	E♭ G F♯
Set 3	major third down, half step up	G♯ E F
Set 4	half step up, major third down	C C♯ A

Once any set is identified as a P form of a three-note set, each remaining set is in an I,
R, or RI relationship to it. To illustrate, call the first set P^0. Then, for set 2, look in the
matrix for the row that begins E♭ G F♯. These three notes will be the first three notes
of R^6 (reading right to left). For set 3, G♯ E F is RI^7; for set 4, C C♯ A is I^1.

These three-note sets are used consistently throughout the work, both melodically
and harmonically. Figure 16.11 begins with three three-note sets aligned vertically
(chords), followed by a melodic set. Note that in the vertical three-note sets, two of the
voices that read horizontally (melodically) are also three-note sets. The third voice consists of three successive notes in half steps; combining any one of these three notes with
the two notes above it produces one of the three-note sets or a variant thereof.[3]

The first vertical sonority includes the notes A F F♯. Check each row of the matrix to determine which row(s) include these as the first three tones (any order). They
are P^7, F F♯ A, and RI^8, A F F♯. Continue checking the second and third chords.

The melodic set for violin, E G♯ G, in measures 15–16 is found as the first three
notes of R^7.

---

[3]Webern's writing, characterized by both short fragments and wide leaps, is often called "pointil-
lism," a term first used to describe a technique in painting in which the picture is made up of a large number
of small dots and strokes. The technique was first used by the French painter Georges Seurat (1859–1891).

ASSIGNMENT 16.6   Complete the analysis of Figure 16.11, and continue with Figure 16.12, a strictly melodic section of the same work.

FIGURE 16.11

Webern, *Concerto for Nine Instruments,* Op. 24, III

FIGURE 16.12

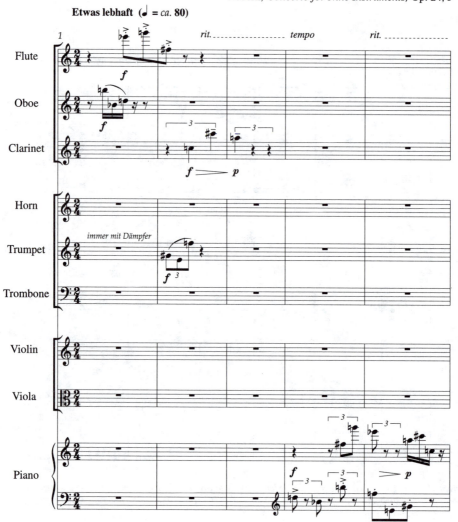

Webern, *Concerto for Nine Instruments,* Op. 24, I

Combinatoriality

Initially devised by Schoenberg, the concept of combinatoriality was later named and augmented by Milton Babbitt (b. 1916). Schoenberg achieved combinatoriality by choosing for the first hexachord (six notes) pitches that would not be duplicated in the first hexachord of its I^5 row. Thus, the tones of the first hexachord P^0 can combine with those of I^5 to form a twelve-tone row. It follows that combining the first hexachords in R^0 and RI^5 will also produce its own row.

This concept can be illustrated from Schoenberg's *Klavierstück,* Op. 33b. In Figure 16.13, the first hexachord each of P^0 and its I^5 version together furnish a twelve-tone row, and therefore can be used together as a row. In addition, combining each of the second hexachords, R^0 and RI^5 will produce a similar row.

FIGURE 16.13

Schoenberg, *Klavierstück,* Op. 33b

The first four measures of Figure 16.14 show the rows P⁰ and I⁵ used separately. In measures 5–10, the upper row is RI⁵ and the lower is R⁰, as bracketed. But also, up to the editorial vertical dashed line, the first hexachord each of RI⁵ and R⁰ combine to form a twelve-tone row. After the dotted line, the second hexachord each of RI⁵ and R⁰ combine similarly.

In studying this score, be sure to eliminate from your calculations the frequent repeated tones, both in immediate succession and in short melodic figures, before the appearance of the next member of the tone row. The X's in measures 5–7 indicate the repeated notes found in the RI⁵ hexachord.

FIGURE 16.14

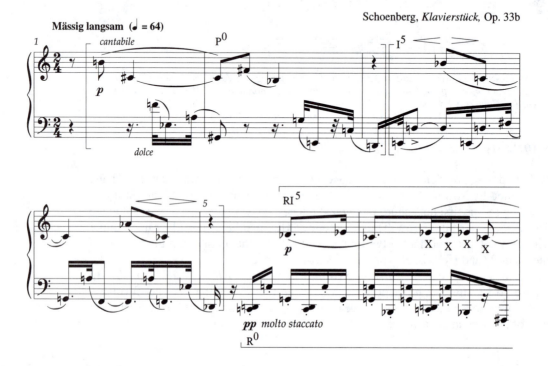

Schoenberg, *Klavierstück,* Op. 33b

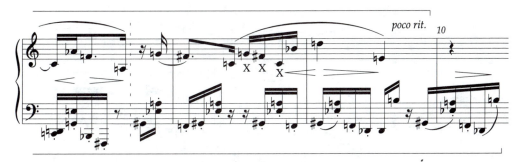

Used by permission of Belmont Music Publishers, Pacific Palisades, CA 90272.

Since this early use involving only P^0 and I^5, other composers, particularly Babbitt, have produced combinatoriality with other forms of the row in the matrix.

ASSIGNMENT 16.8   In the first excerpt (*a*) from Op. 33 b, the first two measures display the four forms of the row shown in Figure 16.13, followed by a pair used combinatorially. In (*b*) the analysis will divulge the use of the other pair.

Schoenberg, *Klavierstück,* Op. 33b

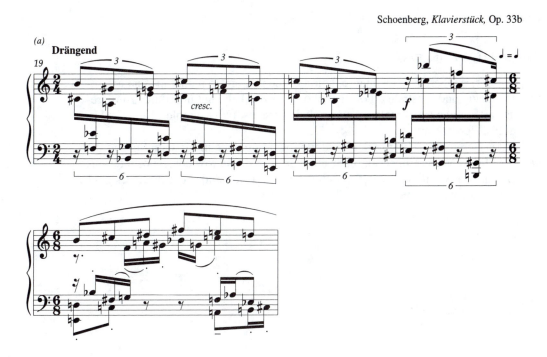

Used by permission of Belmont Music Publishers, Pacific Palisades, CA 90272.

Additional Uses of the Row

The possibilities inherent in the manipulation of the row are so numerous that any attempt to catalog and illustrate all of them would most likely end in failure. To represent this vast storehouse of material, we include here just two examples, each used in an entirely different way.

Alban Berg (1885–1935) often used the row to produce music with links to the tonal past. In his Violin Concerto, order numbers 0–8 of the row consist of intervals of thirds, any consecutive three of which produce a triad, and order numbers 8-11 form a four-note whole-tone scale.

FIGURE 16.15

In the introductory measures of the concerto, the use of the row in producing triadic movement is quite obvious.

FIGURE 16.16

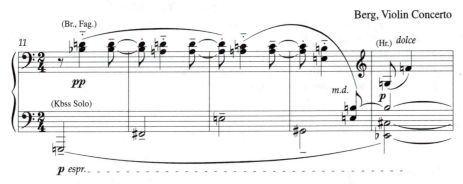

Berg, Violin Concerto

Igor Stravinsky (1882–1971) first made use of row techniques in his seventieth year, and for the next twenty years up to his death, he continued writing in this manner. In one such score, the row consists not of twelve notes but of eleven, and of these, only eight are different in pitch. The first eleven notes of Figure 16.17 constitute the P^0 row. The other three forms of the row follow, each interlocked with the next by overlapping the last note or two of the row as the first note(s) of the next row, as indicated by the brackets.

Note that after the P^0 row, each row has been transposed so that all four rows share the same pitch range, the tritone B–F. Can you identify each row and its transposition?

FIGURE 16.17

Stravinsky, *Cantata,* "Ricercar II"

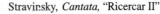

Other Uses of Serialism

Use of serialism for pitches has led some composers to try serializing other factors, such as rhythmic patterns, dynamics, and tempi. In Figure 16.18, durations are serialized. Beginning with the first note in the upper staff, a thirty-second note, the value of each successive note is increased by one thirty-second: 1/32, 2/32, 3/32 . . . ending with 23/32. The lower staff is a retrograde, starting with 23/32, 22/32, 21/32 . . . ending with 1/32, the two rows sounding simultaneously.

FIGURE 16.18

Messiaen, *Cantéyodjoyâ*

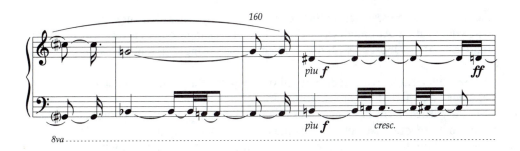

Music since 1950

The term most appropriate to describe in general the nature of composition in the last few decades is "eclecticism." Compositional practices and related techniques described in Chapters 15–16 continue to be an important part of the new music, and the use of serialism, though it reached its zenith in the decade 1955–1965, continues to be a significant element in the music of many composers.

But new practices and concepts began to emerge shortly after the close of World War II, concepts that now appear to be a natural reaction to the complexities and restrictions inherent in serialism, much of this music being far more complex than we have shown in our examples, and often appealing almost exclusively to the intellect at the expense of emotional impact. Once composition reached that state where analysis is of more interest than hearing or performing the score, a reaction was surely inevitable. But in its favor, serialism, along with the exploratory devices of Debussy, must be credited not only with the creation of much significant music but equally with the opening of new pathways at a time when nineteenth-century practices could no longer provide a stimulus for fresh ideas in music composition.

Aleatory Music

The new types of music that most obviously expressed this reaction are known by several names: *indeterminacy, chance music, random music,* and *aleatory music* (or *aleatoric*).[4] All refer to music in which there is a lessening of the restrictions of precise

---

[4]The term was adopted by the French composer Pierre Boulez from the Latin *alea* (game of dice) and the French *aléa* (chance).

pitch, specific melodic patterns, exact rhythms or meters, or any other element of notation in music composition. Although each of the four terms supposedly has its own meaning, all are used rather loosely, with different composers using different terms to express the same concepts.

In any case, indeterminacy can apply to all or any part of a work, or to one or more of its elements (pitch, rhythm, and so forth), in any combination.

Probably the earliest form of chance music is the "jamming" by a jazz combo, free improvisation by several instruments simultaneously, based on a given tune and chord progression, though even earlier, the Baroque practice of realizing a figured bass produced results that were not totally predetermined.[5] Chance music, however, gives the performer, and sometimes the conductor, the choice of what to play, when, and for how long, from a group of composed or implied possibilities, or improvisation on any of these possibilities, or any combination of scored music and improvisation. Conventional instruments, electronic instruments, prerecorded tapes, and human voices may join in the chance or improvisatory ensemble. Works in conventional style (to be played as written) often include sections in aleatoric style.

Since aleatoric music will vary from performance to performance, analysis is not possible in the traditional sense; we can look at a score and try to predict what might occur, but with few exceptions, the actual music will never be committed to paper.[6]

Music without Notation

The most violent reactions to the extremes of traditional notation were compositions based either on no notation whatsoever or on notation without specific meaning. Playing a piece of music without notation implies improvisation, which, of course, is the direct opposite of completely controlled notation, whereas nonspecific notation implies the necessity of symbols newly created for the purpose.

Figure 16.19 is "a composition" written "for ensemble" and is from a large collection of similar events.[7]

---

[5]Mozart is said to have experimented with throwing dice to determine compositional choices.

[6]We have already seen a form of indeterminacy in Figures 15.24 and 15.25, Ives's *Central Park in the Dark* (1906), the indeterminacy of the strings playing against the piano's ragtime. Ives can also be credited with first use of a row, *Tone Roads No. 3* (1915), though a row is simply repeated throughout the composition against a background not using the row.

[7]The term "event" in avant garde music is commonly used to indicate the duration of a complete unit of activity. This example is a single event; larger works may consist of several events

FIGURE 16.19

Stockhausen, *From the Seven Days*

MEETING POINT

everyone plays the same tone

**lead the tone wherever your thoughts
lead you
do not leave it, stay with it
always return
to the same place**

English version ©1968 by Universal Edition A.G., Wien. © Renewed. All Rights Reserved. Used by permission of European American Music Distributors Corporation, sole U.S. and Canadian agent for Universal Edition A.G., Wien.

In another nonnotated event by John Cage, *Variations III (For One or Any Number of People Performing Any Actions)*,[8] the player is furnished with forty-two plastic discs to be dropped on a flat surface. Those not touching another are removed, after which the performer, noting the number touching and their relationships, performs "suitably" before going on to another group.

Progressing (or regressing) from these extremes to the absurd are such works as an "organ concerto" for which the performer sits at the console and shaves with an electric razor, the sound amplified for the enjoyment of the audience, and a "piano burning," the climax to an aleatory evening, at which the audience congregates outside the hall to listen to the random sound of snapping strings and exploding fireworks prepositioned in the instrument. Obviously, there are no bibliographical references to these happenings.

Graphic Scores

Notated aleatoric music often makes use of *graphic notation,* symbols of any kind, usually unique to a particular music composition. This notation, therefore, is found in many guises, three of which are seen in Figures 16.20, 16.21, and 16.25. When graphic notation does not express a specific pitch or metric value, it serves, in a way, the same purpose as eighth-century neumes. (Review *Elementary Harmony,* fifth edition, page 37.)

[8]New York, Henmar Press, 1963.

In Figure 16.20, each square is equivalent to MM 88, a specific metrical concept. Symbols in the squares indicate the activities for each of these periods of time. As with most such scores, it is necessary that a list of symbols and their meanings be included.[9] In this work, for example, a number indicates how many sounds to make or, if in a circle, how many to make at once (no particular sounds). The symbols ♪ and ♩ indicate "short" and "long" grace notes; ♩ . . . . indicates a sustained note. Arrows indicate whether to play high or low notes. Thirty-seven symbols are listed by the composer.

FIGURE 16.20

Feldman, *In Search of an Orchestration*

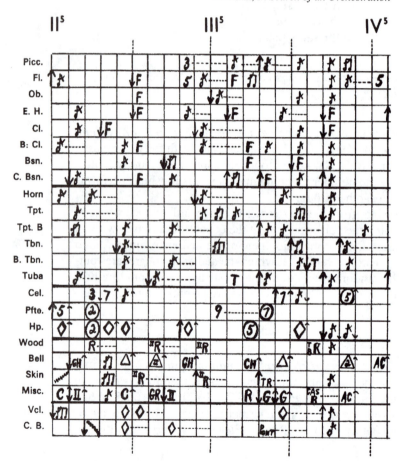

[9]See Smith Brindle, *The New Music,* for an eleven-page list, beginning on page 188, of "some new notation symbols." The list is probably far from complete.

Walaciúski's notation in Figure 16.21 refers to performance at the keyboard, including use of the palm of the hand on the strings, percussive sounds on wood or metal inside the piano, and percussive sounds other than on the piano.

FIGURE 16.21

Walaciúski, *Allaloa*

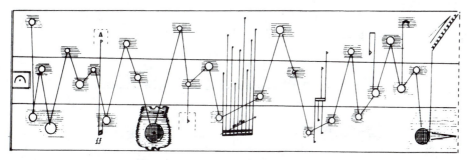

Graphic Staff Notation

The current trend is away from such extremes. Aleatoric ideas are expressed in more conservative ways, usually combined with conventional staff notation as in Figure 16.22, measured but with only approximations of pitch, and in Figure 16.23, without measured time but with specific pitch.

FIGURE 16.22

Penderecki, *Ecloga VIII* (for six male voices)

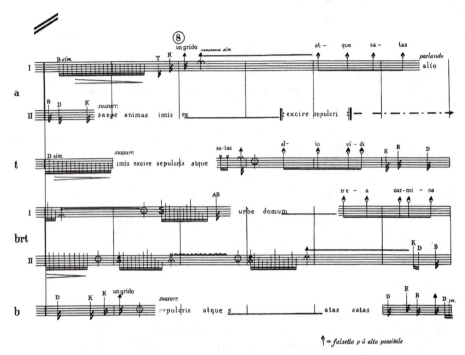

It can be said that regardless of their musical accomplishments, the aleatoric composers have contributed much to music composition by freeing it from its rigid adherence to rhythmic and pitch values, just as serialism freed music from its dependency on the major-minor tonal systems.

New Sound Sources

In all the preceding examples, we have studied those factors that differentiated twentieth-century writing from that of earlier eras. Yet, no matter to what degree they have differed, they still have had one constant characteristic in common. In any era, the sources of musical sound have been the same: the vibrating string, the vibrating air column, and the vibrating membrane. Therefore, the kind of sound for which composers write has been basically the same (though of course with constant refinements and improvements) from the time when man first blew on a reed, plucked a taut string, or struck a stretched skin.

FIGURE 16.23

Crumb, *Madrigals,* Book I, iii,
"Los muertos llevan alas de musgo"

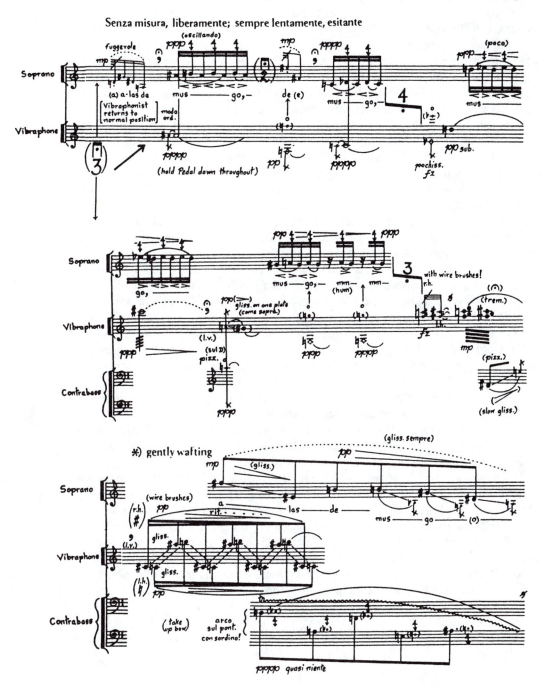

The twentieth century provided, for the first time in music history, new resources in sound itself. There are two varieties of such sounds: (1) electronic manipulation of natural sound and (2) electronic production of new sounds.

The first development in this area, known as *musique concrète,* combines old sound sources, including various forms of noise, with manipulation of those sounds by various techniques through the use of the tape recorder. A conventional sound or group of sounds is recorded on tape. The taped sound can be manipulated in many ways—for example, by changing the speed of the machine or by reversing the tape. Tapes can be cut up and spliced together to achieve desired effects, and sounds from other sources can be superimposed upon existing taped sounds. These procedures, among others, provide a composer with almost unlimited possibilities for imaginative musical creation. There is no score for such a composition; the final tape is the score itself. No notation is required, since the composition will be heard only when the tape is played on a machine. The effect of this kind of music is enhanced by stereo reproduction of the sounds on the tape using two and often more than two speakers.

Electronic music takes advantage of the fact that a vacuum tube or transistor is capable of producing electrical oscillations, which can be converted to sound by a loudspeaker. These sounds can be organized and controlled, as in the electronic organ, to the point where they can fairly realistically duplicate existing acoustic sounds, such as those produced by orchestra and band instruments. But they can also produce a wide range of sounds never before heard by human ears. These sounds are produced on a synthesizer, a machine that not only produces tones but also can modify them in an almost unlimited number of ways. In addition to a wide variety of timbres, it is able to produce microtonal pitches, resulting in the possibility of creating scale formations with almost any number of desired equal tones to the octave. These sounds, along with white noise, a mixture of many simultaneous frequencies, are combined and juxtaposed in countless combinations on magnetic tape. Other sounds from nature, as in *musique concrète,* are often included as part of the texture of the completed composition.

Electronic music is performed in several ways: (1) by a playing of the completed tape alone; (2) by playing the tape along with an instrument or a voice, or with an ensemble, with a conventional score for the conventional performers; and (3) by using the synthesizer as one of the instruments of the ensemble, played by a soloist with or without simultaneous performance of prerecorded tapes.

Electronic music is usually subject only to aural analysis since the tape for the improvisation *is* the score. Stockhausen has provided a graphic score for an early electronic work, Figure 16.24 (in his words, "the first Electronic Music to be published"). On the upper part, the horizontal lines represent pitches ranging from 100 to 17,200 Hz. The vertical lines indicate the outer limits of pitches, and overlapping areas represent simultaneous sets of pitches. Duration of sound is indicated in tape speed, 76.2cm per second, and in the lower section, intensity is shown in decibels. All these factors are explained in detail in the published score.

FIGURE 16.24

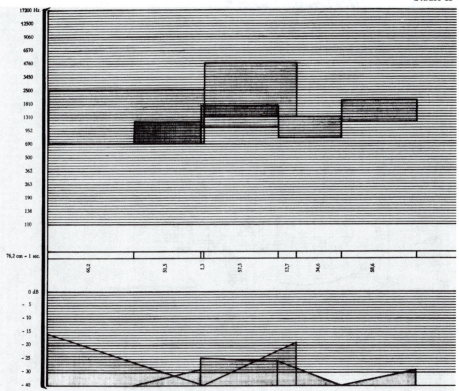

Figure 16.25 is an excerpt from a work for symphony orchestra. Although most of the composition is written with conventional orchestra scoring, an aleatory section appears midway in the work. Part of its notation is shown on page 470. The aleatory section makes use of both conventional instruments and electronic sounds. Our figure shows the score for the electronic sounds, and other pages provide aleatory passages for each section of the orchestra. In a performance of "Electronic Events," the conductor chooses which event or combination of events will be sounded and indicates these by hand signals, two of which are shown. The duration of the performance is

FIGURE 16.25

Merrill Ellis, *Kaleidoscope*

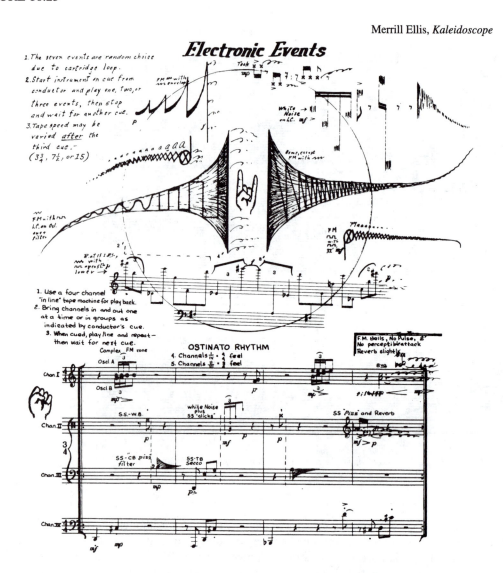

also at the discretion of the conductor. Successive performances of this work, then, will usually differ greatly from one another.

The circle at the top of the page represents a prerecorded endless tape loop containing several "events" as pictured around the circle. At the given hand signal, the tape is played, beginning at random at any point on the circle, or a live performer at the keyboard of a synthesizer may choose any point on the circle and improvise according to the diagram at that point. Among the many notational devices shown, we will describe a few: (1) the hornlike symbol at the left represents crescendo of a tone, rise in pitch, addition of pitches to be sounded simultaneously, and a modulating timbre, indicated, reading left to right, as a change from a "sine" wave to a "square" wave; (2) white-noise sounds at the upper right are indicated in only approximate pitch locations; (3) conventional notation at the bottom of the circle is combined with electronic instructions. A different hand signal will cue in one of the prerecorded ostinato patterns at the bottom of the score.

Computer music takes electronic music a step further. Here, the machine is the composer. The human element is the programmer who prepares for the computer a codification of the "styles" or "rules" within which the computer will do its work. The machine then produces random sounds within the programmed framework, and these sounds are recorded on tape. According to the information fed to the computer, it can compose "original" music varying in style from simple "pop" tunes to the most complex display of electronic sound combinations.

Recent advances in computer technology take electronic music a step further in two ways. (1) Digital wave-form synthesis programs use numbers to approximate the shape of a sound wave. These numbers are converted to electronic signals forty thousand times each second and can be played through a speaker. Composers can create entirely new sounds in this way. (2) In computer-assisted composition, a program stores rhythmic and melodic patterns created by a composer and then selects their temporal organization.

Multimedia is an art form combining several varieties of aural and visual stimulation simultaneously. Its basis is usually electronic music, using a tape, performance at a synthesizer, or both, combined with almost any other presentation of events, including projections—motion pictures, pictorial slides, random colors, laser configurations, and so forth—as well as dancers, instrumental or vocal soloists, staged effects, or whatever the composer's imagination can produce. The practice can be said to date from Scriabin's *Prometheus: Poem of Fire* (1910) for orchestra and a "color organ" of the composer's invention.

Epilog

It is understandable that the abstract and nonemotional qualities of much of twentieth-century music composition has found little favor with the general listening public. Accustomed to three centuries of music featuring predictable harmonic succession and individual tones that are easily recognizable as either consonant or dissonant, the average nonprofessional concert attendee has found music compositions without those features incomprehensible in varying degrees.

Still, in spite of such negative reaction, today's composers continue their efforts as before, bolstered in part by approval from members of academia and other professional musicians. In so doing, they hold out the hope that eventually a musical style acceptable to themselves and to the public will be achieved. But at the turn to the twenty-first century, others are seeking more immediate general acceptance without sacrificing musical integrity. There appear to be two approaches to that goal: through simplicity in the extreme and through carefully applied principles of pre-twentieth-century music. The descriptions that follow are at best merely samplings of the techniques. Inspection of scores and references to the bibliography in Chapter 14 are necessary for fuller comprehension.

1. Minimalism

In contrast to the complexities of earlier music of the twentieth century, minimalism features the simplest of harmonic and melodic materials combined with repetition, sequence, and ostinato. As an example, rhythmic patterns may be presented repetitiously with occasional variations over an extended length of time. Tonally, a single melodic line may be treated in a similar manner. In more than one part, for example, the parts may be similar although each part begins at a different point in the meter. Often, these parts are performed at slightly different tempi, causing one line to gradually get ahead of another line. Over time, a continually changing texture is heard.

The best known of the minimalist composers are John Adams, Philip Glass, and Steve Reich.

2. Return to Pre-Twentieth-Century Music

Neoromanticism. Not an actual return to nineteenth century romanticism, neoromanticism seeks to incorporate melodic and harmonic elements in contemporary music in such a way as to avoid the abstract and totally dissonant quality of much of the twentieth century's earlier music. The music of David Del Tredici and Henryck Górecki are representative. The quantity of the sales of Górecki's recording of Symphony No. 3 was astounding, an indication of a demand for aurally accessible contemporary music.

Early music: Gregorian chant up to the Baroque period. Inspiration derived from this period implies that its influence would be principally on the composition of choral music. Of particular interest is that the rhythm of its individual parts is usually determined by the poetic rhythm of its text. This concept of rhythm in choral music has already been explained in *Elementary Harmony* under the title "Another Metrical Concept," page 343. In the present volume, the same principles are shown for both sixteenth- and twentieth-century secular vocal music in Figures 15.8 and 15.9.

In twentieth-century music, this rhythmic feature is often found together with the elements of minimalism described earlier. A typical composer of this music is Arva Pärt.

These few descriptions of contemporary practices indicate that change, as it always has, is taking place in the concepts of music composition. Although most of the accomplishments of the early and middle years of the twentieth century are not ignored, neither are they now used exclusively, even in a single composition. Rather, in most current practice, any combination of serialism, electronics, and indeterminacy, and any systematic or nonsystematic principles of harmonic and contrapuntal development may be found. Added to these is the increasing use of pre-twentieth-century materials, such as triadic harmony in conjunction with major, minor, and modal resources. As the new millennium proceeds, experimentation seems to be the order of the day, rather than consolidation of the achievements of the preceding century. Consequently, the present volatile state of the art may continue for some time before the true accomplishments of the twentieth century are known and a rational and comprehensive theory of its music can be developed.

As an interested observer or participant in these changing concepts, you are urged to listen critically to that which composers have to offer, and to take advantage of the numerous writings on the subject to aid in your understanding and appreciation of the fast-moving developments in recent and current music activity.

The Essentials of Part-Writing

conventional procedures

These essentials represent the basic procedures of part-writing. In no sense are they intended to include the countless variations in part-writing techniques that can and do exist.

The Single Chord

Approximate range of the four voices

Soprano: d^1–g^2

Alto: a–c^2

Tenor: e–g^1

Bass: G–d^1

Triad Position. In *open position,* the distance between the soprano and the tenor is an octave or more. In *close position,* the distance between the soprano and the tenor is less than an octave. The distance between adjacent voices usually does not exceed an octave, although more than an octave may appear between bass and tenor.

Usual doubling The tonic, subdominant, and dominant tones in a key can ordinarily be doubled freely. To go beyond this generalization, some common doubling procedures are listed here:

Diatonic major and minor triads

1. Root in bass: Double the root.
2. First inversion: Double the soprano note.
3. Second inversion: Double the bass note.
4. Exception: Minor triads, root or third in bass. The third of a minor triad is often doubled, particularly when this third is the tonic, subdominant, or dominant note of the key.

Diminished triad (usually found in first inversion only): Double the third; however, when the fifth is in the soprano, the fifth is usually doubled.

Augmented triad: Double the bass note.

Seventh chord: Usually all four voices are present. In the major-minor seventh chord, the root is often doubled and the fifth omitted.

Altered triad: Same doubling as nonaltered triads; avoid doubling the altered note unless that note is the root of a chord.

Chord Connection

The objective of part-writing is the connection of a series of chords in such a way that each of the voice lines is an acceptable melodic line and that any pair of voice lines sounds well together. The general procedures listed here should always be a consideration when working with any of the more specific procedures that follow shortly.

1. Move each voice the shortest distance possible.
2. Move the soprano and the bass in contrary or oblique motion if possible.
3. Avoid doubling the leading tone, any altered tone (including $\sharp\hat{6}$ and $\sharp\hat{7}$ in minor), any nonharmonic tone, and the seventh of any seventh chord.
4. Avoid parallel fifths and parallel octaves between voices, and the augmented second in a melodic line.

The more specific conventional procedures that follow help to ensure the production of satisfactory melodic lines while avoiding the objectionable items listed above. But they do not rule out the use of more creative melodic lines, the procedures for which are unique in any given situation (review page 245 in *Elementary Harmony*).

Triads with Roots in the Bass

These procedures refer to two successive triads, each with its root in the bass.

Repeated Roots   When roots in the bass are repeated, the two triads may be written in the same position (open or close) or they may be in different positions. Triad position should be changed in the following circumstances:

1. When necessary to keep voices in correct pitch range
2. When necessary to maintain a voice distribution of two roots, one third, and one fifth
3. To avoid large leaps in an inner voice

Roots a Fifth Apart

1. Retain the common tone; move the other voices stepwise.
2. Move the three upper voices in similar motion to the nearest triad tones.
3. Move the third of the first triad by interval of the fourth to the third of the second triad. Hold the common tone and move the other voice by step.
4. At the cadence, the root of the final triad may be tripled, omitting the fifth.

Roots a Second Apart   Move the three upper voices in contrary motion to the bass.

Roots a Third Apart   Hold the two common tones; the other voice moves stepwise.

General Exception   When it is impossible or undesirable to follow conventional procedures, double the third in the second of the two triads; however, if this third is the leading tone or any altered tone, double the third in the first of the two triads.

Triads in Inversion

One of the Two Triads Is in Inversion   Write to or from the doubled note first, using oblique or contrary motion if possible, and then fill in the remaining voice.

Both Triads Are in Inversion   Each triad must have a different doubling to avoid parallel octaves and/or fifths, or the same doubling may appear in a different pair of voices. Avoid doubling the leading tone or any altered tone. Approach and leave each doubled tone as above.

Nonharmonic Tones

A nonharmonic tone temporarily replaces a harmonic tone. Approach and leave any nonharmonic tone according to the definition of the nonharmonic tone being used. Consider an accented nonharmonic tone as one of the chord tones, so that when it resolves the chord displays conventional doubling.

Seventh Chords

The seventh of a seventh chord, its note of approach, and its note of resolution constitute a three-note figure similar to these nonharmonic tone figures: passing tone, suspension, appoggiatura, and upper neighbor. The seventh usually resolves down by step.

Chromatic Tones

Chromatic tones are defined as tones not members of the key and scale in which the music is sounding.

1. Raised (sharped) tones usually ascend stepwise, and lowered (flatted) tones usually descend stepwise.
2. A chromatic tone may leap to any other tone in a repeated triad.
3. A raised tone may descend a half step to the seventh of a seventh chord.
4. When a lowered tone is the root of a chord, it moves as any chord root.
5. When a chromatic tone is followed by a diminished seventh chord, any movement from that tone is possible.

Instrumentation

ranges; clefs; transposition

Range

For each instrument, the range written in whole notes is satisfactory for use in the exercises in this text. The lowest note for each instrument is given, and a dotted line connects the upper whole note with the actual highest note in that instrument's range.

Clef

Each instrument regularly uses the clef or clefs found in the musical illustrations under "Range." Exceptions or modifying statements are found under the heading "Clef."

Transposition

Unless otherwise indicated under this heading, pitches given under "Range" sound concert pitch when played (concert pitch: $a^1 = 440$ vibrations per second: the note a^1 on the piano keyboard is concert A). All transposing instruments sound their name when written C is played; for example, a clarinet in B♭ sounds B♭ when it plays a written C.

String Instruments

Violin

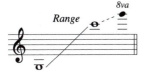

Viola

Clef. Alto clef is used almost exclusively. Treble clef is used occasionally for sustained high passage.

Violoncello (Cello)

Clef. Bass clef is ordinarily used. Tenor clef is used for extended passages above small A (not shown). Treble clef is used for extreme upper range.

Double Bass (Bass Viol, Contrabass)

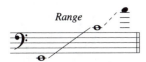

Transposition. Notes sound an octave lower than written.

Woodwind Instruments

Flute

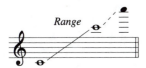

Oboe

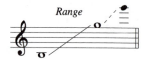

English Horn (Cor Anglais)

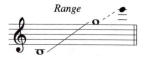

Transposition. Notes sound a perfect fifth lower than written. Use signature for the key a perfect fifth *above* concert pitch.

Clarinet: B♭ and A

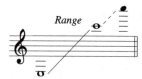

Transposition

1. Clarinet in B♭. Notes sound a major second lower than written. Use signature for the key a major second *above* concert pitch.
2. Clarinet in A. Notes sound a minor third lower than written. Use signature for the key a minor third *above* concert pitch.

Bassoon

Clef. Bass clef is ordinarily used. Tenor clef is used for upper range.

Saxophone: E♭ Alto, B♭ Tenor, and E♭ Baritone

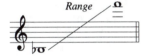

Transposition

1. E♭ alto saxophone. Notes sound a major sixth lower than written. Use signature for the key a major sixth *above* concert pitch.
2. B♭ tenor saxophone. Notes sound a major ninth (an octave plus a major second) lower than written. Use signature for the key a major second *above* concert pitch.
3. E♭ baritone saxophone. Notes sound an octave plus a major sixth lower than written. Use signature for the key a major sixth *above* concert pitch.

Brass Instruments

Horn (French Horn)

Clef. Treble clef is commonly used.
Transposition. Horn parts are written in F, E, E♭, and D.

In F: Notes sound a perfect fifth lower than written.

In E: Notes sound a minor sixth lower than written.

In E♭: Notes sound a major sixth lower than written.

In D: Notes sound a minor seventh lower than written.

Traditionally, horn parts have been written without key signatures, requiring accidentals to be placed before notes as needed. In recent practice, key signatures are given.

Trumpet or Cornet: B♭ and C

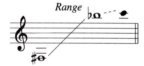

Transposition

1. Trumpet or cornet in B♭. Notes sound a major second lower than written. Use signature for the key a major second *above* concert pitch.
2. Trumpet or cornet in C. Nontransposing—sounds as written.

Trombone

Clef. Both tenor and bass clefs are commonly used.

Tuba

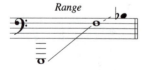

Index of Compositions

Subject Index